ATTITUDE AND ATTITUDE CHANGE

WILEY FOUNDATIONS OF SOCIAL PSYCHOLOGY SERIES

Series Editor: **DANIEL KATZ**, University of Michigan

BOOKS IN THE SERIES

Attitude and Attitude Change

HARRY C. TRIANDIS

Department of Psychology
University of Illinois

JOHN WILEY & SONS, INC.

NEW YORK • LONDON • SYDNEY • TORONTO

Library of Congress Catalogue Card Number: 76-140555

ISBN 0-471-88830-3 (cloth)
ISBN 0-471-88831-1 (paper)

Printed in the United States of America

10 9 8 7 6 5

Series Preface

The phenomenal growth of social psychology during the past thirty-five years has occured both in depth—in the development of its root system of experimental studies—and in breadth—in its branching out to embrace the social realities covered by the more traditional social sciences. In 1935, the first handbook of social psychology (edited by Carl Murchison), even with its many chapters from anthropology and demography, comprised a single volume. In 1969, the second edition of the Lindzey *Handbook* included five volumes. How then can we communicate to the various interested publics the findings and concepts of this far-flung enterprise? The handbooks with their summaries of the literature and their extensive bibliographies fulfill the needs of the specialist, but what about other audiences? The traditional method of a single text for a single course entails great difficulties in communicating the basic knowledge in the field to students or to other interested readers.

In this series we propose an alternative to the traditional methods by providing a number of separate volumes based on the major areas of interest for social-psychological research. Each book, although considerably shorter than a text, permits a more thorough treatment of a subarea than a text chapter. Several of these volumes provide the critical blocks of material for an introductory course, and particular books furnish the basis for an advanced course. The objective is to avoid the single textbook's scanty coverage of important issues and, also, to avoid the handbook type of treatment, which is too detailed and cryptic for the needs of the broader audience. Moreover, reader motivation will improve with the investigation of a single problem area that is broad enough to represent meaningful patterns of relationships and yet sufficiently delimited to permit a depth of study.

Interestingly, the field itself is developing in this direction. Researchers are concentrating their efforts on a related series of problems and are foregoing both grand theory and scattered pieces of empiricism. They are accumulating knowledge through their communication and contact within the given subareas of the field. If findings are to be replicated, if their determinants are to be systematically explored,

v

if they are to be generalized to other settings, then the frame of reference must encompass the relevant work of others in the same vineyard. Empirical studies show that scientific communication for active researchers takes place along these lines. It is less a matter of systematic perusal of all the journals and more a matter of informal communication among those with common research interests, through the exchange of preprints, letters, and discussion. Although this does not provide for the theoretical integration of all of social psychology, it does lead to the cumulative building of knowledge in a given subarea. This systematic accumulation is a prerequisite for scientific development and for later more comprehensive theory construction.

This series takes advantage of these research developments, especially as they are linked to the continuing problem areas in social psychology. It provides the student, the teacher, and the interested consumer of social science with a systematic account of what is known in fields such as social motivation, attitude structure and change, group processes and interpersonal behavior, social influence, the psychological aspects of social systems, balance theories, interpersonal perception, and attitude measurement. The series permits the instructor to select the areas that he considers of greatest importance for coverage in general and specialized courses in social psychology.

Daniel Katz

University of Michigan

Preface

It is difficult to write a textbook that can be used by undergraduate students taking their first course in social psychology, by students in a specialized course on attitudes, and by beginning graduate students who wish to become acquainted with attitude theory and research.

My own views on how the book should be used are as follows. Undergraduates, using it as part of their social psychology course, will read it to obtain an overall view of the field. Students who use this book for a course on attitudes will want to examine the *Suggested Readings* that accompany each section. If the book is used in combination with books of readings and with a few excursions into specialized articles, it can cover the field most adequately. Graduate students will want to use this book as a springboard or as a guide for their reading. The references at the end of the book are exhaustive. The *Suggested Readings* often cite books that cover certain topics in depth. Actually, this book is structured so that the student can be selective or thorough in reading the material.

I am biased in favor of "active learning." I believe that students learn most when they perform projects, write papers, talk to each other, and argue about controversial topics. To facilitate this type of learning I have included here a large number of *Projects for Advanced Students.* These projects request the student to read one of the current controversies in the attitude literature or to examine one of the more recent promising developments. An ideal way to teach a course is to ask several students in a small section to write the same paper and to debate differences in their conclusions. Another way to teach is to give credit for each completed project and to let the students earn credits by completing as many of these projects as they wish. The instructor's job, then, becomes one of counseling the students, guiding them, and correcting their papers. Good students tell me that this is a very exciting way to learn.

The writing of this book was greatly facilitated by the academic year (1968-1969) that I spent at the Center for International Studies at Cornell University. I arrived at the center with a first draft of the book, and started working on another book—*The Analysis of Subjective Culture*—which is concerned with the cultural determinants of attitudes, roles, norms, and values, and deals with both the antecedents and the consequences of these concepts in the context of theories of social behavior. As I worked on the subjective culture book, it became clear that the present volume could be restructured to fit into a more coherent theoretical framework. Once the framework proved itself, by providing some cohesion to the attitude literature, it was successfully applied to the more general problem of analyzing subjective culture. In short, working concurrently on the broader book on subjective culture and the more focused book on attitudes proved helpful to both.

I am grateful to the Cornell Center for International Studies for providing the setting in which this "communication" between the two books could take place. I thank the Director of the Center, Douglas Ashford, and his staff, who made numerous facilities and services available to me during my year at Cornell.

I am indebted to W. J. McGuire for his superb summary of the attitude area in Lindzey and Aronson's *Handbook of Social Psychology,* which was available to me in preprint form. The present volume was edited by my wife, Pola, who curbed my inclination for writing "academese." Helpful critical comments were obtained from Robyn M. Dawes, who read the first three chapters of the first draft, and Daniel Katz, Keith M. Kilty, Norman Miller, Martin Fishbein, and Henry Teune who read the second draft. I thank all of them. Their comments improved the book.

Harry C. Triandis

Contents

List of Tables

ATTITUDE AND ATTITUDE CHANGE

Wildebeast
septic lung
radio 4

I

Introduction
and Underlying Processes

Mr. Brown is a skilled factory worker in an almost all-white neighborhood. Mr. Smith is a black accountant who is married and has two children. How is Mr. Brown going to feel about Mr. Smith? What is he likely to think about him? How is he likely to behave toward him? The answers to these questions concern Mr. Brown's *attitudes* toward Mr. Smith.

This book deals with attitudes. It discusses why we have attitudes, what different kinds of attitudes we might profitably consider, what determines attitudes, and what changes attitudes. It examines some of the consequences of attitudes.

Many of the important problems of the latter third of the 20th century concern attitudes. Perhaps the biggest problem is that the rich nations are becoming richer while the poor nations are becoming poorer in a world that is progressively getting smaller. We have the technical knowledge to change the world, but most of us do not have the attitudes that can bring about that change.

The next most important problem is that unless we change our attitudes toward many of our fellow men there is the possibility of a nuclear war, which would mean the end of all living things—except, perhaps, some hardy viruses. Mr. Brown's attitudes toward Mr. Smith are an element in intergroup conflict that is widespread in many parts of the world. Conflict often occurs when people hold different ideologies (religions, political views), possess different quantities of goods, or belong to different racial or cultural groups. In the past, conflict was highly undesirable; in the future it can mean total destruction. We must learn to live in harmony, to bridge the barriers that create conflict, and to develop new societies that utilize conflict creatively. Just as the atom can be harnessed to produce electricity or can be unleashed to produce an explosion, so conflict can be harnessed to produce creative solutions to social problems or to destroy mankind. It is easier to unleash than to harness conflict, because harnessing requires a detailed understanding of how attitudes are generated and changed. We do not yet have this knowledge, but progress has been made. This book reflects the state of this knowledge as of mid-1969.

1

Other problems may, in the long run, prove equally important. The disruption of the ecology by man reflects in part his attitudes toward his environment, toward his neighbors, and toward himself. The more we have, the more and more garbage, refuse, and pollution we create. If we have one set of attitudes, we do not let this disturb us; with another set of attitudes we control it.

Although the study of attitudes is worthwhile, no one must think that knowing all there is to know about attitudes can immediately solve all of these problems. A view of this kind would be oversimple and naive. There are long-established traditional patterns of behavior and complex problems of agriculture, engineering, economics, health, and law, to mention but a few, that are interwoven with attitudes and that support them and make them difficult to change. The study of attitudes is only one facet of a complex puzzle. But the puzzle is there, and this book can be a key toward the beginning of its solution.

Definitions

Consider first a set of situations that have some social objects in common; then consider a set of social behaviors that a person emits in the presence of these situations. If there is similarity among these social behaviors, we infer that the person has an *attitude* toward the social objects that are present in the social situations. For example, if we observe a number of social situations in which "Negroes" are present and a set of social behaviors that are mostly positive (or negative), we would infer that the person has a positive (or negative) attitude toward Negroes. In other words, attitudes represent "consistency in response to social objects" (Campbell, 1963).

Allport (1935, 1954a) has covered in detail the history of the use of this concept in social psychology. As early as 1918, social psychology was *defined* as the scientific study of attitudes (Thomas and Znaniecki, 1918). As can be expected with a term that has been used by many psychologists and sociologists over such a long period of time, its definition has varied. The common element that runs through most definitions, however, is "the readiness to respond" to a situation. This readiness can refer to "mental attitudes" (Spencer, 1862) and the ability to "interpret" correctly what is being said, as a result of holding those attitudes. At other times the reference is to "motor attitudes" (Lange, 1888), which are states of readiness to respond in a motor task. Allport's (1935) definition is still highly influential:

"An attitude is a mental and neural state of readiness, organized through experience, exerting a directive or dynamic influence upon the individual's response to all objects and situations with which it is related" (Allport, 1935).

A definition that includes many of the central ideas used by attitude theorists would be as follows: "An attitude is an idea charged with emotion which predisposes a class of actions to a particular class of social situations." This definition suggests that attitudes have three components:

(a) A cognitive component, that is, the *idea* which is generally some category used by humans in thinking. Categories are inferred from consistencies in responses to discriminably different stimuli. The category *cars* can be inferred, for example, by determining that people make similar responses to Fords, Chevrolets, etc., and other stimuli that they are capable of discriminating. Statements of the form "cars are . . ." "cars have . . ." are also part of this component.

(b) An *affective* component, that is, the emotion which charges the idea. If a person "feels good" or "feels bad" when he thinks about the category we would say that he has a positive or negative affect toward the members of this category. For example, if he feels good when he thinks about cars he has a positive affective component toward them.

(c) A behavioral component, that is, a *predisposition to action*, such as driving, using, buying, or admiring cars.

A person who does not have the concept of car also would not have an attitude toward cars. When seeing a car he probably would place it in one of his already existing categories (for example, monster) and might have an attitude toward this object, but not toward *cars*. The cognitive representation of the category is the minimum condition for having the attitude. In addition, the cognitive category must become associated with pleasant or unpleasant events or desirable or undesirable goals. When this happens, the category becomes charged with affect. The more pleasant the events, and the more frequently they occur in the presence of the category, the greater is the amount of affect that becomes attached to the category. Similarly, the more desirable the goals that can be reached through the category

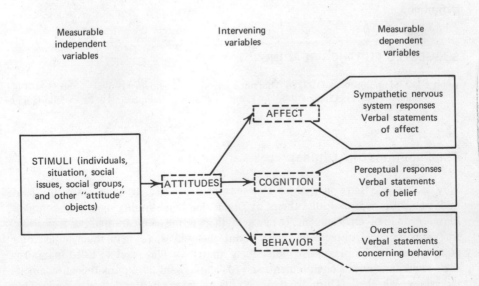

FIGURE 1.   A schematic conception of attitudes (after Rosenberg and Hovland, 1960).

(and the more certain that if one has the attitude object he will reach desirable goals), the more the affect. For example, a student who regards possession of a car as a sure means to heterosexual success in school, is likely to have a more positive attitude toward cars than a student who sees himself being successful with or without a car.

Rosenberg and Hovland (1960) represented attitudes as in Fig. 1. The stimuli are grouped in a category that represents the attitude object. The attitude has three aspects, and each aspect is measured by a variety of subject responses.

Although the three components are generally closely related, there are circumstances that can produce inconsistent components. For example, a person who has just been in an automobile accident may have a negative affective component (feels "bad" when he thinks about cars), but he may realize that he cannot get around in his town without using cars and, therefore, has a positive behavioral component—is predisposed to use them.

PROJECT FOR ADVANCED STUDENTS

Review several definitions of the concept attitude. Examine the definitions of Bogardus (1931, p. 62), Thurstone (1931, p. 261), Rokeach (1967, p. 530), Doob (1947), and Chein's (1948) objections to Doob's approach. Consider Campbell's (1963) argument that psychologists use 80 concepts that share the operational definition of the concept attitude. According to him, all of these concepts deal with phenomena that are acquired and that modify later responses of the organism. Decide for yourself how attitudes should be defined. Defend your choice of a definition.

SUGGESTED FURTHER READINGS

Allport (1935) in Fishbein (1967a); Thurstone (1931) in Fishbein (1967a); Doob (1947) in Fishbein (1967a); Chein (1948) in Fishbein (1967a); Campbell (1963) in Jahoda and Warren (1966).

The Functions of Attitudes

Why do people have attitudes? The reason is because attitudes (a) help them understand the world around them, by organizing and simplifying a very complex input from their environment, (b) protect their self-esteem, by making it possible for them to avoid unpleasant truths about themselves, (c) help them adjust in a complex world, by making it more likely that they will react so as to maximize their rewards from the environment; and (d) allow them to express their fundamental values. We shall return to these points in later chapters of this book. This approach involves the so-called "functional analysis of attitudes," because it is concerned with the functions performed by attitudes "in the economy of personality." [The major theorists are Smith (1947), Smith, Bruner, and White (1956), Katz and Stotland (1959), and Katz (1960).]

These writers have argued that attitudes may *express* some aspects of an individual's personality. Smith, Bruner, and White (1956), for instance, speak of persons with a history of meager energy and a low fatigue threshold. These persons may display a lack of interest in the affairs of the world which may be reflected in indifference attitudes toward most attitude objects relevant to international affairs. Here the attitudes express a physiological condition of the individual.

More importantly, attitudes help us adjust to our environment, by providing a certain amount of *predictability*. We have an established repertory of reactions to a given category of attitude objects. Once a social object has been classified in that category, we can employ our existing repertory of reactions. This saves us from deciding again, starting from first principles, what our reaction should be to a particular attitude object. To the extent that our system works, it adds predictability to the events of our social environment. If we have classified the attitude object correctly and the object behaves the way similar objects have behaved in the past, we can employ our previous experience as a guide and usually be correct about the outcome.

Our attitudes also help us to *adjust* to our environment by making it easier to get along with people who have similar attitudes. The people who really count, in our social environment, tend to have attitudes that are similar to ours, and often we bring our attitudes in line with the ones held by these important people. Smith, Bruner and White (1956) also point out that one of the functions of attitudes is to provide some *externalization* of inner problems. For example, a young man who has a strong unresolved fear of rejection by powerful figures expresses this inner conflict in greater than average hatred toward fascism, nazism, etc. Similarly, a young man who hates his father may adopt attitudes that are generally inconsistent with those advocated by most authority figures in his society.

In a similar line of argument, Katz (1960) discussed four functions that attitudes perform for the personality: (a) instrumental, adjustive-utilitarian, (b) ego-defensive, (c) value-expressive, and (d) knowledge function. The *adjustment function* is derived from the tendency to maximize the rewards in the external environment and to minimize the penalties. For example, a worker may support a political party that he believes will help him economically. *Ego-defensive functions* are served by attitudes that allow the individual to protect himself from acknowledging uncomplimentary basic truths about himself. *Value expressive functions* are involved when the expression of the attitudes gives pleasure to the person, because the attitudes reveal some of the basic values he holds dear. *Knowledge functions* are based on the individual's need to give structure to his universe, to understand it, to predict events, etc. Thus, Katz's discussion is basically an elaboration of the views expressed by Smith et al.

Behavior as a Determinant of Attitudes

One way of answering the question of why people have attitudes is to argue that they need to give meaning to their behavior. People "explain" their behavior to themselves by convincing themselves and others that the social objects that benefitted from the behavior are intrinsically good and worthy of such positive action. For example, a businessman may support a particular political program because he feels that this support will increase the number of his clients. Having done this, he convinces himself and tries to convince others that the political program has great merit. In the process, his attitude gradually becomes positive toward this program.

Traditional thinking about the direction of causality in attitude theory has assumed that attitudes cause a person's behavior. The view just described postulates the opposite direction of causality—the behavior causes the attitude.

Breer and Locke (1965) present extensive laboratory evidence in support of their theory that the beliefs, attitudes, and values of a group of people are determined by their task experiences. If members of a given culture receive rewards in situations in which they act as individuals their "individualism" will increase; if they receive rewards in situations in which they act as members of a group, their "collectivism" will increase.

Similarly, if they frequently succeed in tasks in which there is a leader they will tend to become more "authoritarian," and if they frequently succeed in tasks in which there is no leader, they will tend to become "equalitarian." After experiences of the first kind the subjects of Breer and Locke's experiment showed a significant unfavorable change in their attitudes toward "discussion groups" and "groups in general"; after experiences of the second kind, the subjects showed a significant favorable change in their attitudes toward these two attitude objects.

By exposing some subjects to greater frequencies of success than others, Breer and Locke (1967) were able to change some of the attitudes and values of subjects toward *effort, luck, control, fatalism, time,* and *mastery over nature.* They suggest that situations that have a 50-50 chance of being rewarding lead to greater effort and to a higher evaluation of "hard work." Situations that are too difficult or too easy do not have this characteristic. They make an intriguing suggestion, that the situation of the lower, middle, and upper classes corresponds to the difficult, intermediate, and easy condition of their experiment. In their experiment, people in the hard (lower) and easy (upper) conditions (classes) are more likely to believe in *luck*, but in the medium condition (middle classes) they believe in *effort*; people in the easy condition (upper classes) were more likely to view the control of the environment by man as appropriate, but those in the other conditions saw acceptance of the environment the way it is as more appropriate. The correspondence of these laboratory findings to sociological studies of attitudes is most suggestive.

Summary

Although there are many definitions of the term attitude, two themes are common to most of them: (a) an attitude is a predisposition to respond; and (b) an attitude is represented by consistencies in the responses of individuals to social situations. Those who develop procedures for the measurement of attitudes have adopted restricted definitions, and those concerned with theory development have adopted broad definitions that allow the analysis of the functions performed by attitudes in "the economy of the personality." Typically, those concerned with measurement have defined attitudes as unidimensional constructs (for example, the degree of positive or negative affect), and those who have been concerned with theory building have employed a number of components. The present writer has adopted a middle-ground position (Triandis, 1964b, 1967) which employs three components, but provides for the explicit operational measurement of each one.

STUDY QUESTIONS

1. Explain what is meant by the functional approach to the study of attitudes.
2. Now that you have learned about the functional approach, do you want to change your mind about your own definition of attitudes, as you wrote it out in answer to the previous study question?

SUGGESTED FURTHER READINGS

Smith (1947) in Fishbein (1967a); Katz (1960) in Fishbein (1967a).

Basic Underlying Processes

In the previous section we stated that attitudes are inferred from consistencies in the responses of persons to social situations having some social object(s) in common. This is a rather abstract definition which needs to be broken down into components.

1. What is a social object? Any person, product, or creation of a person or social event can function as a social object. "President Nixon," "Piccasso's paintings," an "automobile," a "poem," a "party given by a campus fraternity," the "fraternity itself," the "Republican party," "Liberia," and "modern art" are all examples of social objects.

2. What kinds of response consistencies do we observe? (a) People tend to associate social objects with other social objects in consistent ways. For example, "President Nixon" is more closely associated with the "Republican party" than he is with "modern art." These consistencies in "thinking" about social objects are part of the attitudes toward them. In fact, the attitude of a Mr. Smith toward Nixon and the Republican party are likely to be similar, although the attitudes toward Nixon and modern art may be quite dissimilar. (b) People tend to "feel" consistently about an attitude object. Those who admire President Nixon are likely

to "feel good" in his presence, to consider him "honest," "clean," "fair," etc. If we attach electrodes to the skins of these people while we present them with the sentence "Nixon is a crook" we will observe a physiological arousal similar to the arousal observed in an angry animal. (c) People tend to "act" consistently toward the attitude object. For example, if they show respect toward a person, they also are likely to "cooperate in a political campaign," to "obey," to "invite to dinner," etc., this particular person.

These consistencies in "thinking," "feeling," and "acting" suggest the existence of an attitude. However, such consistencies are by no means extreme. There are attitude objects to which people react in a very simple, consistent way and other attitude objects toward which their reactions are extremely complex. In addition, there are people who look at the world in simple terms or in complex terms.

Specifically, certain attitude objects are responded to in an undifferentiated way. With the exception of artists, MODERN ART as an attitude object is likely to involve simple and consistent responses. Those who like it and think well of it, feel good about it and act consistently toward it—they go to see it, pay money for it, and speak in favor of it. Those who dislike it think that it is associated with "a bunch of incompetents," feel angry or indifferent about it, and act accordingly—they avoid it, speak against it, ridicule people who pay money for it, etc. By contrast MY MOTHER, or MY SON, as attitude objects, may produce rather differentiated responses, particularly when these attitude objects include both good and bad characteristics. The more information one has about an attitude object the more likely he is to perceive both good and bad aspects of it (Scott, 1969) and, hence, may tend to show more complex responses to it. A person might recognize, for example, that his son is "ugly," but he finds him nevertheless "most lovable" and, although he wants to "spend a lot of time with him," he may recognize that this is not good for him and so he does the opposite. In other words, with attitude objects of this kind there may not be a perfect consistency in the thinking, feeling, and acting aspects of the responses.

To summarize, an attitude can be conceived as having three interrelated components: (a) a cognitive component—described by the person's categorizations, and the relationships between his categories—(b) an affective component—described by the way the person evaluates the objects which are included in a particular category; and (c) a behavioral component—which reflects the behavioral intentions of the person toward the objects included in a particular category. We now analyze each of these components.

The Cognitive Component

There are potentially an infinite number of just noticeable differences in the human environment. In the area of color discriminations alone, color engineers estimate that there are 7,500,000 discriminable colors (Brown and Lenneberg, 1954). Since that fine a discrimination of the environment is beyond the capacity of human attention, man typically treats many discriminable stimuli as instances of the same thing. In other words, he categorizes stimuli. Since it simplifies the task of responding to the environment, categorization has considerable survival value. However, it involves a great loss of information (Allport, 1954b; Bruner, 1958). Misinformation also may be added since, when a stimulus is placed in a category, it is assumed to have the same associations with other categories that the typical members of the category have with these other categories.

Language has a key function in categorization. When a language provides a term for a particular category, it facilitates the use of this category by those who speak it. Some languages have richer vocabularies for certain domains of concepts than others (Klineberg, 1954).

Categories may be conceived as being organized according to both a horizontal dimension of discrimination (for example, poodle, collie, terrier) and a vertical dimension of level of abstraction (for example, poodle, dog, animal).

Categories are often defined by other categories that are called *attributes*. American political figures, for instance, might be classified into four categories by means of the attributes Democrat-Republican and Liberal-Conservative. These two attributes produce four categories.

Humans must learn to react to their environment differentially, because the environment reacts differentially to them. For example, unless a child differentiates the small lion in the zoo from his pet cat, he may have an unfortunate experience with the lion. Also, it is impossible to consider all the details in every situation. It is clearly more economical to talk about "the animals in the zoo" than to list all of them.

In addition to these two dimensions of cognitive organization, it is important to consider the dimension of centrality of the concepts. Rokeach (1967, 1968) has shown that concepts differ in "centrality." There are certain beliefs that deal with the individual and for which there is unanimous social support. For example, the belief "My name is Triandis" is very central with this author. There is no public dispute of this statement. There are other beliefs that are somewhat less central. They also deal with the self but there is no social support for them. For example, the belief "my mother loves me" is less central and, therefore, this writer can be less sure about it than he can be about the belief "my name is Triandis." Authority beliefs are even less central. For example, the belief "The philosophy of Lincoln is basically sound and I am all for it" is a statement that is less central than the previous ones. It is an authority belief, because it centers around an authority figure. Further removed from the central beliefs are peripheral beliefs, for example, "The United States should have remained neutral during the 1956 crisis of the Suez Canal." The least central are those beliefs that are inconsequential, for example, "Elizabeth Taylor is more beautiful than Mia Farrow."

Although Rokeach describes centrality, other authors (for example, Sherif et al., 1965) write much about ego-involvement. Highly central beliefs are very ego-involving. It may be better to employ the term centrality, because it implies that the change of a belief high in this characteristic also will change many other beliefs, but the change of a peripheral belief may have an unimportant effect on the organization of the cognitive system. Nevertheless, the two terms can be used interchangeably, and it should be clear that central or highly ego-involving beliefs are more difficult to change than peripheral or uninvolving beliefs. For example, it took almost 100 years for the scientific world to accept the theory of evolution, but the theory of relativity was accepted in just a few years. This difference does not reflect a difference in the validity of the two theories, but only a difference in the centrality of the beliefs that had to be changed in order to accept each theory. Very few people have central beliefs relevant to Einstein's theory, but many people did (and still do) have central beliefs relevant to Darwin's theory.

The content of categories is greatly influenced by culture (Triandis, 1964a). In Japanese, the status of the speakers in a conversation is very precisely defined, but the substance and the rest of the context are left highly ambiguous. In other words, Japanese interpersonal categories include information that is not present in American interpersonal categories and exclude some information that is. Each culture defines its categories somewhat differently. Even when two languages use essentially the same word for a particular category, they may include somewhat different social objects in that category. For example, "sympathetic people," in English, are supposed to be people who are affected by the state of another. In the languages of the Latin group (Italian: simpatico; French: sympathique, etc.) they are "nice, pleasant, charming people." The latter connotation is not precluded in the English meaning, but it is certainly not dominant.

STUDY QUESTIONS

1. List some properties of the cognitive component of attitudes. Describe each of these properties. Suggest how they may be measured.
2. What are the implications of differentiation and centrality for the reactions of people to information? Make some guesses, then check them, if you have time, by doing the next project.

PROJECT FOR ADVANCED STUDENTS

Examine the definitions of differentiation, complexity, unity and organization supplied by Zajonc (1954, 1960b). Study the definitions of differentiation salience, time perspective, information support, and complexity found in Smith, Bruner and White (1956) and the definitions of domain differentiation, attribute centrality, attribute articulation, affective salience, and ambivalence found in Scott (1966, 1969). Examine Scott's (1969) data on the measurement of such aspects of the cognitive component of attitudes, and the interrelationship among these measures. Then attempt to present your own theory of the structure of natural cognitions. Indicate why you think your theory is better than the theories of the authors quoted above.

If you wish to write a still more advanced paper, read Weick's (1968) discussion of several kinds of cognitive links and attempt to assess the importance of these links for theories of attitude change.

FURTHER READING

Triandis (1964a); Weick (1968).

The Affective Component

Once a category has formed, it is possible for it to become associated with pleasant or unpleasant states, and through conditioning it can acquire the property of arousing positive or negative states in the individual. The way the person feels about an attitude object is often determined by the previous association of the attitude object with pleasant or unpleasant states of affairs.

Another important connection among categories is the relationship between a category and valued (or disvalued) outcomes. Peak (1955) has suggested that the attitude toward a particular object depends on the instrumental relation between the object and our goals. Thus, we experience positive affect toward objects that help us reach our goals and negative affect toward objects that hinder us or lead us to undesirable goals. Thus, INTEGRATED HOUSING may be viewed by a particular person as related to certain undesirable outcomes (for example, reduced property values) as well as to certain desirable outcomes (for example, equal opportunity or justice). A person's affect toward INTEGRATED HOUSING is determined by the perceived probabilities of a connection between INTEGRATED HOUSING and various outcomes, as well as the satisfaction score associated with each outcome. Specifically, the affective loading toward the attitude object (A) is connected with the probabilities of the outcomes that are salient $(P_1, P_2, \ldots P_u)$ and the evaluation (E) of each of these outcomes by the equation:

$$A = P_1 E_1 + P_2 E_2 + \cdots + P_n E_n$$

This equation has also been used by Rosenberg (1956), Carlson (1956), and in a modified form by Fishbein (1961). The latter considered the "beliefs" about the object (B) and the evaluative aspect of these beliefs (E). According to Fishbein, if a person thinks that there is very high probability (say +3 on a -3 to $+3$ scale) that a Negro would be *musical*, and he values this characteristic very much (say +5 on a -5 to $+5$ scale), then his affect would be $(+3) \times (+5) = 15$. If he perceives additional probable connections between the category Negro and various characteristics, they would contribute additional terms to the above equation. The equation then will have n terms, where n is the number of characteristics that Negroes may have. Fishbein believes that 5 to 9 characteristics contribute most of the affect for most attitude objects. It should be clear that the numbers obtained from this procedure are arbitrary and depend on the scales used.

The Behavioral Component

In our discussion of the cognitive component we have suggested that subjects respond to the myriads of stimuli in their environments by first categorizing them and then relating their categories to others. Some of these categories are affective, or in other words, involve emotion. Other categories are normative, that is, they involve ideas about what is correct behavior toward members of a given category. For example, a person may categorize a painting by period, artist, the museum in which it is housed, the school of which it is a product, the country in which it was created, etc. Associated with categorizations of this kind are certain emotional states, pleasant or unpleasant. In addition, there are associations with certain ideas about what is correct behavior. These norms typically develop in small groups or subcultures. They are ideas about what is correct behavior for a member of *this* group—my family, my school, my club, and so forth. Thus, one group may express its pleasant emotional state, in connection with a certain category of paintings, by the norm "attempt to buy it at an auction," but another group may have a very weak norm about buying, but a very strong norm about talking in favor of such objects. A third group might have norms consistent with doing both.

Most persons do not have strong norms about buying expensive works of art simply because they cannot afford them. Most civilized groups probably would not develop the norm "to destroy" a work of art, even for art that is highly negative in evaluation (unpleasant affect). In other words, a positive emotion will not *necessarily* lead to norms of approach, and a negative emotion will not *necessarily* lead to a hostile norm. This is not to say that consistency among the three components is not the general rule. In general, the cognitive, affective, and behavioral components are consistent. One can guess that, when the 16th century Portuguese soldiers practiced marksmanship by shooting at the magnificent Hindu statues at the Elephanta caves (outside Bombay, India), they did so because they (a) considered them pagan (non-Christian) art; (b) they had a somewhat negative affective reaction to the sculpture (it was too different from what they were used to); and (c) they developed a norm about "correct" behavior for members of their particular group that was consistent with (a) and (b).

Two Major Dimensions. The major dimensions that underlie behavior toward any kind of attitude object are *positive* versus *negative affect* and *seeking* versus *avoiding contact*. This system of dimensions results in a typology of behaviors that may be described simply as going *toward, against,* or *away* from the attitude object. Figure 2 shows this conceptualization and includes some behaviors to illustrate how they would be positioned in this two-dimensional space.

Any behavior can be conceived as involving (a) a certain amount of seeking or avoiding contact and (b) a certain amount of positive or negative affect. For maximum contact, consider the behaviors "to kiss" and "to use knife against"; for minimum contact consider the behavior "to run away from"; for maximum positive affect consider "giving one's life to save the life of another" and for maximum

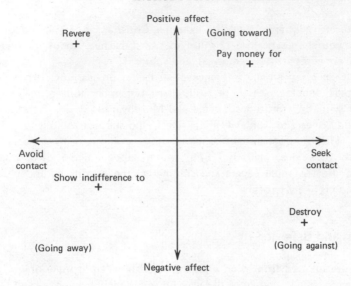

FIGURE 2.   The two basic dimensions of behavior toward attitude objects.

negative affect consider "planning to throw an incendiary bomb at him." Clearly, different behaviors involve different mixtures of the two qualities (contact and affect). This appears to be the case on empirical grounds (Triandis, Vassiliou and Nassiakou, 1968) as well as logically.

A person's behavioral intention, that is, what he would do toward an attitude object, is very closely related to norms of behavior, that is, what people think he should do. In several studies, correlations on the order of .60 have been observed between behavior norms and behavioral intentions (Bastides and Van den Berghe, 1957; Triandis, Vassiliou and Nassiakou, 1968). This is a very high correlation coefficient, since in most psychological studies correlations of .30 are rather typical.

PROJECTS FOR ADVANCED STUDENTS

1. Write an essay on the relationship of attitudes and values. Sample, first, some definitions of the concept value by examining Allport, Vernon, and Lindzey (1960), England (1967), and Rokeach (1968). List some differences between attitudes and values (*Clues:* they differ in level of abstraction, the degree to which they are enduring, and the degree to which cultural influences instead of individual experiences determine them). List some similarities (*Clue:* they both involve the notion of affect). Explore some anthropological perspectives (Kluckhohn and Strodtbeck, 1961) and some psychiatric implications (Diaz-Guerrero, 1963; Diaz-Guerrero and Peck, 1967; Rudin, 1968). Explore the relationship of personality

variables to attitudes and values (for example, Christianson, 1959; Scott, 1960). At this point you should be in a position to say something about the relationships among the concepts attitudes, motives, and values.

2. Write an essay on the influence of attitudes on learning. It has long been thought that people learn more easily, and remember longer, material that is consistent with their attitudes. Levine and Murphy (1943), Jones and Aneshansel (1956), and Jones and Kohler (1958) have found support for this idea. But Waly and Cook (1966), Brigham and Cook (1969), and others have not found any support for this idea. Malpass (1969) found support under certain specifiable conditions. Review these papers and summarize the conditions under which this phenomenon is likely to occur.

Attitudes and Behavior

Attitudes are inferred from what a person says about an attitude object, from the way he feels about it, and from the way he says he will behave toward it. To what extent are what he says, how he feels, and how he intends to behave consistent with what he actually does? This is a problem that is loosely referred to by social psychologists as the problem of the relationship between attitudes and behavior.

One naive view considers the relationship between attitude and behavior as very strong. In fact, the relationship is rather weak, and in a widely quoted study by LaPiere (1934) no relationship of any kind was observed. In the early 1930s, LaPiere traveled through a portion of the United States with a Chinese couple. They stopped at 66 hotels and motor inns and 184 restaurants and were refused service only once (in a third-rate California motor inn). Six months after the trip, LaPiere sent a letter to the establishments that they had visited, as well as to a control group of similar establishments that they had not visited. He asked if the establishment would give service to Chinese guests. Only 128 of the establishments answered his letter. Of those answering, 92 percent indicated that they would not accept Chinese as guests. Similar results were obtained by Kutner, Wilkins, and Yarrow (1952) in restaurant visits of a white-Negro party.

It would be naive, however, to conclude from these results that there is no relationship between attitude and behavior. What should be understood is this: attitudes involve what people *think* about, *feel* about, and how they would *like to behave* toward an attitude object. Behavior is not only determined by what people *would like* to do but also by what they think they should do, that is, social *norms*, by what they have usually done, that is, *habits*, and by the *expected consequences of the behavior*.

Imagine the hotel clerk who is suddenly confronted with a smiling, presentable Chinese couple, speaking excellent English, carrying good luggage, and asking to be served. His first impulse may very well be to serve them; furthermore he is in the habit of admitting guests, and the consequences of this behavior are likely to be rewarding (he will get more income) while the probability of punishment (loss of other customers) is remote. Although there are some norms among certain groups of people about not serving Orientals, there are also hospitality norms that would favor serving them, and as a result the Chinese couple would be admitted.

If the same clerk had to answer LaPiere's letter he would be faced with a different stimulus. First, instead of *this* pleasant, smiling, well-dressed Oriental, it is *any* Oriental, including those who would justify the clerk's most uncomplimentary stereotypes. Second, he does not have many Oriental customers, hence, he is not in the *habit* of admitting them. By committing himself in print to admit Orientals "in general" he exposes himself to *consequences* over which he does not have control. Furthermore, the social *norms* may apply to Orientals in general, but are not necessarily applicable to that particular "nice" Oriental couple. In other words, when the particular Chinese couple applied for service most factors tended toward acceptance; when the clerk answered the letter most factors tended toward nonacceptance. Other weaknesses of this study include the fact that it is not known whether the same person admitted the Chinese couple and answered the letter, nor whether the 92 percent rejection rate would have been as high if the 49 percent of the institutions that did not answer LaPiere's letter had answered it.

The problem is best conceived as follows: when we measure someone's attitude, we usually obtain information about a class of people—for example, blacks, Orientals—or a class of objects—for example, federal aid to education. The judgment that the subjects make involves really *one* element—blacks, Orientals, or federal aid to education. By contrast, when we measure a particular behavior toward a particular person, or a particular issue, there are probably seven or so elements influencing the behavior (Miller, 1956). It is no longer just an Oriental; it is *this* Oriental who is short, male, smiling, has a blue tie, wears glasses, and speaks excellent English. In short, the subject who responds has attitudes not only toward Orientals, but also toward short people, males, smiling people, people who wear blue ties, people who wear glasses, and people who speak excellent English. Each of these attitudes may have a different function, and his behavior will be determined by several of these attitudes. Furthermore, as Kiesler et al. (1969) have pointed out, it is probable that when taking a paper-and-pencil test some attitudes are salient, and when in a social situation some different attitudes may be salient. Unless we measure most of the relevant attitudes, we shall have little success in predicting behavior.

One way to think about the relationship between attitudes and behavior is to use an analogy. Consider, on the one hand, the extent to which your refrigerator is full of food and, on the other hand, your decision (behavior) to eat at home or at a restaurant. An empty refrigerator does not necessarily mean that you will eat at a restaurant, since you could eat canned food, but it would strongly predispose you to eat out. Conversely, a full refrigerator does not necessarily mean that you will eat at home because there may be other reasons for eating at a restaurant, for example, social pressures from your friends, your habit of eating at a restaurant once a week, the superiority of restaurant food, etc. In other words, a full refrigerator is neither a sufficient nor a necessary cause of eating at home. Analogously, attitudes are neither necessary nor sufficient causes of behavior. They are "facilitative causes" in the same sense that a full refrigerator and the possibility of having food spoil might press you to decide to eat at home.

Since attitudes are neither necessary nor sufficient causes of behavior, are they worth studying? Just consider what would happen if your major purpose was to predict whether a person would decide to eat at home or at a restaurant. You surely would want to know, among other things, how much food he had at home. Thus, the answer is self-evident.

To summarize the present argument, behavior is a function of (a) attitudes, (b) norms, (c) habits, and (d) expectancies about reinforcement. When all four factors are consistent, there is consistency between attitudes and behavior; when the four factors are inconsistent, there is much less consistency.

This formulation was tested by Sugar (1967), who asked college students (a) whether they liked to smoke (affect toward smoking), (b) whether their friends believe it is all right to smoke (norm), and (c) whether they usually smoked (habit). On another occasion, while the subjects participated in an unrelated experiment, the experimenter in charge casually offered them a cigarette. When the three predictors used in Sugar's experiment were consistent among themselves, the behavior was predicted with great accuracy: in 33 out of 38 cases where attitudes, norms, and habits were consistent, the behavior was consistent. When the three predictor variables were inconsistent, the accuracy of the prediction dropped. The strongest single predictor variable was habit, followed by norm, and the least important predictor was attitude. On the other hand, the combination of attitude and other factors predicted 81 percent of the observations of behavior. To put it differently, when only the cases that accepted the cigarette are considered, in 82.5 percent of the observations, habit, norms, and attitudes were consistent with the observed behavior; when the cases that did not accept the cigarette are considered, there is a diffusion of the reasons—habit is most powerful, and typically people who report that they usually do not smoke also say that they do not like to smoke. (Sixty-eight percent show both negative habits and attitudes.) Thirty percent of those who did not accept the cigarette stated that their friends believe that it is *not* all right to smoke. Since there is overlap between these two groups, this accounts for most of the cases who refused the cigarette offer. In sum, attitudes alone do not predict behavior; attitudes together with norms and habits do.

PROJECT FOR ADVANCED STUDENTS

You may wish to write a paper on a recent important theoretical development concerning the relationship between attitudes and behavior. Fishbein (1967b) has adapted Dulany's (1967) theory concerning the relationship between cognitions and behavior to the area of the relationship of attitudes and behavior. You may wish to study this theory and an empirical test of it (Ajzen and Fishbein, 1970).

Another paper of interest would be one that examines the conditions under which a person acts on his attitudes. McArthur, Kiesler, and Cook (1969) have found that behavior is more likely to be consistent with attitudes when a person thinks of himself as the sort of person who does "that sort of thing." If you write this paper you also should read Freedman and Fraser (1966), which suggested this idea to McArthur et al.

Rotter (1967) emphasizes different kinds of expectancies of reinforcement (reward). He distinguishes *specific* from *generalized* expectancies. The specific expectancies are tied to the particular situation, but the generalized are closer to personality traits. For example, one of the generalized expectancies relevant to whether a person would or would not support social change is a person's *internal* versus *external* control. Those who have an internal control expectancy believe that what happens is the result of their own behavior; those who have an external control expectancy believe that what happens is because of luck, chance, and fate. The internals are more likely than the externals to join organizations that support social change such as unions and the civil rights movement. Rotter argues that the probability that a particular behavior will occur depends on the expectancy of the occurrence of reinforcement, following the behavior, in the particular situation, and the value of this reinforcement in that situation. He lists a variety of sources of reinforcement—social approval, consistency between a person's own private views and his behavior, etc. Thus, the consistency between private views and behavior is considered a source of reinforcement, but the force produced by this source may not be sufficient to overcome the forces produced by other variables, for instance, social approval, so that behavior/attitude consistency may or may not be observed.

An equally important source of apparent inconsistency between attitudes and behavior can be found in considering the "difficulty" of a social act. Obviously, it is much easier to say "Hi!" to a person than to marry that person. The first behavior is on the extreme end of the continuum involving small sequences, but the second behavior usually has very considerable consequences. This point is particularly emphasized in a situation in which A and B are a white and a black person. In American society it is clearly much easier to say "Hi!" than to intermarry.

This argument, about the importance of the threshold of a behavior was clearly stated by Campbell (1963). He pointed out that the LaPiere study involved two situations with very different thresholds: it is harder to refuse a well-dressed Chinese in a face-to-face setting than it is to refuse the Chinese as a group in a letter. Campbell further argues that LaPiere's study has no relevance as far as the problem of inconsistency is concerned. Inconsistency would have been observed if those who refused face-to-face accepted by questionnaire or those who accepted by questionnaire refused face-to-face.

Support for this analysis can be found in a number of studies. Leventhal, Singer, and Jones (1965) presented fear-arousing communications to several groups of students which were designed to convince them that they should obtain tetanus shots. After receiving the communications, 31 percent of the subjects in the low fear group and 60 percent of the subjects in the high fear group indicated that they intended to get shots. By contrast, in the no fear (control) group only 18 percent of the subjected indicated an intention to get shots. An additional treatment was given to half the experimental and to half the control group subjects in the form of specific recommendations on how to get to the student health service (including a map) and what routes to follow to and from the library. The results showed that none of the subjects in the control groups took the shots; only 3 percent of the subjects in the fear groups took the shots; yet 28 percent of those subjects who were in the fear groups *and* received specific recommendations took the shots.

One interpretation of these findings is that the specific recommendations given to the subjects made the behavior easier, or lowered its threshold, in Campbell's sense.

Consistent with the LaPiere findings, the Leventhal et al. findings can be summarized by saying that attitudinal statements show large amplitudes—people say they will do either good or bad things toward others, but when it comes to the actual behavior there is less amplitude—people do not do all the good or all the bad things that they said they would do. A large study of the behavior of the police in three American cities (Reiss, 1969) found much prejudice toward blacks and almost no discrimination. Again, the predisposition to discriminate is there, but the actual behavior does not occur, presumably because of the official policies of the police commissioners. But when these policies are less salient, as for example in a riot, we can expect police brutality because the predisposition is already there.

Further support for Campbell's argument can be found in a study by Naidoo (1966) in which different thresholds for verbal and behavioral acts actually were observed. Naidoo asked students whether they would accept a black student as a friend, as a neighbor, etc. She also placed her white female subjects in situations in which they interacted with blacks and whites who agreed or disagreed with them. After the discussion the subject had the option of either agreeing with the white or with the black confederates of the experimenter. Finally, the subjects were casually asked by the black confederate to go with him to the student union "for a cup of coffee." The subject's acceptance or rejection of this invitation was noted. Naidoo found a much larger percentage of the white girls rejecting a black in the paper-and-pencil verbal task, than in the face-to-face situations. Specifically, Naidoo found that only 20 percent of her subjects would accept blacks as their neighbors, as kin by marriage, etc., on a paper-and-pencil test (Triandis' Behavioral Differential). About 40 percent of the subjects described blacks on paper-and-pencil tests (Osgood's Semantic Differential) as good, clean, and honest. About 57 percent of the subjects indicated that they would engage in formal behaviors involving acceptance with blacks, such as cooperate in political campaigns, invite them to their club, etc. (this result was also obtained on a paper-and-pencil test, namely, Triandis' Behavioral Differential). No less than 62 percent of these subjects indicated they would prefer the black instead of the white confederate as a partner in a similar experiment. Fully 86 percent accepted the coffee invitation to go to the union for a cup of coffee. The paper-and-pencil instruments, then, reveal more prejudice than do superficial behaviors such as accepting a coffee invitation.

Campbell would argue that it is easier to reject a Negro in a paper-and-pencil test than in real life. But there is an additional factor: in some of the paper-and-pencil items the subjects are asked whether they would engage in extremely intimate social behaviors (for example, marry) but most of the behavioral tests involve behaviors that are quite formal or superficial. When superficial questions are asked on questionnaires (for example, cooperate in political campaign) the percentages that accept blacks are similar to the percentages obtained with the behavioral tests. In Naidoo's study there was no correlation between the attitude measures and agreement with the black confederate, which is consistent with Berg's (1966) finding that verbal racial attitudes did not predict agreement with a black or white confederate in a situation involving autokinetic judgments. The autokinetic effect occurs when a person is placed in a dark room in which there is a small source of light. Usually, the light is seen as moving. Since the light is stationary the extent of the illusion can be studied. Typically, subjects are strongly influenced by judgments made by other people in this ambiguous situation (Sherif, 1935). Berg expected a person to be influenced more by a white than by a black confederate, if the judgments of the two confederates were in conflict. The prediction was not supported by the evidence. In both the Naidoo and Berg studies the laboratory situation (agree with black or with white) involved no social norms, previous habits, or consequences. Therefore, the individual's attitude should have predicted the subject's behavior. The fact that it did not calls for an explanation.

One way of explaining such findings is to argue that the attitude was not relevant for the particular behavior. Attitudes toward blacks have the function of explaining an aspect of the social environment and guiding the subject's behavior in it. But an artificial laboratory situation may not have any relevance concerning this behavior. The presence of the black confederate may be viewed as purely accidental. By contrast, in laboratory studies where the attitude was relevant to the laboratory behavior a high degree of relationship was observed (Davis and Triandis, 1965).

Davis and Triandis (1965) obtained the attitudes of 220 white students toward Negroes and civil rights issues. They then invited groups of subjects, homogenous with respect to their attitudes, to participate in caucus groups in which they formulated positions concerning civil rights legislation. The caucus groups were then split, and pairs of white subjects negotiated civil rights laws with pairs of Negro confederates of the experimenters. The behavior of the white subjects was predicted from their attitudes with correlations of the order of .40.

Linn (1964/1965) did a study that further illuminated this point. He asked female Wisconsin students to respond to questionnaire items that involved the willingness to pose with a Negro of the opposite sex for pictures that were to be used for different purposes ranging from laboratory work to a nationwide campaign for racial integration. Four weeks later the students were asked by a fictitious psychological testing company to volunteer to help develop a semiprojective personality test. During an interview with the representatives of this company the subjects were asked to pose for pictures with a Negro. Linn found that many more subjects gave verbal responses indicating willingness to pose with Negroes than agreed to do what they said they would do. The subjects explained the inconsistencies in their behavior by suggesting that thoughts of the reaction of parents and "people back home" changed their mind when it actually came to posing for the pictures. The data suggest that one actually might act counter to his attitudes in order to conform to social pressures.

When such conflicts between attitudes and norms are not present, attitudes are reasonably good predictor of behavior, for instance, for consumer behavior (Katona, 1960) and voting behavior (Campbell, Converse, Miller, and Stokes, 1960). The behavior of mothers toward their children is also predictable from their attitudes toward permissiveness and punitiveness concerning their children's sex and aggression behavior (Sears, 1965).

As an example of a clear relationship, examine Fig. 3 which reproduces a graph from a study by Nisbett (1968). The figure shows the relationship between the evaluation of ice cream and the grams of ice cream eaten by three kinds of subjects—overweight, normal, and underweight. Observe that the relationship is close to linear for the normal and underweight subjects, and approaches an S curve for the overweight. The complexity of these curves, however, should warn us against assuming that the relationships between verbal and nonverbal attitudes will

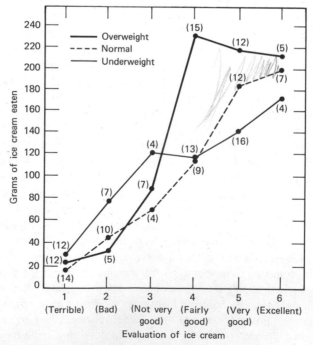

FIGURE 3.   Grams of ice cream as a function of ratings of its taste (numbers in parentheses denote *n* for each point).

always be linear. In fact, Nisbett's study shows that responsiveness to taste is a function of the weight of the subjects, and suggests that there may be individual differences in responsiveness to attitudes—some may respond more extremely, dependably, and reliably than others. This is a hypothesis that needs further study.

Another consideration is whether the person *can* do what is consistent with his behavior. A student might be very interested in football, but attendance at a particular game might be impossible because it takes place during his mother's birthday and he would like to visit his hometown during that weekend. Holman (1956) asked 253 students how worthwhile they considered attendance at football games. He also presented a list of games and asked them whether they intended to attend. Presumably, such predictions of attendance take into account whether the subject *can* attend. For example, if he does not have the money to go, he would indicate that he would not attend. After the football season was over, Holman asked his subjects to indicate the football games that they had attended. The correlation between the subject's prediction and attendance was .80; attitude and attendance correlated only .41; attitude and the subject's prediction correlated .33. The multiple correlation of actual attendance and attitudes plus the subject's prediction of attendance was .96. Thus 92 percent of the variance of attendance can be predicted, but attitudes contribute only 17 percent of the variance in a prediction of this kind. Behavior is situationally determined to a much larger extent than it is determined by attitudes. Notice that the subject's prediction of attendance in Holman's study is conceptually related to the behavioral component of attitudes much more than it is related to the other components. Similarly, the worthwhileness of attending football games is related to the affective component. From Holman's study we would expect that the behavioral component might be a better predictor of behavior than the other components. This was the case in the studies by Davis and Triandis (1965) and by Ostrom (1969). Ostrom obtained the attitudes of subjects toward the church and then related them to answers to questions concerning the number of times per year the respondent had attended church and the number of dollars he had given to the church. To obtain a behavioral measure of attitudinal interest, Ostrom allowed his subjects to tear a part of their questionnaire and hand it in with their name, supposedly to obtain "additional information about the church." Both the attendance and the giving-of-money questions and the tearing-of-the-questionnaire behavior were predicted from the behavioral component of attitudes somewhat better than they were predicted from the other two components.

STUDY QUESTIONS

1. What is the relationship between the three components of attitude?
2. What is the relationship between attitudes and behavior? Which variables moderate or modify this relationship?

SUGGESTED FURTHER READINGS

LaPiere (1934) in Fishbein (1967a); Linn (1964/1965), also in Rosnow and Robinson (1967). Fishbein (1967b).

Attitudes and Other Variables

A summary of the relationships among attitudes and other variables should be helpful to those who are interested in theoretical issues. Others may wish to skip this section.

Attitudes consist of three types of components: affect, cognition, and behavioral intentions. Behavioral intentions are related to overt action; but overt action also is dependent on habits, norms, and other attitudes than the attitudes that are directly relevant to the behavior toward a particular attitude object.

Habits get established through learning processes, such as the ones you learned in your introductory psychology course. Norms of social behavior depend on messages received from others. The ten commandments are an example of proscriptive norms. Some norms are ambiguous and others are very clear; some deal with behavior in relation to specific positions in a social structure and are called *roles,* and others apply to everyone in a given society; some prescriptive norms are very specific and tell you exactly what to do and others are quite general. Behavioral intentions depend on the way a person feels about the attitude object and also on the expectations of the person concerning what will happen if he behaves in certain ways. There is evidence that these expectations include ideas about the consequences of behavior; some of these consequences are pleasant and some are unpleasant. If you hit your boss, for instance, you might feel better and you probably will be fired. The behavioral intention will reflect both the expectations (How probable is it that you will feel good? How probable is it that you will be fired?) and the value of the outcomes (How pleasant does it feel to "feel good"? How unpleasant is it to be fired?). Some theorists have suggested that we should multiply each expectation with each value and sum all the products. The sum of these products would be reflected in the person's behavioral intentions. Of course, expectations depend on previous experiences and the confirmations of expectations on earlier occasions. The value of the outcomes will vary from person to person depending on the kinds of motives and values that the person has adopted as a result of his history of rewards and punishments.

Affect is acquired through classical conditioning, when a category is paired with pleasant or unpleasant events. Cognitive structures are acquired when categories are frequently paired with other categories or events in the particular environment in which a person grows up. Thus, the attitudes of a person involve (a) cognitive structures, (b) affect, and (c) behavioral intentions, all of which depend on the interaction of the individual and his environment. Furthermore, there is much evidence that these three types of components of attitude interact with each other and tend to become consistent; when one changes, say affect, it will tend to change the other two. Also, when a person behaves he changes his cognitions and affect to "bring them into line" with his behavior, so that most of the cognitive elements found in a person at a given moment of time tend to be consistent.

In addition, the person's attitudes depend on the kinds of anchors that he uses to understand his environment. We constantly compare ourselves with others who are in similar positions in the social structures in which we belong. If we bring to a situation "inputs" of a certain level (for example, education, experience, fame) we expect to get out of it "outputs" (rewards, prestige, salary) that are at least as high as the rewards received by others who bring comparable inputs to the situation (Adams, 1965). We are satisfied when our environment provides us with rewards that are comparable to the rewards received by comparable others. In short, our attitudes depend on the relationship of our perceived inputs and outputs relative to comparable others.

An illustration comes from the field of civil rights. Marx (1967) did a study based on public opinion data collected from a national sample of Negroes. He employed an 8-item index of "militancy" based on the responses of the subjects. For example, militants were those who (a) disagreed with the statement "Negroes who want to work hard can get ahead as easily as anyone else," (b) wanted to see more demonstrations, and (c) thought the government in Washington "was pushing integration too slow." This index was found to be quite valid, in a number of checks of its validity. Marx then investigated the characteristics of the militant Negroes. He found that the more militant had more education, were more likely to be employed, had higher prestige in their occupations, had more income, were higher in social class, tended to participate in social organizations to a larger extent, read more books and magazines, and were better informed than the less militant. These data suggest that *relative deprivation* was the most important determinant of militancy—the higher their social level, the more the Negroes were aware of what they were being deprived and the more militant they became. An uneducated black sharecropper in Mississippi does not feel as concerned about civil rights violations when he compares his fate with that of a white sharecropper as does a professional who compares his fate with that of white professionals.

This discussion has not yet covered all important points, hence, we use another example to illustrate the level of complexity of everyday experience and to show how the concepts we have just defined and interrelated help us to understand it.

The subject of our example is Mr. Brown, the skilled factory worker, in an almost all-white neighborhood, with whom we opened the chapter. We are concerned with his attitudes toward Mr. Smith—a black accountant who is married and has two children.

First, consider the complexity of the stimulus. The categories black, accountant, good family man, resident of my town, citizen of my state, an American, and many others apply to the stimulus. The subject's attitudes towards Mr. Smith must reflect, in part, his attitudes to each of these elements. In addition, the subject has *ideals,* for example, what is an ideal neighbor? Now, to the extent that Mr. Smith is perceived as being close to the ideal, he causes a positive affective state in our subject.

Our subject may be influenced by some of his neighbors, who believe that "Mr. Smith will cause property values to fall" and, hence, may have norms of unfriendly behavior toward Mr. Smith. For these neighbors, the beliefs about Mr. Smith imply certain behaviors and become concepts about proper behavior toward him. If our subject has a high tendency to comply to social norms (an individual differences variable), then he probably will behave in an unfriendly manner toward Mr. Smith, too. He, for example, may refuse to sign a petition in favor of a particular political action simply because Mr. Smith asked him to; he may not invite Mr. Smith to his house, he may caution his children about playing with Mr. Smith's children, etc. To the extent that he is conscious of his behavioral intentions, this may change his cognition of Mr. Smith, and also his affect.

Now suppose that Mr. Smith does something nice toward our subject. This will change the affect, via conditioning, and this will have an influence on the behavioral intentions and the cognitions. The final attitude will depend on the relative strength of the influences from the values, experiences, and norms, and it will reflect the way the category, Mr. Smith, is related to other categories.

The final section of this illustration concerns an example of what might happen if our subject were required to act toward Mr. Smith. Suppose that Mr. Smith sends our subject a delicious cake, which our subject eats and enjoys. This will change his affect, since he has a pleasant experience in connection with Mr. Smith. Then, assume that Mr. Smith invites our subject to dinner. The invitation itself will produce a further increment in positive affect and will require a reorganization of the cognitions to make them consistent with beliefs, such as "Mr. Smith is a nice neighbor." The changed affect and cognition will press the behavioral intentions toward change.

However, our subject who is an unskilled worker may not be in the habit of accepting dinner invitations. Once or twice in the past, when he accepted an invitation from one of his middle-class neighbors, he felt ill at ease, found very little to talk about with his professional hosts, was not sure of the proper behavior during the dinner, and was even less sure about how to reciprocate. These experiences also have produced expectations that dinner invitations are "painful and embarrassing experiences." Under such circumstances, our subject may decline Mr. Smith's invitation.

The example shows that attitude components may be inconsistent, at least temporarily, and that they are related to behavior in complex ways. Of course, once our subject has declined Mr. Smith's invitation he will find all kinds of reasons to change his cognition and affect to make them consistent with his behavior, so that the final state of affairs will be one in which the components of attitude will again be consistent.

SUMMARY

An attitude is an idea charged with emotion which predisposes a class of actions to a particular class of social situations. It has cognitive, affective, and behavioral components and several kinds of functions: It helps people to adjust, to defend their egos, to express their values, and to understand the world around them. The experiences of people determine their attitudes. As attitudes develop, cognitions become more differentiated, integrated, and organized, and affect and behavioral intentions become associated with these conditions. Attitude is not a necessary or sufficient cause of behavior, but it is a contributing cause. Behavior often changes attitudes, as people develop attitudes that justify their previous behavior. Behavior is the result not only of attitudes but also of norms, habits, and expectations about reinforcement.

PROJECT FOR ADVANCED STUDENTS

Write an essay on the relationship between attitudes and other variables. Begin by looking at a number of theoretical formulations, for instance, those of Rosenberg and Hovland (1960), Katz (1960), Triandis (1967, Fig. 2), Greenwald (1968b), and Ryan (1969). Consider the implications of dissonance theory (Chapter III), of research on the relationship between behavioral intentions and action (for example, Locke and Bryan, 1967) and examine the evidence that, when attitudes are kept constant, then norms control most of the variance of behavior (Sugar, 1967; Fendrich, 1967). Since there is much evidence that people will act in ways that are inconsistent with their attitudes when they are pressured to conform to norms requiring such action (Yarrow, 1958; Campbell and Yarrow, 1961), the theoretical formulation that you develop must allow for phenomena of this kind. Consider also the influence of cultural factors, such as variations in role perceptions (Triandis, Vassiliou and Nassiakou, 1968), and different social theories concerning "proper behavior" (Triandis and Vassiliou, 1967), which are reflected in various kinds of frequencies of behavior in different cultural environments (Feldman, 1968).

II

Attitude Measurement and Methodology

In the previous chapter the concept of attitudes was explained and an introduction to some of the major relationships between attitudes and other concepts was provided. In the present chapter the focus is on the measurement of attitudes.

Before further discussion, however, we should clarify what we mean by the *reliability* and *validity* of a measurement.

Reliability refers to the extent to which we obtain information that is free of measurement error. If an instrument is reliable, the information it provides is stable; also, similar results are obtained when the instrument is used more than once to measure the same thing. It should be clear that all measurement involves some error. When you use your bathroom scale, you are likely to err by as much as one pound. The more refined the measurement, the more likely it is that two repeated measures will not give the same scores. The same is true with attitude measurement. It is a relatively easy matter to establish whether or not Mr. Smith is in favor of school integration. However, if you want to know whether Mr. Smith is more strongly in favor of integration than Mr. Brown, who also supports it, this is a more difficult task, which requires a more reliable instrument.

Validity refers to the degree of relevance of the instrument; a perfectly reliable instrument may have no relevance to what we think it is measuring, but it may have relevance to some other phenomenon. For example, you may ask a student if he likes blacks, and you may believe that his responses indicate his prejudice or acceptance of blacks. Actually, his responses may be a very reliable indicator of what he thinks is the socially desirable answer, and not a measure of prejudice or acceptance of blacks.

In any discussion of attitude measurement it is important to consider the sampling of three aspects: (a) attitude objects, (b) response continua, (c) people. (a) Attitudes may be studied toward a vast array of objects—various types of people, political issues, religious concepts, the self, and so forth. (b) The people studied may be asked questions in a large number of ways. The responses that they give are in large part determined by the form of the question asked by the investigator. (c) Different people may be studied.

Although good sampling is important, it should not be made a fetish. There are situations in which sampling is not important. Consider, for instance, a researcher who wants to find out whether ten-year-olds are of the same height as sixteen-year-olds. Obviously, he can be rather sloppy in his sampling and still determine that sixteen-year-olds are taller than ten-year-olds. In sum, it is possible to obtain important and correct information without sampling, but it depends on the nature of the research question.

Much of the research done by social psychologists involves the assumption that they are discovering "general laws of social behavior," and if that assumption is defensible, the sampling of individuals is of little importance. Similarly, a researcher who is finding a general law of attitude change might discover it when he studies one type of attitude just as easily as when he studies another; hence, sampling of attitude objects may not be crucial. Nevertheless, the "wise" researcher selects two very diverse samples of people—for example, people from different cultures—or two very different attitude objects—for example, one central and another peripheral—and tests his hypothesis four times, instead of once, before he claims that his "laws" are truly general. Unfortunately, the limitations of resources have not made it possible for the majority of the researchers to be "wise."

The discovery of general laws may not require careful sampling, but the determination of the levels of different attitudes among different kinds of people certainly does. The Gallup Poll is an example of a survey intended to represent the total adult population of a particular country. Surveys are undertaken for different purposes, and the sample must fit the purpose. For example, in surveys designed to predict national elections the sample should be confined to eligible voters. Sampling the attitude objects, so that a complete and accurate picture of the particular issues under study can be obtained, is of equal importance. In addition, it is important to sample the questions, or forms of response, since different kinds of questions may result in different kinds of data. There is a need to get the same information by using different kinds of methods to check on the possibility that the data we obtain may simply reflect our methods of measurement (Campbell and Fiske, 1959).

Survey sampling is now a highly sophisticated and extremely technical subject (Kish, 1965). When properly carried out, it makes possible the precise estimation of the errors of measurement associated with a particular sample. The basic concept behind most good sampling is the idea of giving every individual in a given population an equal chance of appearing in the final sample. If we succeed in such an effort, then we can take the average score obtained from a sample and multiply it by an appropriate constant and get a close approximation of the score that we would have obtained had we included every person in a given population in our survey.

Suppose that you want to take a random sample of students in your college. Let's say your college has 1000 students. What you do is the following: first, you list all the students, by picking their names from the files of the registrar of your college. Then, you put a number between 1 and 1000 next to their names. Third, you go to your library and obtain a "table of random numbers." If your library does not have a table of this kind, use the *last* four digits of the telephone numbers in any page of your telephone book. Suppose that you come across number 0127, as you begin reading down the page. This means that you must select the student whose number was 127. You ignore the random numbers that do not fall between 0001 and 1000 and continue picking numbers until you have selected the total number of individuals you wish to have. If you want a 10 percent sample, you would select 100 names by following this process.

If you want to sample a large population, for example, the population of the United States, it is obvious that such an approach would be too expensive. There are several sampling designs that give results approximating those of random sampling. In *stratified* sampling, for instance, you select individuals so that the percentages of people with specific characteristics (age, sex, etc.) in your sample is the same as that found in the United States Census.

This approach avoids biases that might easily occur because certain kinds of people are more easy to study than others. In surveys it is easy, for instance, to miss women who are working, because they are less likely to be at home when the interviewers call. The interviewers may have trouble finding and communicating with certain members of the lower lower class, and they may meet only the butler when they call on the upper upper class subjects. Stratification, by forcing them to have the correct percentages of various types of people, makes such biases less likely.

Another type of sampling design is sometimes called *area probability sampling*. This sampling design begins with random sampling of areas of the country, and continues with the sampling of counties, dwelling units, and so forth, within each area. For example, a country is divided into 100 parts and all of them are sampled randomly. Then each part might again be divided and sampled and the process continued until all the people to be interviewed have been chosen in a random manner. At each stage of sampling a certain amount of error is introduced, but it is possible to calculate this error.

If the aim of the survey is to predict the voting behavior of a population, and the results were, say, 48 percent for and 52 percent against a candidate, with an error of 5 percent, then the sampling was too inaccurate for the purposes of the survey. But if the results were 75 percent for and 25 percent against the candidate, with the same error, they would indicate with considerable certainty that the candidate would be elected. It is possible to reduce the size of the error by increasing the size of the sample.

PROJECT FOR ADVANCED STUDENTS

If you like mathematics and statistics, you may want to write a paper on sampling. Skim through the book by Kish (1965) to get an idea of what is involved and define a small topic that you can cover in a reasonably short time.

SPECIAL PROJECT FOR THIS CHAPTER

The area of attitude measurement is probably the most solid accomplishment of social psychologists. However, learning about it can be dull, unless you *do* something once in a while. For this chapter only, then, we shall suggest special projects that we recommend be done as you read the chapter. We assume that you can use your roommates, classmates, or members of your family, as subjects in these studies.

First project: Draw a random sample.

The Measurement of the Cognitive Component

In studying the cognitive component we can ask a number of questions: What categories does the subject use? What events, stimuli, or experiences are classified in each category? What criteria are used in deciding how to categorize an event or stimulus?

The discovery of the criterial attributes used by people in categorizing experience is an important aspect of psychology. In psychophysics, the relationships between various physical stimuli and the subjects' judgments can be determined. Most of the methods of psychophysics, which are usually covered in an introductory course in psychology, also can be used, with some modification, to study social stimuli, such as *people*. In psychophysics we learn about the correspondence between attributes of the physical stimulus, such as intensity of sound, and psychological reactions, such as judgments of loudness. Analogously, we can vary the behavior of a person on a single dimension of stimulation and can study the reactions of subjects to this behavior. If we do an experiment in which a person speaks at different levels of intensity, and we ask subjects to judge the extent to which he is introverted or extroverted—for example, moral or immoral, upper class or lower class—we are establishing relationships that can be used in understanding social perception. If we use a large number of judgmental continua and find that the responses of the subjects are highly intercorrelated, we can conclude that the subjects employ a limited number of criterial attributes to make their judgments.

One method that is very useful in reducing many observations to a few relationships is factor analysis.

An adequate explanation of factor analysis requires too long a diversion from the present discussion. However, the reader may acquire "a feel for it" by a simple example. Suppose that we obtain the judgments of several subjects when they react to a large number of different people on rating scales referring to whether they would (1) obey, (2) admire, (3) marry, or (4) date the particular people. It is quite likely that when the subjects indicate they would *obey* a person they would also indicate that they would *admire* this person. This would lead to a correlation between the *obey* and the *admire* ratings. The correlation is expressed by a so-called "correlation coefficient," which is an index that may vary from −1.00 to 1.00. Thus, the correlation between *obey* and *admire* may be, say, .80. Now, the fact that a person *obeys* another does not mean that he would be willing to *marry* this other person. On the contrary, there may be a tendency for a reverse relationship between *obeying* and *marrying*, which would then be expressed as a slightly negative correlation coefficient.

Table 1   Hypothetical Correlations among Four Social Behaviors

	Obey	Admire	Marry	Date
Obey	1.00	.80	−.15	−.05
Admire		1.00	.20	.30
Marry			1.00	.90
Date				1.00

Hypothetical Factors obtained from Such Correlations

	Factor I	Factor II
Obey	.95	.05
Admire	.98	.00
Marry	−.05	.90
Date	.05	.95

Table 1 shows the hypothetical correlation coefficients between these four scales. Inspection of this table reveals that the behaviors *obey* and *admire* co-vary; the behaviors *date* and *marry* co-vary; but the behaviors *obey* and *admire* are not particularly related to the behaviors *marry* and *date*. This can be explained as follows: there is a factor of **Respect** that is independent from **Marital Acceptance**. The reason the two are independent is simply that there are many people in the world that a person may respect but whom he might not accept as marital partners because they belong to the "wrong" sex, age, race, etc. Conversely, a person may marry another even though he does not respect him or her (particularly in cultures having arranged marriages). Knowing that a person would obey another, therefore, does not help us predict his marital acceptance of this other; and, conversely, knowing the marital acceptance does not help us predict the respect.

Factor analysis extracts the dimensions that "underlie" a set of observed relationships. Table 1 also shows the way that the factors might appear after the factor analysis has been completed. Factor I is the Respect factor and is closely related to obey and admire. Moreover, Factor II is the Marital Acceptance factor and is closely related to marry and date. These factors can be conceived as the hypothetical variables that underlie the set of relationships. It is easy to understand that factor analysis reduces the complexity of a set of observations by providing hypothetical variables (the factors) that "explain" the observed relationships in a simpler manner. In the present example, instead of four variables there are only two, after the factor analysis.

It should not be assumed that factors have some kind of "eternal truth in them." Actually, in some respects, they are like *averages*; they simply reflect the data that resulted in particular correlation patterns. If the data are poor, the factors are poor.

It is very important to sample adequately the variables and the subjects in any factor analytic investigation. Failure to do so will result in a distorted and incorrect representation of the dimensions underlying a particular study. It is also important to repeat the study several times, with different populations of subjects, different variables measuring the same domain, and under various conditions. Once this has been done, one usually discovers factors that remain invariant across samples of questions, variables, and people. These factors probably do represent the basic dimensions underlying a domain.

This brief introduction to factor analysis is extremely inadequate for an understanding of the procedures. A more extended, yet easy to follow, description can be found in Guilford (1954). A complete description, but one that is difficult to follow without some mathematical sophistication, is given in Harman (1967).

Factor analysis is one way in which to discover the criterial attributes used by a group of people to categorize some aspects of experience. In order to collect data that can be subjected to an analysis of this kind, it is important to have a good sample of stimuli of the type whose attributes we wish to discover and a good sample of response continua.

There is a problem concerning how we might develop an adequate sample of response continua. One way to develop good samples of response continua would be to ask subjects to give their associations to lists of the stimuli, or concepts, we wish to study. For example, if we wish to find what attributes people use in thinking about others, we can present person stimuli and ask people to give us whatever characteristics come to mind (for example, Zajonc, 1960). However, this approach is likely to give a very diffuse sample of response continua.

A more focused approach can be used by adapting a procedure used by Kelly (1955). A particular domain of attitude objects—people, jobs, nations, and so forth, can be explored, a sample of concepts from this domain constituting the basic input. For example, 20 nations might be selected in order to study the cognitive components of a subject concerning international attitudes. Triads of these stimuli are formed, and the subject is asked to indicate which of the three stimuli is different from the other two and why. Given America, Brazil, and Great Britain one subject might pick America because it is "stronger" than the other two, another might pick Brazil because it is "less developed" than the other two, and a third subject might pick Great Britain because it is "smaller" than the other two. When a large number of such triads is presented, it is possible to obtain a long list of characteristics that discriminate one stimulus from the others.

The researcher then forms a grid, the columns of which are the stimuli, and the rows of which are the characteristics given by the subject. He then can ask the subject to check for every stimulus the characteristics that apply to it. The researcher can look at similarities in response patterns both among the columns and among the rows. These similarities reveal broad categories. For example, the subject might respond rather similarly to a number of countries and the researcher may discover that all these countries belong to NATO. This would indicate that this subject employs "membership in NATO" as one of his categories in thinking about nations.

SPECIAL PROJECT

Make a list of six people, jobs, or nations, whichever you prefer. Form the 20 triads that are possible.

For every triad, pick one member who you think is different from the other two and state the characteristic that makes a difference. Ask someone else to do this too, and compare the results. The greater the number of similar characteristics that you and this other person generate, the more cognitively similar you are with this person. This is a way to determine whether you are operating "on the same wave-length" with some other person concerning a particular domain of meaning.

PROJECTS FOR ADVANCED STUDENTS

1. Write a paper on the influence of group membership on the attributes that, generally, are used by people in thinking about concepts in a given domain of meaning. Examine Triandis (1959) to find out how different attributes are used by managers, clerks, and workers in thinking about jobs and people in industry; examine Triandis (1960c) to learn how these attributes are structured.

2. Write an essay on the contributions that multidimensional scaling can make in the area of attitude measurement. Read Torgerson (1958), Messick (1956), Abelson (1955), and Tucker (1964). The last three are reproduced in Fishbein (1967a). Give an example from a recent study by Robinson and Hefner (1967).

3. Explain how facet analysis can be used to confirm that the criterial attributes assumed to exist in a certain attitude domain do, in fact, operate as expected. Read Guttman (1959), and Foa (1965).

4. Explain how feature analysis can be used to confirm that the criterial attributes assumed to exist in a certain attitude domain do, in fact, operate as expected. Read Osgood (1968).

5. Write a paper on some attempts to measure the complexity of the cognitive component of attitudes. In particular, summarize the work of Zajonc (1960c), Scott (1966), and Rosenberg (1956).

Some more ways to measure the cognitive component. Another way to study the cognitive component involves the elicitation of associations produced by the attitude object. However, as already mentioned, these associations are often too diffuse (for example, the stimulus *Night* elicits the association *Day*) to be valuable in attitude research. Various forms of "controlled associations" are more useful.

Triandis and his associates (Davis and Triandis, 1965; Triandis, Kilty, Shanmugam, Tanaka, and Vassiliou, 1968) have developed a number of such techniques.

Consider the nature of the associations of an attitude object with other concepts. The attitude object CIVIL RIGHTS LAWS, for example, may be characterized by its connections to other laws, the various political points of view, and also to a set of characteristics. For example, one possible characteristic of these laws is that they are controversial. Different people may find different strengths in the bond between the concepts CIVIL RIGHTS LAWS and CONTROVERSIAL. Those who find a close connection would have a cognitive component for CIVIL RIGHTS LAWS that *implies* the concept CONTROVERSIAL. It is clear that different people may have different concepts associated with a particular attitude object. Davis and Triandis (1965) employed a procedure that they called the "implicative meaning method" for the measurement of the cognitive component. It presents attitude objects (for example, Integrated Housing) and the implications of such objects. Figure 4 shows an example.

```
┌──────────────────────────────────────────────────────────────────┐
│  If you have INTEGRATED HOUSING then you have:                     │
│  Justice                                                           │
│  improbable ___ ___ ___ ___ ___ ___ ___  probable                  │
│  Slums                                                             │
│  improbable ___ ___ ___ ___ ___ ___ ___  probable                  │
│  More Crime                                                        │
│  improbable ___ ___ ___ ___ ___ ___ ___  probable                  │
│  Better Relations between the Races                                │
│  improbable ___ ___ ___ ___ ___ ___ ___  probable                  │
│                                                                    │
│  FIGURE 4.     Some items from an implicative meaning questionnaire.│
└──────────────────────────────────────────────────────────────────┘
```

A generalization of this approach is the antecedent-consequent meaning method (Triandis et al., 1968). If the researcher wishes to study a subject's cognitive component with respect to certain attitude objects (abstract concepts), such as CRIME, FREEDOM, or DEMOCRACY, the researcher begins by asking him to fill in the following type of sentences: "If you have . . . then you have CRIME," or "If you have . . . then you have DEMOCRACY." These fill-ins constitute the antecedents of CRIME or DEMOCRACY. Similarly, he can ask, "If you have CRIME, then you have. . . ." or "If you have DEMOCRACY, then you have. . . ." Such fill-ins constitute the consequents of these concepts.

If comparisons among subjects are desired, a more elaborate procedure is used. (a) The antecedents and consequents of the concepts are obtained from a sample of subjects similar to the subjects that are to be compared. (b) The most frequent antecedents and consequents are listed in a questionnaire of the form shown in

Table 2. (c) The subjects then are asked to select one of 5 antecedents and one of 5 consequents in each set. Each word is paired in 30 or more sets of the kind shown in Table 2. The sets repeat the antecedents or consequents in different contexts and in such a way that a person may be able to choose a particular antecedent or consequent several times. The number of times an antecedent or consequent is chosen is a measure of its association with the abstract concept under study.

SPECIAL PROJECT

Give the items shown in Table 2 to yourself and to some other person. Did you agree in picking the antecedent and the consequent? If not, why not?

Table 2.   Example of Item for Antecedent Meaning Study

"If you have . . . , then you have FREEDOM"
  Strength
  The Constitution
  Money
  Patriotism
  Restrictions

Example of Item for Consequent Meaning Study

"If you have FREEDOM, then you have . . . ."
  Public disorder
  Life
  Abuse
  Educational facilities
  Irresponsibility

Final Comment on Measures of the Cognitive Component

We have presented a number of different approaches that measure different aspects of the cognitive component of attitudes. Do these approaches give the same results? We do not know. As far as we know they are equally valuable. Their applicability, also, depends on how much we know about a particular set of attitude objects. For example, if we do not know what the attributes might be, it is appropriate to use factor analysis or multidimensional scaling; if we do have a hypothesis about what they might be, it is appropriate to use facet or feature analysis. Future research will tell us whether one is better than the others and how they are related to each other. One point that we made previously can be stressed here. In psychological measurement we often get data that reflect our methods of measurement instead of the specific characteristics of attitude objects. One way to deal with this problem is to measure a theoretical construct in several different ways; if we get consistent results across methods, we can be reasonably certain that what we obtained is not an artifact of our methods of measurement. Scott (1969) used a number of different ways to measure cognitive structure, and he found that the correlations among his measures were consistently between .25 and .30. These correlations are typical in psychological research and reflect acceptable concurrent validity for the measures. A good deal of future research on the measurement of attitude structure is likely to use some of the procedures outlined in the previous section.

PROJECTS FOR ADVANCED STUDENTS

Study the original publications quoted in the text with respect to *one* of the approaches for the measurement of cognitive structure. Write a paper outlining the method in detail and give examples of its application, including evidence concerning its reliability and validity.

STUDY QUESTIONS

1. Define: the reliability of an attitude scale; the validity of an attitude scale.
2. What method did Katz and Braly use to study national and racial stereotypes?
3. What is the difference between the implicative meaning and the antecedent/consequent meaning method of measurement of the cognitive component of attitudes.
4. What is multidimensional measurement?

SUGGESTED FURTHER READINGS

Katz and Braly (1933), Messick (1956), Abelson (1955), Tucker (1964) all in Fishbein (1967a).
Also "A consideration of beliefs and their role in attitude measurement" by Fishbein and Fishbein and Raven (1962) both in Fishbein (1967a).

The Measurement of the Affective Component

The most direct measurement of the affective component involves the utilization of physiological procedures. However, most of the standardized methods of measurement use verbal responses and attempt to measure "the degree of positive or negative affect associated with some psychological object" (Thurstone, 1931). The present section describes these procedures as well as Osgood's Semantic Differential, which is a general method for measuring the connotations of concepts.

Physiological Measures

Westie and DeFleur (1959) showed that prejudiced persons respond differently from unprejudiced persons when they are shown pictures of whites and Negroes in a variety of social situations. They studied the galvanic skin resistance (a physiological measure of arousal), finger pulse, and the duration and amplitude of the heartbeat.

Cooper (1959) reviewed studies that obtained ratings of 20 ethnic groups on six graded preference categories, such as "like intensely," "dislike intensely." Derogatory statements presented in association with the best liked ethnic groups and complementary statements associated with the least liked, showed significantly larger Galvanic Skin Responses than neutral statements. In another study, Cooper obtained the Galvanic Skin Responses first and predicted the preference ranking of nine national groups. A high positive rank-order correlation of .82 was obtained between the rankings of the ethnic groups according to the skin response and the preference response.

Porier and Lott (1967) found that the differences between Galvanic Skin Responses obtained in the presence of Negro and white assistants of the experimenter correlated with the E Scale, a verbal measure of the generalized prejudice of the respondents. In other words, highly prejudiced individuals showed a greater difference in their GSR responses to Negro than to white experimental assistants, than did the nonprejudiced respondents.

PROJECT FOR ADVANCED STUDENTS

Write a selective review of the literature on physiological measures of arousal and attitude. There are a number of techniques, not mentioned above, that appear quite promising. In particular, examine the paper by Hess and Polt (1960) on measuring the size of the pupil to obtain an index of the interest value of visual stimuli. A good place to start your reading is Shapiro and Crider (1969).

Standardized Verbal Specific Methods

This is by far the most popular method of attitude measurement. Edwards (1957a) has summarized the classic approaches to this type of measurement, which were developed by Thurstone (1928), Likert (1932), Guttman (1944), and Edwards and Kilpatrick (1948).

All of these procedures use statements, which are anything that can be said about an attitude object. These statements may be obtained from newspaper editorials, magazines, books, and other materials that deal with the attitude object; or a group of friends may be asked to do some "brain storming" and think of as many statements as possible that refer to the attitude object. Once a pool of these statements has been collected, they should be subjected to screening. Factual, ambiguous, confusing, and excessively long statements should be eliminated. Edwards (1957a, pp. 13 to 14) has provided the following informal criteria for attitude statements:

1. Avoid statements that refer to the past rather than to the present.
2. Avoid statements that are factual or capable of being interpreted as factual.
3. Avoid statements that may be interpreted in more than one way.
4. Avoid statements that are irrelevant to the psychological object under consideration.
5. Avoid statements that are likely to be endorsed by almost everyone or no one.
6. Select statements that are believed to cover the entire range of the affective scale of interest.
7. Keep the language of the statements simple, clear, and direct.
8. Statements should be short, rarely exceeding 20 words.
9. Each statement should contain only one complete thought.
10. Avoid universals such as *all, always, none, never.*
11. Words such as *only, just, merely* . . . should be used with care and moderation in writing statements.
12. Whenever possible, statements should be in the form of simple sentences, rather than compound or complex sentences.
13. Avoid the use of words that may not be understood . . . .
14. Avoid the use of double negatives.

SPECIAL PROJECT

Try to think of 20 attitude statements that refer to a particular attitude object that interests you. Criticize your statements by checking to determine if they meet the above 14 criteria.

Before we discuss the standardized procedures we must make a brief comment on the different kinds of scales that we have in measurement. There are basically four types of scales. The crudest scales are *nominal* scales. These involve only a categorization of some object in two or more classes. For example, when we classify men and women into two categories and examine their answers to a question, for which there is only a *yes* or *no* answer, we relate two nominal scales to each other. Notice that with a nominal scale, order is unimportant and it makes no difference whether we write Men-Women or Women-Men. The next scale is *ordinal* and, as the name indicates, this scale is based on order. If answers to our question can be classified as *Yes, No,* and *Undecided,* the undecided logically belong between the Yes-people and the No-people.

Although an ordinal scale says something about the order of the objects, it does not say anything about the distance between them. For example, suppose you ask people to respond with the categories (a) strongly agree, (b) agree, (c) undecided, (d) disagree, and (e) strongly disagree, to a particular question. The distances between these five response categories may be quite unequal. The distance between "strongly agree" and "agree" might be much larger, for instance, than the distance between "agree" and "undecided." In the case of an *interval* scale, we *do* know the distances. However, the interval scale does *not* allow us to say whether one point on it is twice as high (or large) as another. For that kind of statement we need a scale that has a true zero. A *ratio* scale not only has equal intervals but also a true zero. When you measure the height of people you have a true zero, so you can say that Mr. Smith is twice as tall as his son.

In attitude measurement, some scales are more reliable than others; some are more valid for certain purposes; some are nominal scales, ordinal scales; some are interval scales; and, finally, attitude scales can be constructed with a true zero, thus obtaining ratio scales.

The numbers that we obtain from each kind of scale can be transformed according to certain rules. The rules of transformation that are correct for one kind of scale are not the same as the rules that are correct for another. In general, we can do all transformations required for statistical tests if we have ratio or interval scales; if we have nominal or ordinal scales we must use another set of rules. However, recent evidence suggests that many of the statistical tests that assume interval or ratio scales can also be used with ordinal scales. As Adams, Fagot, and Robinson (1965) have pointed out, it is usually defensible to use most statistical tests with ordinal measurements but the statements that we can make after the use of such tests must take into consideration the nature of the scales that were used. Great caution is needed in what we say about our statistical tests, if the measurement scales were not interval or ratio scales.

Thurstone has provided at least three methods of attitude scaling: paired comparisons, equal appearing intervals, and successive intervals. The first and last of these methods results in an interval scale, but the method of equal appearing intervals results in only an ordinal scale.

Likert's and Guttman's procedures result in ordinal scales that are close approximations to interval scales, and the Edwards and Kilpatrick procedure results in interval scales. Thurstone and Jones (1957) have developed a procedure that results in ratio scales.

A technical discussion of these procedures is provided by Edwards (1957a). In our present introductory discussion we shall describe them only in nontechnical and nonrigorous ways.

The basic principles behind Thurstonian attitude measurement are found in Thurstone's (1927a, 1927b) *law of comparative judgment*, which provides a rationale for psychological measurement. [For a technical exposition of this law, refer to Edwards (1957a, pp. 20-28).] The three Thurstone methods mentioned above, employ subjects who act as judges of the relative favorableness of attitude statements. The judgments made by these subjects are treated statistically to obtain "scale values" for the attitude statements. Then the already scaled statements are presented to the subjects whose attitude is to be assessed.

The Method of Paired Comparison. Given n attitude statements, there are $n(n-1)/2$ possible pairs of statements. If these pairs of statements are given to 100 individuals, all of whom judge which member of each pair is the more favorable to an attitude object, a set of frequencies is obtained that corresponds to the number of times each statement is judged as more favorable than the others. Now consider two statements A and B. If the degree of favorability of these statements toward the attitude object is about equal, frequency with which A is judged as more favorable than B and B is judged as more favorable than A will be approximately equal. The greater the distance between A and B on the favorableness continuum, the more the frequencies of the judgments "A is more favorable than B" and "B is more favorable than A" will be different from each other. For example, to take the extreme case when A and B are items of description that are positive and negative toward the attitude object; A will be viewed as more favorable 100 percent of the time and B as more favorable zero percent of the time. Thus, the frequencies of the favorableness judgments (A better than B, B better than A) can be used as indexes of the distance between two statements on the psychological continuum.

By using information concerning such judgments of which item is more favorable, we can obtain a set of numbers that represent the position of the n statements on the psychological continuum by the following simple arithmetic: the frequencies first are converted into probabilities, by dividing the frequencies by the number of judges. The probabilities are then converted to a statistic called z, by looking up a table that relates probabilities to z values. The method results in n estimates of the position of each of the statements. Estimates then are averaged to obtain the mean "value" of the statement on the particular attitude continuum. The most negative statement is arbitrarily given the value .000; the remaining attitude statements then will have positive values; and the values are on an interval scale. Now 10 to 15 statements are selected that have values at approximately equal intervals.

These statements can be presented in a random order to the people we wish to study. They might then be asked to read the statements and to check the three statements that best express how they feel about the particular issue. Finally, the average of the scale values of these three statements can be computed. This number represents the attitude of the particular individual, expressed in psychological units identical to those used by the judges.

The Method of Equal Appearing Intervals. In this method judges are asked to place the n attitude statements in 11 piles, ordered according to their degree of favorableness to the attitude object. The judges are asked to consider the piles as equally distant from each other, so that intervals between the piles are equal *appearing* intervals. For each of the n statements we obtain a distribution of judgments from the judges. An important purpose is to eliminate "unsatisfactory" items (statements). If the distribution of judgments concerning a statement shows too much dispersion, or is bi-modal, this indicates that the statement is ambiguous (because it is seen by different judges quite differently), and it is eliminated from further consideration. For the remaining statements, the median of the distribution of the judgments can be used as the estimate of their scale value.

Two examples of the kinds of items that might be obtained with this procedure and their corresponding scale values will further illustrate this method. Thurstone and Chave (1929) developed a scale for the measurement of attitudes toward the church, which included the following items. An extremely positive item: "I believe the church is the greatest institution in America today." A rather positive item: "When I go to church I enjoy a fine ritual service with good music." A neutral item: "I like the ceremonies of my church but do not miss them much when I stay away." A rather negative item: "I feel the need for religion but do not find what I want in any one church." An extremely negative item: "I think the church is a parasite on society."

The other example is a scale that measures the "potability of water," developed by Dillehay, Bruvold, and Siegal (1967). Selected adjectives describing water are shown in Table 3. The adjectives were selected to differ by about .5 to 1.0 scale units from each other, so that the reader can appreciate the meaning of these scale units. The scale may be used differently by various experimenters. For example, the subject may be given a drink of water and asked to check the adjectives that best describe it. He will typically want to check two or three of these adjectives (say, tasty, desirable, and enjoyable) in which case his affect toward this kind of water would be the average of the scale values of these three adjectives (in the example, 8.42).

The method of equal appearing intervals results in an ordinal scale. Strictly speaking, one should not average numbers obtained from those scales because their

Table 3   Scale Values of an Adjective Taste Scale, Developed by Dillehay, Bruvold, and Siegel (1967)

Scale Value	Adjective
1.24	horrible
1.78	unfit
2.11	bad
2.46	undesirable
3.14	poor
3.54	inferior
4.25	below par
4.92	can be tolerated
5.95	passable
6.26	OK
7.94	likable
8.63	tasty
9.19	desirable
9.45	enjoyable
10.00	delightful
10.57	delicious

intervals are unknown. On the other hand, if all you want to know is the rank order of individuals on an attitude scale continuum, that is, you only care to know if Mr. A is more favorable toward an attitude object than Mr. B, who is more favorable than Mr. C, it is all right to use this scale. If you want to know also the *degree of difference* between these three people, then you must have an interval scale. The successive intervals method results in such an interval scale.

The Method of Successive Intervals. This method first requires all the steps used by the judges in the method of equal appearing intervals. It involves an additional step, which employs the frequencies of assignment of the *n* statements to the 11 categories as the basis for estimating the distances between the 11 piles. The obtained scale values are on an interval scale, and the statements then may be given to individuals whose attitudes we wish to study. The individuals then are asked to check the three statements which most represent their attitudinal positions. The average value of the three checked statements is the individual's attitude.

Thus, in the three methods that have just been discussed (paired comparison, equal appearing intervals, and successive intervals), judges are employed to obtain the scale values of a set of 10 to 15 attitude statements from an original sample of about 100 statements. The 10 to 15 statements, with values that span the entire attitude continuum, are then given to a sample of individuals whose attitudes we wish to study. Each individual chooses three statements that reflect his attitude, and the average value of these statements is used as a measure of the individual's attitude.

Assumption of the Thurstone Methods. The basic assumption of the Thurstone methods that are commonly used is that the values obtained from one sample of judges will be the same as the values obtained from another sample of judges. It has been shown that as long as the judges are not extremists on the particular attitude continuum, this assumption is generally safe. On the other hand, with judges who are extreme or very ego involved, this assumption is incorrect (Ager and Dawes, 1965). Hovland and Sherif (1952) showed that judges who are deeply involved show displacements in the values of the attitude statements. Specifically, highly favorable judges place only a few highly favorable statements in the favorable piles; they displace the remaining statements toward the unfavorable side of the continuum.

PROJECT FOR ADVANCED STUDENTS

The effects of attitude on the discrimination of opinion statements has generated a considerable literature that you could review as a special project. Read in addition to Hovland and Sherif (1952), Ostrom (1966), Upshaw (1962, 1965), and Koslin and Pargament (1969).

SPECIAL PROJECT

Select a sample of liquids, for instance, tap water with different concentrations of salt or sugar, and ask your friends to use one of the adjectives of the Taste Scale to describe each cup. Is there a relationship between the amounts of salt or sugar that you used in each cup and the scale values of the adjectives?

The Method of Summated Ratings. This method was developed by Likert (1932) and has the advantage that it does not require the use of judges. Thus, attitude statements are given a value by a statistical procedure that employs the data from the sample of persons whose attitudes are being studied.

The Likert method begins with n statements which are given to the sample of individuals who are to be studied. Five response alternatives are allowed: (a) strongly agree, (b) agree, (c) uncertain, (d) disagree, and (e) strongly disagree. The responses of the individuals are first scored "a priori," using the investigator's best judgment of whether the statement is positive or negative toward the attitude object. On the basis of this preliminary scoring, the individuals are ordered from more favorable to least favorable toward the attitude object. Following this step, the most favorable 25 percent and the least favorable 25 percent of the individuals are separated so that they constitute a favorable and an unfavorable group. Such groups should be reasonably pure and should consist of individuals who know where they stand in relation to an attitude object. The responses of the favorable to each attitude statement are compared to the responses of those who are unfavorable. If the attitude statement is good, it will discriminate between the two groups of persons. A statistical test is used to determine whether the responses of the favorable are significantly different from the responses of the unfavorable. Those statements that do discriminate then are used to measure the attitudes of the entire group of individuals.

We must point out here that when one reads in the literature that a researcher has used a "Likert-type item" or "Likert-scale" this does not necessarily mean that he has done an *item analysis,* as described above. Unfortunately, too many researchers are using short-cuts and publish studies that have not been thoroughly analyzed. It is important to read the fine print to determine what they actually have done.

Scalogram Analysis. This is a procedure developed by Guttman (1944) to check on the unidimensionality of a set of statements. Guttman's approach involves the development of a different kind of scale from the scales discussed thus far. This scale has interesting properties, which are not claimed by those who developed the other kinds of scales.

As an example of a scale that has desirable properties, consider a scale that measures weight. If you know that a person weighs 200 pounds, you know at once that he weighs more than one who weighs 180, one who weighs 160, etc. In other words, if you know that a person balances a 200-pound weight, on a balance scale, you need not check to see if he also balances a 180- or a 160-pound weight. Now, if you have a Guttman scale, and you know that a person endorsed a very favorable item, you need not check whether he endorsed a less favorable one; it follows from the nature of the scale that he would endorse the less favorable.

Suppose now that you have some items that constitute a scale of this kind. Then, by asking an individual to respond by agreeing or disagreeing with each of these items, you can place him unambiguously on this scale, the same way that, if you ask a person who weighs 175 pounds, "Do you weigh more than 200, 180, 160 pounds?" and you get the answers, "No," "No," "Yes," you can place him in the interval between 160 and 180 without asking more questions.

If you have a set of attitude statements that form a Guttman scale, an individual who obtains a higher rank (or score) than another individual, must rank just as high or higher than the other individual on *every* one of his answers. To go back to our example, a person weighing 185 pounds would answer the questions of the previous paragraph with "No," "Yes," "Yes"; it is clear that in no case can the heavier person give a No answer to the question "Do you weigh more than. . .?" and the lighter person give a Yes.

Assume now that you have five attitude statements that span the full attitude continuum and five individuals that also span the full attitude continuum. If you rank-order the statements and the individuals so that they are ordered from the most positive to the most negative, you will obtain a pattern of responses (assuming that the individuals are perfectly consistent) like the one shown in Table 4. A parallelogram of "Yes" responses can be seen. The Guttman technique involves the analysis of the responses of approximately 100 individuals to a set of attitude statements. Until the minimum number of inconsistent judgments is obtained, there is a trial-and-error change of the orders of both the persons and the attitude statements. An inconsistent judgment occurs when a favorable person, who has accepted several highly favorable statements, also accepts a statement that is assumed to be unfavorable. Statements that produce too many inconsistent judgments are assumed to belong to a different continuum from that of the majority of the statements, and they are therefore eliminated from further consideration.

The elimination of statements results in a set of about one-half dozen statements that give very few (less than 10 percent) inconsistent answers. Once this set of statements has been obtained, it constitutes the scale. Subjects now can be asked to

Table 4 Theoretical Perfect Response Pattern of Five Individuals to Five Attitude Statements

Attitude Statements:	Very Favorable	Favorable	Indifferent	Unfavorable	Very Unfavorable
The individuals:					
Very pro	yes	yes	no	no	no
Just pro	no	yes	yes	no	no
Indifferent	no	yes	yes	yes	no
Somewhat anti	no	no	yes	yes	no
Very anti	no	no	no	yes	yes

respond to these items by agreeing or disagreeing, and it is possible to place them unambiguously on the attitude continuum.

The Scale Discrimination Technique. The equal appearing interval, summated ratings, and scalogram analysis techniques may be considered as three procedures that accomplish a similar task. The similar task is the elimination of attitude statements that are inappropriate or ineffective. The three procedures use three different criteria for the elimination of statements. The equal intervals procedure eliminates those statements that are not judged consistently and are, in other words, ambiguous. The summated ratings procedure eliminates those statements that do not discriminate between favorable and unfavorable individuals. The scalogram analysis eliminates those statements that do not fall on an unidimensional continuum. The scale discrimination technique of Edwards and Kilpatrick (1948) uses all three of the previously mentioned techniques, thus eliminating statements according to three criteria. The resulting statements should be neither ambiguous nor poor in discrimination and should fall on a unidimensional continuum. One also could use other criteria for the elimination of items. Thurstone used the *relevance* criterion which he obtained by checking how the favorable and unfavorable individuals responded to each item, as is done by Likert. In other words, one could use any combination of the above methods for the elimination of unsatisfactory items.

Discussion of above Methods. A sophisticated comparison of the various methods mentioned may be found in Green (1954) and Scott (1969). Edwards (1957a) also discusses the advantages and disadvantages of the methods in some detail. In this present section, we only point out that the Thurstone technique makes assumptions that differ from the assumptions of the Likert and Guttman techniques in , at least, two important respects:

1. The response characteristics of the items are assumed to be different. Technically speaking, Thurstone items are assumed to be noncumulative (or nonmonotonic); Guttman items are assumed to be cumulative (or monotonic). Suppose that a subject accepts a favorable item on a Thurstone scale; he is not assumed to be acting inconsistently if he rejects a *less* favorable item. On the other hand, the Guttman procedure assumes that the acceptance of an extremely favorable item implies the acceptance of the less favorable items and a rejection of only the indifferent and unfavorable items. The work of Sherif and Hovland (1961) and Sherif and Sherif (1964) on the latitudes of acceptance and rejection of items suggests that the Thurstone assumption is more realistic than the other assumption. In fact, the Sherifs have shown that highly involved (for example, militantly pro-civil rights) subjects reject mildly favorable items (for example, "There should be more discussions between white and Negro leaders") and accept only extremely favorable statements.

2. The Thurstone procedure requires the use of judges, but the other procedures do not. There are disadvantages in the use of judges: (a) We know that unless the judges are moderate in their degree of involvement, their judgments lead to

distorted scale values. (b) It is unclear how much consensus there should be among the judges to establish a satisfactory location for a test item. (c) The subjects and the judges have different tasks. The subjects indicate agreement with the item; the judges locate the item on a judgmental dimension. That sort of shift in the nature of the task may well introduce measurement errors.

It is clear, from the above, that the arguments under (1) favor the Thurstone procedure and that the arguments under (2) favor the Likert or Guttman procedures.

The reliability and validity of the three methods of measurement, just discussed, is usually quite comparable, although in some studies (for example, Poppleton and Pilkington, 1964; Tittle and Hill, 1967) the Likert method of scoring was slightly superior. The validity of the measures, based on criteria of reported behaviors, as used by Poppleton and Pilkington, seems to reflect the superior reliability of the Likert scoring. Tittle and Hill (1967) found consistently slightly lower validities with the Thurstone method than with the Likert or Guttman, with criteria that included objective measurement of the relevant behaviors. Schulman and Tittle (1968) make the interesting point that the Thurstone method seems to eliminate a great proportion of items that refer to the self. They also point out that the greater the proportion of self-reference items, the more satisfactory is the prediction of behavior. The latter point, of course, is consistent with our analysis of the relationship between attitude and behavior, as presented in Chapter I. It appears, then, that the somewhat lower validity of the Thurstone scales may be due to the loss of self-relevant items. It is conceivable that self-relevant items are also responded to with greater reliability.

All three of these methods measure attitudes by a single number, which is located near the midpoint of all acceptable positions, on an attitude continuum. The major contribution of the Sherifs (1964, 1967) is that they demonstrated the importance of the *latitudes* of *acceptance, rejection,* and *noncommitment.* A person has not only a preferred position on an attitude continuum but also a number of other positions which he also finds acceptable. Furthermore, not only does he have one position to which he objects most violently but he also has other positions that are objectionable to him. The Sherifs have demonstrated that the greater the ego-involvement of the subjects, the larger is the size of the latitude of rejection, and the smaller the size of the latitude of noncommitment. The latitude of acceptance is almost unaffected by ego-involvement.

Several implications follow from these findings. Diab (1967) has shown that Arab students, having the *same* preferred position on the subject of "Arab unity," may have widely different latitudes of noncommitment and rejection. Unless these differences are taken into account their behavior in response to communications designed to change their attitudes is not understandable. Conversely, subjects with *different* preferred positions may have similar latitudes of rejection. Thus, subjects who accepted the most moderate statements on Arab unity were similar to the anti-Arab unity subjects. These two kinds of subjects also responded in similar ways to communications about Arab unity. In other words, if only the most preferred position were to be considered, a distinction between the two kinds of subjects would have been made and a difference in their responses to the communication would have been expected. But inspection of the latitudes of rejection and noncommitment reveals the similarity among these two groups of subjects and, hence, explains their similar reaction to the communication. Furthermore, Sherif, Sherif, and Nebergall (1965) have demonstrated that subjects with wide latitudes of noncommitment are more likely to change their attitudes than subjects with narrow latitudes.

Finally, the work on the multidimensional measurement of attitudes (for example, Triandis, 1967) suggests that the measurement of one dimension reveals only part of the total information.

Final Comment on Specific Methods. All of the above-mentioned standardized verbal specific methods are designed for the measurement of the persons's attitudes toward a particular (attitude) issue or (attitude) object. Shaw and Wright (1967) have reviewed the published scales toward a large variety of attitude objects: for example, opinions regarding the upbringing of children, disciplining children, freedom of children, children's activities, educational practices, religious practices, heterosexual practices, health practices, and so on. Other chapters review scales toward social issues, international issues, political and religious issues, ethnic and national groups, and social institutions. Consult this handbook for a description of existing attitude scales toward a large variety of issues and attitude objects.

SPECIAL PROJECT

Use the attitude statements you developed in a previous project to measure the attitudes of a few of your friends. Do a Guttman scalogram analysis of the answers you get from your friends.

General Methods

The methods reviewed in the previous section are designed to measure the subject's affect toward a specific attitude object, or controversial issue. This means that one must employ a different scale, consisting of different items, for each attitude object. Since the development of these scales is time-consuming and the precise measurement of every attitude object is not always required, there have been attempts to develop general scales that are appropriate for a class of attitude objects or for *any* attitude object.

Scales Appropriate for a Class of Objects

We give two examples from among the scales that are suitable for classes of attitude object: (1) Bues (1934) has published scale values of items that may be used to respond to any practice. They range from the item, "It is better than anything else" (11.0), through "My likes and dislikes for this practice are balanced" (6.0), to "Is the worst thing I know" (1.0). Two forms of this scale, each containing 37 items are readily available (see Shaw and Wright, 1967, pp. 124 to 126). (2) Remmers (1960) has published a 17-item scale which measures attitudes toward any proposed social action. It ranges from the item "will bring lasting satisfaction" (10.3) to the item "It is perfectly absurd" (1.0). Two forms are available (see, Shaw and Wright, 1967, pp. 190 to 191).

A Scale Appropriate for all Objects: The Semantic Differential

The most general method for the measure of affect is the Semantic Differential (Osgood et al., 1957). This instrument allows the researcher to present any attitude object, be it person, issue, institution, practice, picture, musical composition, or anything else. A series of scales, bound by polar adjectives, is employed and the subject reacts to the attitude object on this set of standard scales. For example:

                    Integrated Housing

good   ___|___|___|___|___|___|___   bad
passive ___|___|___|___|___|___|___   active
strong   ___|___|___|___|___|___|___   weak

Extensive work done with samples of adjectives by Osgood and his collaborators in more than 20 cultures suggests that three major independent dimensions underlie the judgments made by subjects. They are the following. *Evaluation:* the object is good, clean, fair, honest, beautiful. *Potency:* the object is strong, big, large, powerful, heavy. *Activity:* the object is active, hot, fast, alive. Thus, with a short set of 9 or 12 scales it is possible to measure the connotative meaning, or affect, experienced by the subject toward the attitude object.

Osgood employs the evaluation dimension to measure attitudes. Thus, scoring each of the evaluative scales from −3 to +3, and using four evaluative scales, he can obtain scores that range from −12 to +12. Osgood et al. report, however, that in predicting the scores from Thurstone or Likert scales it is desirable to consider, in addition, the information obtained from the potency and activity scales. A multiple correlation, predicting Thurstone scaled attitude scores from all three semantic differential factors is somewhat higher than the correlation between the Thurstone scaled scores and the evaluative scores.

SPECIAL EXERCISE

In order to get some concrete idea about how the semantic differential may be used, rate four concepts on 6 scales. Mark the degree of association that you feel is appropriate between each of the four stimuli and the six scales. If you feel that the association is extreme use the polar ends of the scales. If you feel that the association is close to zero, or the stimulus could be associated equally well with either pole of a scale, mark the middle interval. Here are the stimuli and the scales.

Stimulus 1. A black American who is a communist

good	_____ _____ _____ _____ _____ _____ _____	bad
weak	_____ _____ _____ _____ _____ _____ _____	strong
clean	_____ _____ _____ _____ _____ _____ _____	dirty
passive	_____ _____ _____ _____ _____ _____ _____	active
fast	_____ _____ _____ _____ _____ _____ _____	slow
heavy	_____ _____ _____ _____ _____ _____ _____	light

Stimulus 2. A black American who is anticommunist

bad	_____ _____ _____ _____ _____ _____ _____	good
weak	_____ _____ _____ _____ _____ _____ _____	strong
dirty	_____ _____ _____ _____ _____ _____ _____	clean
active	_____ _____ _____ _____ _____ _____ _____	passive
fast	_____ _____ _____ _____ _____ _____ _____	slow
light	_____ _____ _____ _____ _____ _____ _____	heavy

Stimulus 3. A white American who is anticommunist

light	_____ _____ _____ _____ _____ _____ _____	heavy
strong	_____ _____ _____ _____ _____ _____ _____	weak
good	_____ _____ _____ _____ _____ _____ _____	bad
clean	_____ _____ _____ _____ _____ _____ _____	dirty
active	_____ _____ _____ _____ _____ _____ _____	passive
fast	_____ _____ _____ _____ _____ _____ _____	slow

Stimulus 4. A white American who is a communist

weak	_____ _____ _____ _____ _____ _____ _____	strong
bad	_____ _____ _____ _____ _____ _____ _____	good
active	_____ _____ _____ _____ _____ _____ _____	passive
heavy	_____ _____ _____ _____ _____ _____ _____	light
clean	_____ _____ _____ _____ _____ _____ _____	dirty
slow	_____ _____ _____ _____ _____ _____ _____	fast

First, add your ratings on the two Evaluative scales. If you put a check mark at the extreme end of the *good* or *clean* scale, mark it +3; if you put a check mark next to the extreme, mark it +2, and so forth. Be careful. We have reversed the scales, and mixed them up in such a way that you have to do this slowly. Your scores will range between −6 to +6 and you should have four evaluative scores, one for each stimulus. Now repeat for the two Potency scales, *strong* and *heavy*. Again, you should end with four scores ranging from −6 to +6. Finally, do it again for the Activity scales, *active* and *fast*.

Second, record your scores in the spaces shown below:

	Your Evaluation Scores		Your Potency Scores		Your Activity Scores	
Communist						
Anticommunist						
	black	white	black	white	black	white

If you have studied analysis of variance, in your course in statistics, you would be able to determine which treatment (color of skin or political views) "controls more of the variance" of your judgments and how much for each of the three semantic differential factors. It is probable that the scores you placed in the three boxes are quite different. If you do not know anything about analysis of variance, you can still observe a bit of the trend in your responses by taking the sums of (the first rows of scores) your two communist scores (SumC) and the sum of (the second row of scores) your two anticommunist scores (SumAC), the sum of (the left column of scores) your two black scores (SumB), and the sum of (the right column) your two white scores (SumW). You can do this, of course, three times, once for each semantic differential factor.

Now compute the difference between the scores as follows:

Difference: (Sum AC) − (Sum C) − (Sum W) − (Sum B) =

[Note: Be sure to remember your algebra. E.G. $(+4) − (−2) = +6$]

Now, if this difference is positive it means that you are paying more attention to the political views than to the color of the skin; if it is negative, it means you are paying more attention to the color of skin than to the politics.

Let us sum up now. In this exercise you have obtained a reading of your attitude toward people who hold certain political views and who have a certain color of skin. Your attitude is expressed by three numbers, corresponding to evaluation, potency, and activity. You have, in addition, learned which of the two traits used in this study are more important for you when you make these kinds of judgments.

Although the semantic differential is a most general instrument, it can also be made quite specific. If one is interested, then, in the attitudes of persons toward jobs, he can employ a specially designed instrument containing adjective scales that describe jobs (Triandis, 1960c). If one is interested in studying only social issues, another set of scales might be used (Davis, 1966). If one is interested in studying only people, still another set may be most appropriate (Davis, 1966). The more specific the set of scales the more comfortable are the subjects when they make their judgments, and the more relevant is the information for the particular problem in hand. For example, Komorita and Bass (1967) used 16 evaluative scales and two concepts: "American foreign policy in Vietnam" and "Draft deferments for married men." After intercorrelating the scales and submitting them to a factor analysis, they found three factors: *Functional Evaluation* (approved, wise, valuable, beneficial, satisfactory); *Pure Affect* (pleasant, attractive), and *Moral Evaluation* (clean, honest, trustworthy, sincere). This means that many subjects who thought the Vietnam policy wise, valuable, beneficial, etc., also thought of it as unpleasant, unattractive, or as insincere and dishonest. It is clear that such subtle points cannot be uncovered with the most general forms of the semantic differential, although specific semantic differentials may probe into quite subtle and intricate aspects of attitudes. On the other hand, there is a great advantage in having a most general instrument applicable to any kind of concept. The fact that the instrument does not have to be standardized every time one is interested in studying a different attitude is a major advantage.

Concepts are logically included in broader, more abstract concepts. For example, the concept, President Kennedy, is included in the concept, American Statesmen, which is included in People, which is included in "all concepts." Those attributes that are applicable to "all concepts" apply to concepts at all levels of specificity. Evaluation, potency, and activity are such general attributes that apply to all concepts.

As we examine domains of meaning that are more specific, we can use more and more specific dimensions, applicable only to objects at greater levels of specificity. The dimension, Democrat-Republican, for example, may apply to most United States Senators, but not to People in General. The greater the level of specificity, the larger the number of attributes that may apply. Also, attributes applicable at a particular level of abstraction apply to all concepts at lower levels of abstraction.

STUDY QUESTIONS

1. Explain how physiological methods are used to measure attitudes.
2. Describe the method of paired comparisons in the measurement of attitudes.
3. Do the same for the method of equal appearing intervals.
4. Do the same for the methods of successive intervals.
5. What assumptions are made by Thurstone in order to obtain values of attitude items?
,6. Describe the method of summated ratings.
7. Describe the principles behind scalogram analysis.
8. Describe the scale discrimination technique.
9. Compare the assumptions of the Thurstone and Likert methods. Which assumptions appear more defensible in the light of more recent research?
10. Give examples of general scales.
11. Describe the semantic differential method of attitude measurement.

PROJECT FOR ADVANCED STUDENTS

There is a very difficult issue in the measurement of attitudes theory that concerns whether or not it is possible to obtain adequate measures of the affective component of attitudes with verbal methods of measurement. Write a paper on this problem. Specifically, consider the fact that the relatively pure methods of measurement of the affective component are physiological; as soon as you use words you introduce some cognitions into the measurement. Examine the paper by Dillehay, Bruvold, and Siegel (1969) and state the implications of the findings of this paper with respect to this issue.

SUGGESTED FURTHER READINGS

Cooper and Pollock (1959), Thurstone (1928) Likert (1932), Guttman (1944) Osgood (1965),

Hovland and Sherif (1952) Sherif and Sherif (1964) Edwards and Kenney (1946), Guttman and Suchman (1947) all in Fishbein (1967a).
For more details on the standardized methods Edwards (1957a) is highly recommended. Also read Green (1954) and Scott (1969).

The Measurement of the Behavioral Component

In the previous chapter we mentioned that the behavioral component of an attitude involves the behavioral intentions of the subject toward the attitude object.

Bogardus (1925) developed a scale that obtains the behavioral intentions of subjects towards various nationalities. The intentions are arranged in a rank order of "social distance" between the subject and a list of nationalities that is presented to him. He is asked to indicate whether he would

> Marry into this group.
> Have members of this group as close friends.
> Have as next door neighbors.
> Work in the same office.
> Have as speaking acquaintances.
> Have as visitors only in my nation.
> Debar from my nation.

The Bogardus scale is ordinal. An interval scale of social distance was developed by Triandis and Triandis (1960), which was later employed in Greece (Triandis and Triandis, 1962), Germany and Japan (Triandis, Davis and Takezawa, 1965), as well as America.

The cross-cultural work employing this scale has required separate standardizations of the scale in each culture. The results suggested that persons from different cultures react to different characteristics of stimulus persons when they make social distance judgments. For example, Greeks show social distance mostly toward people who differ from them in religion; Americans show social distance toward persons who differ from them in race; the Germans and the Japanese show social distance mostly toward persons who are lower class. A review of these studies is found in Triandis and Triandis (1965).

An extension of this work led to the development of the Behavioral Differential (Triandis, 1964b), which is a general instrument that measures the behavioral intentions of subjects toward any person or category of persons. A description of the person to be judged is placed on the top of the sheet, and the subjects indicate their behavioral intentions toward this person on a series of scales. For example:

A Portuguese 35-year-old coal miner

would | | | | | | | | would not
obey this person

would not | | | | | | | | would
ask this person for advice

would | | | | | | | | would not
invite this person to dinner

A typical study is likely to employ about 50 person stimuli and about 20 scales, thus requiring the subject to make 1000 judgments. The stimuli are generated according to factorial designs, that is, all possible combinations of the characteristics under study and different levels of each characteristic are employed. For example, in studying the attitudes of subjects toward several kinds of European nationalities, Triandis and Triandis (1962) employed a preferred nationality (Swede) as well as a nonpreferred (Portuguese); in studying the responses of Greeks toward religion, they employed a preferred (Greek Orthodox) and a nonpreferred (Jewish) religion; in studying responses toward stimuli of different social classes, they presented stimuli that were described as physicians or coal miners. A statistical procedure called analysis of variance allows the estimation of the relative importance of these characteristics in the determination of the judgments made by the subjects.

The sampling of social behaviors requires extensive work. Lists of about 10,000 social behaviors were developed by Triandis, Vassiliou, and Nassiakou (1968) in each culture. They were subjected to a variety of statistical treatments, including the use of factor analysis, in order to obtain a short list of 20 scales that may be used as the standard set of social behaviors in a given culture.

Figure 5 illustrates the format of the behavioral differential. The subjects are asked to place a check mark on the scales that indicate the likelihood of their behavior in relation to the stimulus person described on top of the page.

Factor analyses identified five uncorrelated dimensions (factors). The first four scales of Figure 5 constitute the *Respect* factor, the next four the *Marital Acceptance* factor, the next four the *Friendship Acceptance* factor, the next four the *Social Distance* factor, and the last four the *Superordination* factor.

Although the correlations among the five dimensions are very low, so that we might speak of uncorrelated factors, it is possible to find some correlations among the factors. For example, the typical correlation among the factors is around .3 and sometimes it is as high as .5. Further analyses result in two completely independent dimensions: *intimacy-formality* and *positive-negative* behaviors. It is easy to show that the Respect factor is a mixture of relatively formal, positive behaviors; the Marital factor is a mixture of relatively intimate, positive; the Friendship factor consists of positive behaviors of intermediate intimacy; the Social Distance factor consists of negative, intimate, and the Superordination factor of negative formal behaviors. In short, interpersonal relationships may be described in terms of two fundamental dimensions: positive-negative and intimate-formal behaviors.

The behavioral component of attitudes also can be inferred from observations of the consistencies of a person's behavior in response to situations that have common characteristics. However, there are problems with this approach that may make this work difficult. A person's behavior occurs in part because of his habits, and in part because of norms and roles or his expectations of reinforcement. To measure attitudes from nonverbal behavior we need to "control" for the influence of these variables, and this is quite difficult. More specifically, a person may respond to a set of stimuli and not be aware of what he is doing. For instance, a driver may carry on a complex conversation without realizing that he has been responding to red and

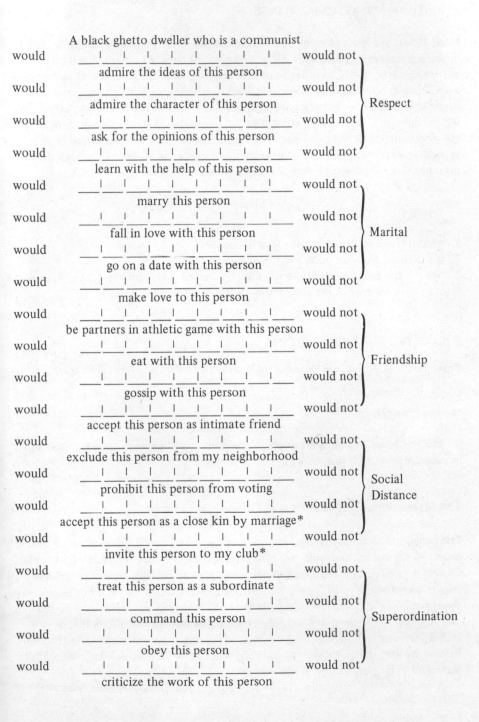

FIGURE 5.   An illustration of the format of the behavioral differential.
*Reverse scoring.

green lights. We do not want such consistencies in responses to lights to lead to inferences concerning attitudes. Or a person might behave quite inconsistently with respect to his attitudes, in order to obtain rewards, to avoid punishment and to gain acceptance from people he likes. This behavior, again, should not be used as a way to measure attitudes. Attitudes are best measured when it is possible to "keep other factors constant," and that is most easily done under controlled conditions. If we can observe consistencies in behavior in spite of extreme variation in habits, norms, as well as expectations of reinforcement, we can employ the behavioral observations to infer the person's behavioral intentions.

STUDY QUESTIONS

1. What is the Bogardus scale of social distance?
2. Is the social distance really unidimensional?
3. What is the behavioral differential? What are the major factors (subcomponents of behavioral intentions) obtained with this instrument?

SUGGESTED FURTHER READING

Bogardus (1925), Triandis and Triandis (1965), Triandis (1964), all in Fishbein (1967a).

SPECIAL PROJECT

Try the items in Fig. 5 on yourself and a couple of other people. Did you agree in your judgments? If not, why not?

The Measurement of Norms and Roles

The remarks that completed the previous section suggest that it is important to obtain measures of norms and roles in connection with the measurement of attitudes. Closely related to the behavioral component are the social norms that influence a person's attitude. Typically, the correlation between measures of what people say they *should* do and what they say they *would* do is .60 or larger (Bastide and van den Berghe, 1957; Davis and Triandis, 1965). The behavioral differential, described in the previous section, can be used to study norms by modifying the instructions. Instead of asking the subject to indicate what he *would do*, we ask him what he *should do* (Triandis, Vassiliou, and Nassiakou, 1968).

A closely related instrument is the role differential. It has the same format as the behavioral differential, but the stimuli are roles, for instance, father-son, son-father, client-saleslady, or laborer-foreman. By convention, the first entry of a role pair is the actor and the second is the person acted upon. This instrument has been used extensively in studying cultural differences in the perception of roles (Triandis, Vassiliou, and Nassiakou, 1968; Triandis, McGuire, Saral, Yang, Loh, and Vassiliou, 1968; Loh and Triandis, 1968).

There is considerable correspondence between the dimensions of the behavioral component of attitudes and the dimensions that underlie social norms and roles, as determined by these instruments. The same two dimensions (positive-negative affect and intimacy) were obtained in studies of role relationships. In addition, the dimensions of superordination-subordination and hostility appeared in these analyses. Different kinds of roles are located in different positions in the four-dimensional space determined by affect, intimacy, subordination, and hostility. For example, family roles demand high positive affect, much intimacy, and no hostility; boss to subordinate roles some affect, intermediate intimacy, high superordination, and low hostility; conflict roles (for example, policeman-demonstrator) low affect and intimacy, high superordination, and some hostility.

Indirect Methods

One of the major disadvantages of the direct methods of attitude measurement, like those of Thurstone, Likert, and Guttman, is that they are rather transparent. The subject knows that his attitudes are being measured. When the subject is aware that he is being studied, he is likely to modify his responses in order to (a) please a respected experimenter; (b) make trouble with the study of a disliked experimenter; (c) appear open-minded or "enlightened"; (d) give a good impression, and so forth. None of these influences is conducive to accurate measurement.

Some of the procedures described in the previous sections, provide a certain amount of disguise of the intentions of the experimenter. For example, the semantic differential is usually presented as a method for the "measurement of the meaning of words." A variety of other indirect methods is also available, of which Campbell (1950) has provided an excellent review. Of particular interest here are disguised measures, such as ambiguous pictures to which individuals respond. Their responses are then subjected to a thematic frequency count.

Doll play techniques, in which the respondent is asked to "make a dramatic scene or scenes of the world as you like it to be" have been found to measure intergroup attitude in meaningful ways.

A sentence completion test has been successfully used to measure racial attitudes. In this test, critical sentences such as "Skin color . . . ," "Some lynchings . . . ," "Negro body odor . . . ," etc., are interspersed with neutral items, such as "Maybe . . . ," "I feel . . . ."

Information tests, estimations of group opinion, tests of critical thinking, and perceptual or memory tests that are susceptible to distortion because of respondent attitudes may be used as attitude measures. Here, systematic errors, or the persistent selectivity of performance are made the bases for the attitude measurement. For example, to measure religious attitudes, respondents may be asked to react to an item like the following: "During the 1941 to 1945 period church attendance increased greatly. During the 1945 to 1965 period it has: (a) declined slightly, (b) tended to increase still more, (c) stayed at its high peak, (d) returned to its prewar level, (e) fallen to its lowest point since 1920."

Very little research on indirect measures has followed Campbell's review, so that it is still too early to tell whether these procedures have higher validity than the direct measures, as claimed by their proponents. On the other hand, it is clear that these procedures have lower reliabilities than some direct measures. A major program of research (Cook and Selltiz, 1964) is now underway which considers and evaluates a number of these measures. Among the measures tested in this program, are the ratings of the favorableness of statements (Selltiz, Edrich, and Cook, 1965) and the judgments of the plausibility of statements (Selltiz and Cook, 1966). Subjects with differing attitudes differed systematically in their ratings of unfavorable and intermediate items that referred to the position of the Negro. Pro-Negro subjects rated these statements as more unfavorable than anti-Negro subjects. It is less clear that ratings of plausibility can be used to predict the subjects' attitudes. In the latter test, the subject rates a statement on the degree to which it is a good argument for the side that it supports. Judgments of this kind were only slightly related to other measures of attitude.

Some indirect procedures appear extremely promising. For example, DeFleur and Westie (1958) had white subjects view a number of colored photographic slides showing a young Negro man and young white woman, or a young white man and a young Negro woman, in a social setting. The subjects described the pictures and answered specific questions about them. Following this phase, the subjects were told that another set of these slides was needed for further research, and they were asked if they would be willing to be photographed with a Negro of the opposite sex. Finally, the subjects were given "a standard photograph release agreement." They were asked to sign, giving permission for the use of the slides for different purposes—ranging all the way from "laboratory experiments where it would be seen only by qualified social scientists" to "a nationwide publicity campaign advocating racial integration." This approach provides a highly realistic, behavioral measure of the subject's attitude toward interracial contacts.

Another promising method is the one developed in Canada by Lambert et al. (1960). As stimuli they used a tape of a speech recorded by the same bilinguals (in French and English). Their Canadian subjects were then asked to evaluate the personality characteristics of the speakers. The comparative favorableness of the evaluations of the French and English guises appears to be a measure of the favorableness of the subjects toward French and English Canadians.

Webb et al. (1966) have reviewed a large number of *unobtrusive measures* that are quite promising as disguised procedures for the measurement of attitudes. For example, we might systematically record the frequency of positive and negative comments made by visitors to an art gallery. We also might determine which sections of the floor get worn out. The most attractive paintings will elicit positive comments, and the floor in the room in which they are hanging will wear out faster. Thus, attitudes toward paintings can be indexed by both popular comments and by the wear of the gallery floors.

When subjects are extremely involved in a particular issue, as happens when the attitude object is a central concept in the subjects' cognition, it is possible to observe the way in which they made judgments and to infer their attitudes. This was discovered by Sherif and Hovland (1953) who asked blacks to judge items relevant to the measurement of attitudes toward Negroes. Since the concept "Negro" is rather central for black students, such subjects were said to be "ego-involved."

Ego-involved subjects use very few categories when they are given the task of sorting items into "as many categories as you want." On the other hand, less-involved subjects use more categories. In short, the less involved differentiate more finely among various attitudinal positions.

Sherif and Sherif (1964) and Sherif, Sherif, and Nebergall (1965) used this phenomenon to measure involvement with the attitude object. Their procedure asked their respondents to sort attitude statements into as many piles as they desired and, for this reason, it is called the "own categories procedure." Persons who are extremely ego-involved with the particular attitude issue place statements in fewer categories. The Sherifs have also asked individuals to sort statements in "accept," "indifferent," and "reject" categories. Involved people generally place only a few statements in the "accept" category and put most of the statements in the "reject" category.

The Sherifs related this work to standard Thurstone scaling of the statements and found that for highly involved individuals the "latitude of noncommitment" is relatively small but that the "latitude of rejection" is relatively large. The latitude of rejection can then be used as a measure of involvement. The "own categories" method has the advantage that it measures the individual's attitude without his awareness. His task is simply to sort the statements into as many categories as he desires, but the way he sorts them is used to learn his position on the issue. On the other hand, it is probable that individuals can be classified in only a rough way according to their attitudes by this method.

STUDY QUESTIONS

1. What is the normative component of attitudes?
2. Describe *two* procedures for the measurement of a subject's ego-involvement with an attitude object.
3. What are indirect measures of attitudes used in research? Give examples of these measures.

SUGGESTED FURTHER READINGS

Campbell (1950), Cook and Selltiz (1964), both in Fishbein (1967a).

Some Methodological Issues

The measurement of attitudes requires a highly sophisticated technology, which has been covered very briefly in the previous pages. The direct methods of measurement are subject to several influences that may modify the results: some subjects tend to distort their responses in ways that are socially desirable (Edwards, 1957b) although the importance of this bias has been both miscalculated and exaggerated (Norman, 1967); some subjects tend to agree with ambiguously phrased attitude items (these subjects have an *acquiescence response set*); some subjects respond in one way when the wording of the item is of a particular form and in a different way when the wording is in slightly different form (semantic bias). Some subjects have a "positivity" response set, and they tend to agree with positively worded statements, but others have the opposite tendency and tend to agree with negatively worded statements. Sophisticated measurement requires the matching of items for their social desirability, careful phrasing, and the balancing of the items so that agreement with the item does not by itself raise the value that we attribute to a person's attitude.

The measurement of various components, employing similar formats of measurement, shows that the information obtained from the measurement of each component overlaps with the information obtained from the other components, but there are also aspects that are unique to each component.

In the final analysis, it is necessary to employ a variety of methods of measurement, each measuring the same component. In addition, some measures at the direct level should be supplemented with measures at the indirect level. It is then possible to employ statistical procedures that separate the effect of the measurement procedure from the content of what is being measured (Campbell and Fiske, 1959). However, these issues are too detailed for treatment in the present introductory text. For a more detailed discussion, refer to Dawes (1971).

STUDY QUESTIONS

1. What kind of biases enter into the measurement of attitudes?
2. How can these biases be overcome?
3. Why does the author recommend multiple measurement of each of the components of attitude?

SUGGESTED FURTHER READINGS

Guilford (1954) and Campbell and Fiske (1959), both in Fishbein (1967a).

PROJECT FOR ADVANCED STUDENTS

One of the central issues of attitude measurement is whether one takes direct measures, for instance, the ones of Thurstone, Likert, Guttman, Osgood, and Triandis, or indirect measures, for example, the ones reviewed by Campbell (1950). A good review of unobtrusive measures can be found in Webb, Campbell, Schwartz, and Secrest (1966). Read the original sources as well as Webb et al. and try to answer for yourself the following question: Under what conditions does a social psychologist employ the various kinds of measurements?

SPECIAL PROJECT

Use the items that you developed earlier, including the items that you criticized and found inadequate, in a sorting procedure with instructions to your subjects to use as many categories as they like in sorting these statements into piles. Now pick a subject that you think might be extreme on this attitude. Ask him to do the sorting. If your hunch was correct, he will use fewer categories (piles) in doing this task than your other friends.

III

Attitude Theory

In the first chapter we discussed attitudes as contributing causes of behavior. To understand them we focused on both their structure and consequences. Our discussion of the relationship between attitudes and behavior was sufficiently complete (Chapter I) that we need not return to it. On the other hand, our discussion of attitude structure was too brief; hence, we begin this chapter by examining again the organization of attitudes. Attitudes are acquired and changed as a result of both internal processes that go on in the heads of people, and external processes, some of which are sociological. We begin with the internal, and in the next two chapters we shall focus mostly on the external influences.

The Structure of Attitudes

The Relationships among the Three Components of Attitude

There is evidence that the three components of attitude are highly interrelated. Rosenberg (1956), for example, specifies that (a) the greater the perceived link between an attitude object and a person's values, and (b) the more salient these values, the more affect will this person experience. Similarly, Fishbein (1965) shows that the greater the connection between an attitude object and certain beliefs about it, and the greater the affect associated with these beliefs, the greater is the affect toward the attitude object.

On the other hand, there is also evidence that suggests that the three components should be conceptualized and measured independently. Illustrative is a study by Gardner, Wonnacott, and Taylor (1968) which examined the perception of French Canadians by English Canadians. A 39-scale semantic differential was used to study the stereotypes of the subjects. A very clear pattern of stereotypes emerged: the French Canadians were viewed as exceptionally *talkative, excitable, proud, religious, sensitive, colorful, emotional,* and so forth. A "French Canadian Attitude Scale" was also used, which had previously been scaled to measure affect toward the French Canadians. The semantic differential scales and the measure of affect were then subjected to a factor analysis. The first factor had a high loading on the affect scale and the characteristics *hospitable, generous, sociable, pleasant,* and *kind*. It is, then, clearly an *Affective* factor. The second factor had a zero loading on the affect scale, but had high loadings on all the scales that constituted the French Canadian stereotype, mentioned earlier. In addition to this community-wide stereotype, mentioned earlier, there were two kinds of stereotypes associated with positive or negative images of the French Canadians. These could be seen in the third and fourth factors. The third factor had a negative loading on the affect scale and high loadings on *stupid, uncultured* and *ignorant*; and the fourth factor had a positive loading on the affect scale and high loadings on *reliable, dependable,* and *rugged*. Here, then, we have both a separation of the affective and cognitive components and also factors that show the form of the cognitive component for subjects who are positive as opposed to subjects who are negative toward the attitude object.

PROJECT FOR ADVANCED STUDENTS

A controversy in the current literature concerns whether measures of the affective, cognitive, and behavioral component of attitudes are highly inter-correlated and may be assumed for all practical purposes to be measures of the same thing, or are relatively independent and should be considered as separate entities. There is considerable disagreement among social psychologists on this issue, with the present writer strongly favoring separate measurement. The evidence is mixed. Fehling and Triandis (1969) found through factor analysis that, when measures of the cognitive, affective, and behavioral components of interpersonal attitudes are placed in the same analysis, the dimensions that are extracted are independent and correspond to the three kinds of components.

This is not always the case, as can be seen from a study by Woodmansee and Cook (1967). When the categories under investigation are very specific, factor analyses will lead to factors that represent mixtures of the three components.

Consider a hypothetical study that investigated attitudes toward black militants, with a set of scales which measured the affective, cognitive, and behavioral components of attitudes. The subjects can only respond toward the stimuli that are presented to them; if they dislike (or like) *all* the stimuli, they will show very little variation in their ratings and, hence, one affective measure will have a small chance to correlate with another and to produce an affective factor. This is also true of the cognitive and behavioral scales. On the other hand, if the subjects can discriminate between militand black A and militant black B they will show variations in the way they respond to them. If some subjects like one better than the other, in different combinations, there will be a factor consisting of all the reactions of the subjects toward Mr. A and another factor consisting of all the reaction to Mr. B. In short, the restriction of range of the attitude objects in an investigation of this kind is likely to result in Mr. A and Mr. B factors that will merge the affective, cognitive, and behavioral aspects of the attitude objects.

It is therefore preferable to investigate independently the affective, cognitive, and behavioral ratings of subjects to a variety of attitude objects and then to examine empirically the extent to which the three kinds of ratings are interrelated. This approach was used by Triandis et al. (1967) who reviewed studies in which it is shown that, with American and Indian subjects, the *Respect* dimension of the behavioral component is related to the affect component (with correlations of the order of .75), but the other dimensions of the behavioral component are weakly related to the affective component (about .50). On the other hand, in Japan, it is the *Friendship* dimension of the behavioral component that is related to affect (about .66), but the *Respect* dimension is weakly related (.48).

Ostrom (1969) found considerable consistency among the three components, but also some uniqueness for each of the components. In sum, the components of attitude are highly interrelated, but each of them operates to some extent in a unique way and contributes specific information that increases our understanding of attitudes.

Examine the evidence for yourself and write an essay summarizing your conclusions.

Factor Analytic Studies of Attitudes Toward Many Social Objects

In the previous sections the focus was on a person's attitudes toward one social object. What happens when we measure the attitudes toward several social objects and correlate these attitudes?

Ferguson (1939) used factor analysis and found that certain attitude objects form clusters, in the sense that people respond to these objects in similar ways. Thus he found a factor (cluster) that he called *religiosity* which was related to opposition to the theory of evolution and birth control and to positive attitudes toward various religious concepts. He found a second factor that might be called *tendermindedness* because it is characterized by opposition to war and to severe treatment of criminal and capital punishment. Of course, it is not certain that the same factors would appear today, but a more recent study by Comrey and Newmeyer (1965), which sampled a much wider range of attitude objects, discovered similar factors. In addition to *religious* and *nonpunitive* attitudes, these authors discovered a cluster of attitudes concerned with *welfare,* characterized by liberal political preferences, an opposition to weak federal government, and an opposition to anti-unionism, a cluster of *nationalistic* attitudes, for instance, favoring service to the country, and opposition to pacifism, world government, and population control, and *racial tolerance,* consisting of attitudes that favor rapid social change and education for adjustment. The five clusters can be conceived as the branches of a tree, the trunk of the tree is the dimension of radicalism-conservatism.

The radicalism side of this dimension is associated with welfare attitudes and racial tolerance attitudes; the conservatism side is associated with punitive attitudes, nationalism, and religious attitudes. Figure 6 shows a map of social attitudes which summarizes Comrey and Newmeyer's study.

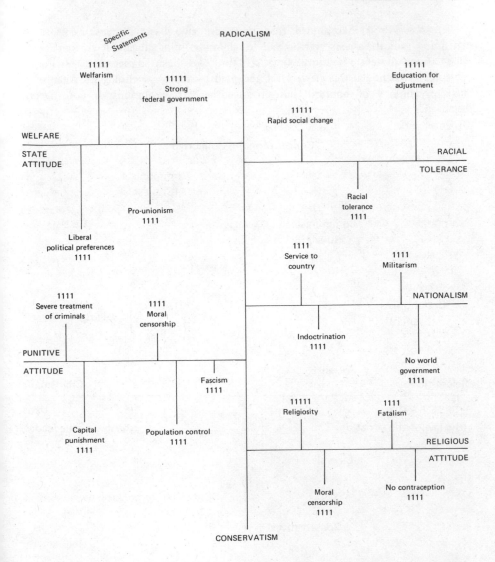

FIGURE 6. A map of social attitudes.

There is evidence that radicalism is favored by people who are younger (less than 40 years of age), of higher intelligence and education, who have more information, have done more traveling, are Jewish or Unitarian, and admire scientists, inventors, writers instead of leaders, athletes, financiers, or entertainers. In the United States, Catholics and fundamentalist Protestants are more likely to be conservative than liberal. This implies that certain fundamental social attitudes are intimately related to demographic characteristics.

Eysenck (1960) has argued that there are two basic dimensions of social attitudes: radicalism-conservatism and tough-tender-mindedness. He further argued that these dimensions correspond to the two basic dimensions of human personality, although this view is not accepted by many psychologists. Analysis of his "psychology of politics" has produced a certain amount of controversy.

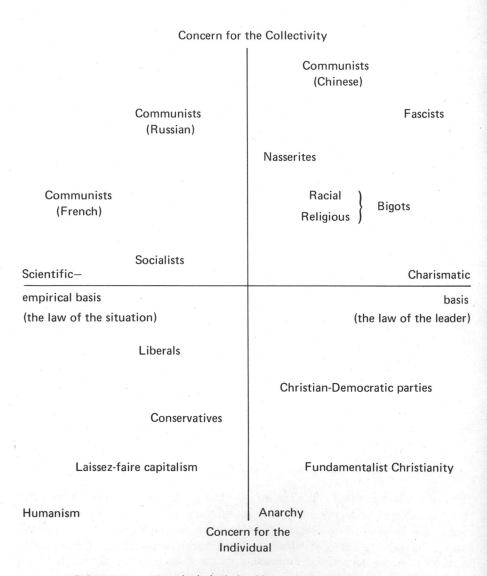

FIGURE 7.   Hypothetical relationships among political philosophies.

Eysenck claims that his two dimensions (radicalism-conservatism and tough-tender-mindedness) separate the major political positions. On the radicalism dimension, the communists are most radical, then the liberals, then the conservatives and fascists. On the tough-tender-mindedness dimension, the communists and fascists are similar, the conservatives intermediate, and the liberals are the most tender-minded. This view has been challenged by many, including Rokeach, who found that the British communists agree only with the anti-religious tough items and reject the remaining tough items.

The present writer believes that the basic dimensions of political attitudes are related to the "management of change." One view of change is that it must be instituted according to scientific discoveries and to the empirical verifications of scientific theories; therefore, the "laws of the situation" should govern change. The other view is that change must come from the guidance of a great genius, leader, or prophet. Thus, the authority of the leader should govern change. The other dimension of the management of change is concerned with the focus of change. Should change be directed at improving the individual or the collectivity? Clearly, there are laws that do little for the individual's well-being but that do help the survival of the collectivity—the city, the state, the alliance, and so on. Viewed in this perspective, the position of the political parities may be as indicated in Fig. 7. There is no direct empirical support for this view, but it appears to deal with the really fundamental differences of political behavior. Indirectly, there is a fair amount of support from the work of those who have concerned themselves with the measurement of attitudes and personality. Further research is needed in this area.

PROJECT FOR ADVANCED STUDENTS

The traditional views about attitude structure, reviewed in the earlier parts of this section, have been challenged by Kerlinger (1967) in two fundamental ways: Kerlinger's theory holds that (a) the assumption that attitudes are unidimensional is incorrect; (b) the assumption that attitudes are bipolar is only true under special conditions and is by no means a general characteristic of attitudes. In other words, he rejects both the notion that attitudes can be conceived as varying along a single dimension and the notion that they vary from extreme *pro* to extreme *con* the attitude object.

Write a critical assessment of Kerlinger's theory.

STUDY QUESTIONS:

1. What is the radicalism-conservatism dimension of social attitudes?
2. How are the attitudes toward a variety of attitude objects structured?

SUGGESTED FURTHER READING

Comrey and Newmeyer (1965).

Summary

Every discriminable category to which people react may provide the basis for an attitude. Since there are millions of these categories, they are usually organized by humans into larger and more abstract categories. These more abstract categories provide the basis for some of the fundamental social attitudes. These attitudes are also organized into larger wholes, and these larger wholes correspond to the fundamental values held by a group of people.

When measuring attitudes, we usually focus on an intermediate level of abstraction. For example, the attitude toward the *church* may be an expression of some fundamental value, such as man's good or evil nature, but it also may be conceived as an organizing attitude for several more specific attitudes, for example, the attitudes toward priests, ministers, church-going people, atheists, and so on. Thus, we have a structure of attitudes that resembles a tree: the leaves are the millons of concepts that we use to perceive and conceive our world; the branches are different kinds of attitudes, at various levels of abstraction. Finally, the trunk system represents the basic values.

The Dynamic Aspect

General Comments

Suppose a communication reaches an individual and in some sense "changes his attitudes." Does this mean that all of the components of his attitude change, or can there be an effect on only one component? Very little research has been directed, thus far, at clarifying this problem. The scant evidence that does exist suggests that the effects of various kinds of communications are not the same on the cognitive, affective, and behavioral components.

Consider a study by Davis and Triandis (1965) in which there participated 300 white, male, naive introductory psychology students. The study obtained measures on a large number of attitude objects, including the students' evaluations (measured by the evaluative factor of the semantic differential) and behavioral intentions (measured by the behavioral differential) toward Negroes who were in favor of strong civil rights legislation. Approximately a month later, the naive subjects were invited to an experimental negotiation with Negro confederates of the experimenters. The Negro negotiators took a very strong pro-civil rights stand and presented their arguments in excellent English, supported by statistics, clear logic, and effective arguments. For many of the naive subjects this was their first experience with a well-educated Negro. After the negotiation, they rated the Negro negotiators on the same semantic and behavioral differential scales employed in the pretest. The results showed that even the most prejudiced of the white naive subjects changed their evaluations of the Negro negotiators (the probability of getting this result by chance was less than one in a thousand experiments). On the other hand, the behavioral intentions of the naive subjects, although shifting somewhat toward the positive side of each scale, did not reach statistical significance. More specifically, although the experiment increased the tendency of the subjects to report that Negroes who are pro-civil rights are "good," "clean," and "fair," it did not change their stated intentions to "accept in my neighborhood," "not treat as subordinate," and "eat with," or "admire the ideas of," "elect to political office," and "be commanded by such persons."

The second illustration comes from a study by Vassiliou, Triandis, and Oncken (1968). The three components of attitude of Americans toward the Greeks were measured both before and after reading an ethnographic essay discussing Greek culture. The data suggested that learning occurred and changed the cognitive component of these attitudes. However, there was no evidence of change in either the affective or the behavioral components. We are tempted to generalize that cognitive changes are "easy," but affective changes are more difficult, and behavioral changes are the most "costly." However, this is a speculative generalization and should be subjected to empirical tests.

One way to understand, theoretically, some of these results is to consider the "cost" of behavior versus the "cost" of affect. It is more costly for the organism to emit actions than to feel good or bad about an attitude object. In Chapter I we mentioned Campbell's conception of behavior having different thresholds. The threshold of action varies with different kinds of actions. We may feel positive about an issue but not be positive enough to act. Conversely, we may feel very negative about an issue, but acting in opposition may be too costly. If we conceive of affect as the energizing component and of cognition as the directive component of behavior, the behavioral intention may require not only some cognitive elements in support of the action but also a substantial amount of affect consistent with the action before strong resistance or inhibitions are overcome.

The foregoing argument suggests that the three components of attitude may change at different rates and in different degrees. However, there are strong tendencies toward consistency among these components. These tendencies can be found at three levels: (a) consistency among cognitive elements, (b) affective-cognitive consistency, and (c) affective-cognitive-behavioral consistency.

Attitudes change through direct or indirect experience. Direct experiences with the attitude object usually change all of the components of attitude; indirect experiences typically change the cognitive or behavioral components, since they are usually informational or normative. Perceptual theories are directly relevant to understanding how we experience the attitude object; learning theories are directly relevant to understanding how we learn to make "attitudinal responses" to the attitude object. The course of attitude change also is influenced by the particular functions that each attitude performs for the individual.

We have already discussed how attitudes and behavior are related, thus, our next review will be concerned with the relationships among the components of attitude, that is, with the so-called "consistency theories." After this review we shall examine perceptual theories, learning theory, and finally functional theory, as it applies to attitudes.

Theories of Cognitive Consistency

Introduction. In recent years, a number of important theories have been proposed that incorporate some variation of the theme that inconsistency among cognitive elements is unpleasant to the subject and subjects will naturally attempt to reduce these inconsistencies. An excellent review of the status of these theories can be found in McGuire (1966).

The earliest of these theories was proposed by Heider (1946), who argued that if a person p likes another person o who likes an object x, there will be a tendency for p to like x. Notice here that we have three elements—p, o, x—which may be connected with a positive link (for example, p likes x) or a negative link (p dislikes x). A balanced state of affairs occurs when all three links are positive (everybody likes everybody else) or when there are two negative links (for example, p dislikes x, o dislikes x, and p likes o). On the other hand, when only one of the three or all three links are negative, the system is under strain because it is unbalanced. When this happens, there will be a tendency to change some of the links in the direction of balance. For example, when p likes x and o dislikes x while p likes o, there will be a tendency for one of these links to change sign. Balance can be restored if p learns to dislike x or if p manages to persuade o to like x, or if p decides to dislike o. Which of these links will change depends on the strength of the links. Figure 8 shows examples of balanced and unbalanced systems. [Heider's system was applied by Newcomb (1953, 1956) to communicative acts and was generalized by

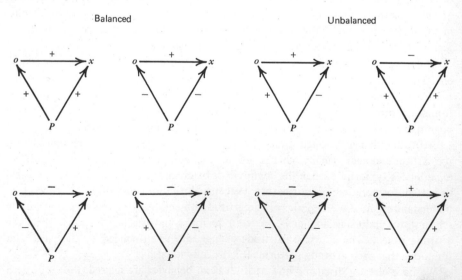

FIGURE 8.   Balanced and unbalanced states.

Cartwright and Harary (1959) to structures of any number of elements. Abelson and Rosenberg (1958) generalized it further so that it dealt with cognitive consistency among any cognitive elements.]

Extensive support for this point of view has been provided by presenting hypothetical social structures, such as "Jim likes Joe, Joe likes John, Jim dislikes John," to subjects who are asked to (a) learn them, (b) rate how pleasant they are, (c) estimate how likely they are, or (d) estimate whether they are likely to change over time. The data suggest that subjects learn the balanced structures more easily than they do the unbalanced ones and that they rate the balanced as (a) more pleasant, (b) more likely, and (c) less likely to change than the unbalanced.

An illustration of a study of the latter type is Burnstein's (1967) who asked 916 subjects to decide which, if any, of nine hypothetical social structures were likely to change over time. The structures consisted of two individuals who either liked or disliked each other, and who either favored or were against Goldwater and Johnson during the 1964 election campaign. The balanced structures were viewed as less likely to change than the unbalanced. Restructuring usually resulted in balanced structures and was done in such a way that the least possible number of changes were made. The relationships that were altered were usually interpersonal, rather than the relationship between the individuals and the political candidates. There were more changes from a negative to a positive interpersonal relationship than there were changes in the other direction. This has been called the "positivity bias" [for a review of studies on this bias see Feather (1967), p. 154] and is described as a tendency toward positive rather than negative interpersonal relations. When the hypothetical individuals disagreed about politics, the pro-Goldwater subjects achieved balance by changing initially anti-Goldwater attitudes of the hypothetical individuals to pro-Goldwater attitudes and pro-Johnson attitudes to anti-Johnson attitudes, while the pro-Johnson subjects showed the reverse effect.

One explanation of these results is that there are differential costs associated with positive and negative interpersonal relations. A mildly positive relationship is the least costly: it involves few obligations and is unlikely to produce negative reactions. A very positive relationship, of course, can be costly. A good friend can ask much of you, even your risking your life to save him! But in most social psychological experiments, the positive relations are probably perceived as being mild. On the other hand, even mild negative relations might be quite unpleasant. Not saying "hello" to a passing acquaintance might bring a torrent of abuse. The cost is even greater if the relationship is negative enough to go to court over an issue.

This study demonstrates the existence of a bias toward cognitive balance. In addition, it shows that other cognitive biases are also operating. These include biases toward minimal change, positivity, reciprocity (if Jim likes Joe, Joe likes Jim; if Jim dislikes Joe, Joe dislikes Jim) and "wishful thinking" (pro-Goldwater subjects seeing the anti-Goldwater hypothetical person change his attitudes and the pro-Johnson subjects similarly seeing the anti-Johnson hypothetical person change his attitudes to agree with their own attitudes.)

The tendency toward wishful thinking is explicitly included in a theoretical model proposed by McGuire (1960a, 1960c). McGuire assumes that an individual's beliefs or expectations are related to each other according to the rules of formal logic. On the other hand, there is also a tendency for the individual's beliefs to be consistent with his desires and wishes. The individual attempts to minimize the inconsistencies among his beliefs as well as the inconsistencies between his beliefs and his desires or wishes. When the individual is made aware about his inconsistent beliefs, he experiences discomfort which results in attitude change. This is the so-called Socratic Effect (McGuire, 1960c). It is possible to increase the salience of the logical or the wishful system, and this will result in different kinds of cognitive change. The experimental evidence concerning McGuire's theory gives partial support to this formulation, but further research is needed to account for some inconsistencies between experimental findings and theoretical predictions. For a review, see Insko (1967, pp. 105 to 110).

An example dealing with our Mr. Brown, from the first chapter, may help. Let us assume that Mr. Brown holds the belief, "Negroes moving into neighborhoods cause property values to drop," and also the belief, "Negroes are moving into my neighborhood in large numbers." If we multiply the subjective probability of these two beliefs, we will, other things being equal, obtain the subjective probability of the belief, "Property values will drop in this neighborhood." However, since Mr. Brown's desires are also involved in this situation, the extent to which he does not desire blacks to move into this neighborhood will influence his belief that they are moving into it; probably even one black family will be perceived as "*many* Negroes moving into my neighborhood." In sum, people follow the laws of logic and probability in thinking about issues, but their wishes, values, and personality may distort some of these beliefs.

How is an individual to react when someone he likes disagrees with him? According to balance theory he will either change his attitudes toward the object of the disagreement, or he will change his liking for the other person. However, these are not the only courses of action. Steiner and Rogers (1963) investigated a situation in which subjects found their judgments contradicted by a respected associate of the same sex. The subjects resolved the imbalance by (a) conforming with the associate's judgments, (b) rejecting the associate as less competent than he had been thought to be, (c) underrecalling the extent of the disagreement, and/or (d) devaluating the importance of the topics under discussion. They found that females made less use of rejection and were more likely to tolerate the conflict than were males. There was a strong tendency for particular subjects to use one of the four means of reducing imbalance but not all four. In short, some people develop a habit to conform, others to reject, still others to underrecall, and some learn to devaluate the issue. It is reasonable to assume that when persons are rewarded in childhood for conforming, or rejecting, or for making any of the other responses, they develop a tendency to use that particular method for the resolution of imbalance.

There are other ways of handling cognitive conflict. The individual can (a) simply *"stop thinking,"* or (b) *bolster* one element by thinking of all the reasons why he is "right." As an illustration, the smoker who hears about the connection of smoking and lung cancer may think of how "enjoyable," "relaxing," "helpful in social relations," and "less dangerous than driving a car" smoking really is and, hence, find the risk of cancer "quite acceptable." He can (c) argue that respected people are like him; for example, "my doctor smokes"; (d) *differentiate,* for example, "there are cancer-producing cigarettes and noncancer producing ciga-rettes"; or (e) *transcend* the inconsistency by finding a higher level reason for the inconsistency, for example, "it would ruin the economy if everybody stopped smoking." Abelson (1959) has provided an extensive discussion of these forms of conflict resolution.

A major individual-differences variable relevant to the reactions to inconsisten-cies is cognitive *complexity.* Scott (1962) defined this variable as the number of independent dimensions the individual brings to bear in describing a particular domain of phenomena. He measures it by asking subjects to sort objects according to various criteria. For example, in a study of the way nations are perceived, he asked them to sort nations on the basis of (a) their importance in world affairs, (b) their belonging together, etc. The greater the similarity in these sortings between two criteria, the less complex is the subject in thinking about nations. Another method is to present a group of nations and to ask the subject to sort them into as many groups as he wishes. If he uses many groups, this would be an indication of cognitive complexity. Cognitive *flexibility* can be measured by asking the subjects to expand the groups they created in the original sorting. Scott found that the greater the cognitive complexity, the greater was the cognitive flexibility, and the more extensive the information the person had about nations. In another study (Scott, 1963) he found that cognitively complex persons were less affected by imbalance than cognitively simple persons.

Telling a person that he will have to talk with a highly critical peer increases his "social anxiety." Opinions are less differentiated and less organized under high social anxiety. Consistent with Scott's findings, Sears (1967) found that arousal of social anxiety increases opinion change. Sears also had expected persons suffering from chronic social anxiety to avoid interpersonal conflict and, hence, to change very little. The data did not support this expectation.

Which aspects of the cognitive system are most likely to change? The more sure a person is concerning a cognitive element, the less likely he is to change the element. If a cognition is closely related to a strong emotion, it would be less likely to change (Abelson and Rosenberg, 1958). If a cognition is grossly distorted by wishful thinking, it should be more vulnerable to change (McGuire, 1960a). The least "bolstered" of two cognitions would be more likely to change (Festinger, 1957; Rosenberg, 1960c; Zajonc, 1960a). If "ego" is one of the inconsistent cognitions, that element is less likely to change than the other elements (McGuire, 1966).

Each cognitive element may be thought of as having a positive or a negative sign. In addition, the various elements are linked to each other. When the link is implicative, or causative, we shall consider it positive; when the link is of the form "A does *not* imply B," we shall consider it negative. Abelson and Rosenberg (1958) consider a change in the sign of the link easier than a change in the sign of the cognitive element. Weick (1968) has reviewed evidence which suggests that *connected balance* is the most preferred outcome of a cognitive reorganization. *Unconnected balance* is a condition in which all the elements are not connected to each other, but those that are connected are in balance. Unconnected balance is less satisfying than connected balance, but more satisfying than *connected imbalance*, which is in turn more satisfying than *unconnected imbalance*.

STUDY QUESTIONS

1. Is there any evidence that the cognitive component of attitudes can change while the other components do not change?
2. Explain the concept of "cognitive balance."
3. Review a study that shows the presence of different kinds of cognitive biases.
4. How is cognitive complexity related to attitude change?
5. Which cognitive elements are more likely to change when a cognitive structure is under strain?

SUGGESTED FURTHER READINGS

Heider (1946), McGuire (1966), Cohen (1960), Abelson and Rosenberg (1958), Newcomb (1953), Cartwright and Harary (1959), Abelson (1959) and McGuire (1960). Most of these papers have been reproduced in Fishbein (1967a).

Affective-Cognitive Consistency. There is evidence of consistency among the affective and cognitive components of attitudes. For example, Porier and Lott (1967) used as a measure of affect the subjects' Galvanic Skin Response (GSR) and as a measure of cognition their responses to a self-report attitude scale. They found a correlation between the two measures. Specifically, they found higher levels of GSR in white subjects who came in contact with a black experimenter than with a white experimenter, when the subjects were high in a self-report measure of prejudice.

There also is evidence that when affect and cognition are inconsistent, there is a tendency for one or the other to change. If a communication changes a person's cognitive component, there will be a tendency for the affective component to change. Similarly, an experience that changes a person's way of feeling about the attitude object will tend to change his cognitions about it.

Inconsistencies between affect and cognition, of course, do not always produce attitude change. If the person receives a communication that changes his cognitions, he may restructure these cognitions so that new distinctions are made among them, and his affect may not change. A person who dislikes Negroes, when hearing of some good deeds performed by certain Negroes, may make the distinction between "good Negroes" and "most Negroes" and will continue feeling negatively about "most Negroes"; since there is little cognitive change, there is no affective change. Or a person may have a positive experience that changes his affect toward Negroes but that has only a small effect on his cognitions because the cognitions are "reinterpreted." For example, previously Negroes were bad and loud, and loud was associated with being obnoxious. After the positive experience, Negroes are now good, although they are still loud, only now loud is associated with "swinging," "fun to have around," etc. In other words, it is *possible* for one component to change without producing a change in the other but, *in general*, when one component changes the other does also.

Most categories are related to each other in cognitive structures of considerable complexity. For example, most attitude objects may be regarded as the means for attaining valuable goals. Attitudes are related to each other in complex structures in which one concept leads to another. Consistent with our discussion of attitudes and values (Chapter I) is the idea that categories can be rank-ordered from very concrete to very abstract. The abstract are generally more inclusive. The category Mr. John S. Smith refers to our subject's neighbor who is an accountant. Therefore, when the subject responds to Mr. Smith, he is in part reflecting his attitude toward accountants as well. However, accountants are also "professionals." The attitude our subject has toward professionals will have some influence on his attitude toward accountants. All of these categories, in the case of our subject, may be components of his category "Americans," and the latter category may be part of his concept "man." Attached to each of these categories are both connections to other categories (for example, Smith is tall; accountants are hardworking; professionals are very intelligent; Americans are efficient; man is a language-using animal) and varying amounts of affect.

A person's cognitive structure may be conceptualized as consisting of less than 100,000 meaning categories (this guess is based on the vocabularies used by educated people). Each of the categories is linked to one or more other categories, and the categories may be ordered according to their level of abstraction. Each category is linked with other categories according to the rules of logic. These rules include negation (A is not B), inclusion (A is included in B), conjunction (A and B), disjunction (A or B), implication (if A, then B), and so on. Some of these cognitive links are of great interest. Consider, for example, the concept of implication. If A is the attitude object and B is a value, and if there is an implicative relationship involving these elements, the subject's affect toward A depends on the strength of this value and the strenth of the implicative relationship.

Carlson (1956) showed that attitudes toward "open occupancy" can be changed by linking the movement of Negroes into white neighborhoods with a person's values, such as "equal opportunity for personal development," "being experienced," "being broad-minded," and "being worldly-wise." In other words, Carlson showed that cognitive changes creating linkages of this kind result in affective changes toward "open occupancy," creating a new attitude with a new cognitive component, and a different quantity of affect.

The converse effect also can be shown: if affect is changed, it results in changes in the subject's cognitions. Rosenberg (1960b) showed that this can be done by hypnotizing a person and suggesting to him that he will feel differently about the attitude object.

Some other studies that are consistent with the theory were published by Abelson and Rosenberg (1958) and Rosenberg and Abelson (1960). The latter showed that the attitude changes that are observed in such experiments follow the principle of least effort, in other words, people make the least number of necessary cognitive changes in order to restore balance in their affective-cognitive systems.

Stimulus Pooling. Suppose that two attitude objects have affective values A and B. If we have an attitude object that combines the two, what will be its affective value? That is, if we know a subject's affect toward REPUBLICANS and also toward PHYSICIANS, can we predict his affect toward REPUBLICAN PHYSICIANS?

Several models have been proposed to handle this problem. The simplest model is the one involving averaging. Anderson (1962) presented adjectives describing a person, such as good-natured, bold, humorless, etc. The affective value of the adjective was known and each adjective was chosen to represent one of three levels of affect. Three adjectives at three levels of affect resulted in $3 \times 3 \times 3$ or 27 combinations, that is, 27 descriptions of a person. The subjects responded on a 20-point scale of "likeableness" after hearing the adjectives. For 75 percent of the subjects tested, the simple averaging model provided an excellent fit with the obtained responses. Even for the subjects who deviated from this model, the deviations were rather small. Anderson and Jacobson (1965) obtained further support for an averaging model under a variety of conditions. Nevertheless, small but real discrepancies from the averaging model were observed. Anderson's research program has attempted to discover the source of such discrepancies from additivity (Anderson, 1966), but thus far with limited success.

Another model is provided by Fishbein's summation theory. According to Fishbein (1961, 1965), an individual's affect toward an attitude object is related to his beliefs about this object and his affect associated with these beliefs. An individual holds many beliefs about any given object; all categories that are associated with the category in which the subject places the attitude object constitute these beliefs. The individual attaches affect to each of these categories. His affect toward the attitude object depends on the sum of his affect toward all these related categories.

Fishbein has argued that some beliefs are higher in the individual's hierarchy of beliefs than others and that they should have a greater influence on affect than the beliefs that are lower in the individual's hierarchy. He has also stated that approximately seven beliefs may be sufficient to provide most of the affect. An implication of his theory is that the idiosyncratic beliefs elicited from an individual will be more suitable for predicting his affect than a set of beliefs provided by the experimenter. Hackman and Anderson (1968) found partial support for these implications although, contrary to Fishbein's theory, a set of "standard" beliefs supplied by the experimenters predicted the subjects' affect better than the beliefs elicited by the subjects themselves.

When the Fishbein model is applied to the problem of stimulus pooling, it predicts that if the affect toward objects A and B is slightly positive, the affect toward the combined A *and* B will be even more positive than the affect toward either of the two stimuli. Conversely, if the affect toward A and B is slightly negative, the affect toward the combined A *and* B would be more negative than the affect toward either object. Kerrick (1958) obtained results that clearly support this model. Fishbein and Hunter (1964) and several others obtained support for such a model.

PROJECTS FOR ADVANCED STUDENTS

1. Manis, Gleason, and Dawes (1966) have pointed out that most of the studies that obtained an "extremity effect," for example, the one just described, have used measurement procedures which assumed that the response scales were of equal intervals but, in fact, the scales had only equal *appearing* intervals. Review this argument and their data, as well as the evidence presented by Dawes (1965). Present your conclusions concerning this controversy.

2. Review a number of mathematical models that have been proposed to account for stimulus pooling. In addition to the ones mentioned above, examine the model by Dustin and Baldwin (1966) that explicitly takes account of the overlap in the meaning of the two elements that enter into a composite judgment. Osgood and Tannenbaum (1955) have proposed a *congruity* model that weighs the elements of a composite by their polarities, and predicts that the most polarized elements will change the least. Rokeach and Rothman (1965) have proposed that the elements should be weighed by their perceived importance. Triandis and Fishbein (1963) have compared the congruity model with Fishbein's summation model and have found the latter to be superior. Fishbein and Hunter (1964) have further supported the summation model. On the other hand, Anderson (1965) finds more support for an averaging than for a summation model. Podell (1966) argues that Anderson's results may be because of the fact that his subjects made too many judgments and became fatigued; his results support summation theory. Triandis, Tanaka, and Shanmugam (1966) compared congruity, summation, and a weighted average model, with subjects from America, Japan, and India. Brewer (1968a) found that the greater the number of elements the less the rate of increase in the evaluation of the compound stimulus. Chalmers (1969) proposed that as the subject is exposed to more information about another person, he weighs the new information, using weights that are a function of the previous information. Which model do you consider most satisfactory, after your review of the evidence?

The Congruity Principle. Suppose that you feel very strongly about THE DAILY WORKER and you have rather weak attitudes concerning MODERN ART. How are you going to feel about the communication: THE DAILY WORKER IS IN FAVOR OF MODERN ART? Osgood and Tannenbaum (1955) suggested that your attitude toward this communication will fall somewhere between your attitude toward the two elements. Specifically, since you feel strongly about the newspaper and have no particular opinion about modern art, you will experience this communication as falling closer to your attitude toward the newspaper than toward modern art. The principle is a mathematical statement of the shifts in the attitude toward the two elements that consititute the communication (Fig.9). Tannenbaum (1968) has shown that there is considerable research concerning attitude change in which this principle has provided excellent theoretical predictions.

Let us represent the affect toward concept 1 by the symbol a_1, the affect toward concept 2 by the symbol a_2, and so on. Imagine that we obtain this affect by looking at the way a person rated a concept (THE DAILY WORKER or MODERN ART) on a scale that ranged from +3 (good) to −3 (bad). Let us say that a person rated the DAILY WORKER −2 and MODERN ART +1. To understand how the principle works, we need two kinds of symbols: (i) the absolute value (omit their signs) of the rating, which is represented by two vertical lines, $|a_1|=2; |a_2|=1$; and (ii) the algebraic value of the ratings which, of course, includes the actual signs $(a_1) = -2$ and $(a_2) = +1$. We need one more symbol: the change in the affect of concept 1 which we can represent by D_1 (D stands for difference of concept 1). Now the formula is very simply

$$D_1 = \frac{|a_2|}{|a_1|+|a_2|} \ (a_2 - a_1)$$

and $$D_2 = \frac{|a_1|}{|a_1|+|a_2|} \ (a_1 - a_2)$$

If we substitute the values that we have already mentioned we have

$$D_1 = \frac{1}{1+2} \ [1-(-2)] = \frac{1}{3}(1+2) = 1$$

$$D_2 = \frac{2}{1+2}(-2-1) = \frac{2}{3}(-3) = -2$$

In short, the change in the affect toward the DAILY WORKER is only one unit, from −2 to (−2 + 1) = −1; the change in value of MODERN ART is 2 units, from +1 to (+1 −2) = −1. The conflict is resolved after the communication at −1 and, of course, −1 is between the original values of −2 and +1.

In Figure 9, we have represented the affect toward the two objects on a scale that varies from -3 to +3. We also show the point of resolution of the conflict. It is clear that THE DAILY WORKER changes less than MODERN ART. The change reflects their polarities; since the newspaper occupies a more extreme position on the attitude scale, it changes less.

A number of interesting predictions have been based on the congruity principle.

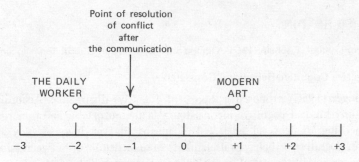

FIGURE 9.   Cognitive shifts according to the congruity model.

Tannenbaum and Gengel (1966) predicted and demonstrated that a change in affect toward a given concept will generalize to produce a change in affect toward a source which previously made an assertion about that concept. Tannenbaum (1966) obtained evidence indicating such a change, as well as a change in affect toward an additional concept about which the source had made an assertion. Tannenbaum (1967) reviewed a number of these studies and also focused on the question of how to reduce attitude change.

Interest in the reduction of attitude change can be traced to the Korean War during which a number of American prisoners of war were "brainwashed" and apparently accepted the "communist philosophy" which was presented to them by their camp superintendents. McGuire (1964) summarized an elaborate theory that deals with a person's inoculation against persuasion. According to this theory, a person who has never . . . been exposed to arguments that are counter to his own beliefs (as happens with beliefs that McGuire calls "cultural truisms") does not develop any defenses against attitude change. The analogy with inoculation against infection is explicitly made by McGuire. He argues that one way to prepare a person to avoid attitude change is to expose him to arguments that are inconsistent with his own beliefs and then to refute these arguments. Such a "treatment" gives the person the means to resist persuasive attempts. In a series of studies, which carefully varied a number of parameters, McGuire showed that his theory received support.

STUDY QUESTIONS

1. Describe Rosenberg's procedure for the change of the affective component. What were the results of such changes?
2. What is Fishbein's attitude theory?
3. What is the congruity principle?
4. Present and compare three models that account for stimulus pooling phenomena.
5. What studies of attitude change support the congruity model?

FURTHER READING

Rosenberg (1960b), Fishbein (1965), Osgood and Tannenbaum (1955), Tannenbaum (1967).

Affective-Cognitive-Behavioral Consistency

Festinger (1957) proposed a theory of cognitive dissonance. According to this theory, any kind of cognitive inconsistency is uncomfortable and the organism will do something to "get rid of it." This means that an inconsistency among the affective, cognitive or behavioral elements of an attitude, or between two cognitive elements, or any other sort of cognitive inconsistency will produce pressures toward consistency. Festinger defined cognition very broadly, as involving "any knowledge, opinion, or belief about the environment, about oneself, or about one's behavior" (p. 3). cognitive dissonance occurs where there exists a "relationship between two cognitive elements in which the obverse of one follows from the other" (p.13). The existence of dissonance gives rise to pressures to (a) reduce dissonance and (b) to avoid increases in dissonance. Manifestations of the operations of these pressures include (a) behavior changes, (b) changes in cognition, and (c) circumspect exposure to new information. "The magnitude of the dissonance between any two elements is a function of the importance of the elements" (p. 16).

It had been known, even before the formulation of dissonance theory (Kelman, 1953; Janis and King, 1954), that when a person behaves in ways that are inconsistent with his attitudes, he tends to change his attitudes to make them consistent with his behavior. In the Kelman study, schoolchildren were induced to write essays favoring a particular type of "comic book" which was different from the type that they actually preferred in order to gain prizes. The study showed that the comic books that were praised became more attractive. Festinger (1957) argued that the attitude toward the comic books was in conflict with the behavior of writing these essays, and it thus resulted in cognitive work. If the person can find some external justification for having done what he did, then there may be little dissonance. For example, if he receives a large prize, or avoids a considerable punishment, or gets the approval of the teacher, or can find a reason for his behavior that is consistent with some other attitude, then the dissonance can be dissipated. But if these avenues are not available to him, he is likely to change his attitude to make it consistent with his behavior, that is, he will like the type of comic books he praised in his essay more than he did before writing the essay.

This dissonance theory interpretation of Kelman's results is not the only theoretical explanation of what happens. McGuire and Millman (1965) compared dissonance theory predictions with predictions from self-esteem theory, according to which "people behave so as to maximize their self-esteem" (p. 477). One could argue that the two theories have the same status, since one can be translated into the other. For example, behaving so as to maximize one's self-esteem is equivalent to minimizing the discrepancy between the real and ideal self. Presumably, being cognitively consistent is a value in our society and, hence, when behaving to reduce cognitive dissonance, one is increasing his self-esteem because he feels more consistent, hence, more valuable.

Janis and King (1954) have demonstrated that role playing can influence attitudes. Subjects who were induced to engage in role playing that was inconsistent with their private attitudes tended to change their attitudes to make them consistent with their behavior. The authors explained these results by arguing that their subjects rehearsed and generated new arguments under the role-playing condition that changed their attitudes. Festinger (1957, Chapter 4) explained these results differently, arguing that when the subjects play a position opposite to their own, they experience cognitive dissonance, and attitude change occurs to reduce this dissonance. However, the two explanations are not necessarily contradictory. Greenwald and Albert (1968) showed that subjects do indeed discover new arguments and value their own arguments very highly, a phenomenon consistent with the original Janis and King explanation. It is possible that both the new self-generated thoughts and the perception of their behavior as inconsistent with the original attitude contribute to attitude change.

Numerous other explanations of this phenomenon are possible. An alternative dissonance explanation would point to the greater effort of the role players. Or the subject might come to identify himself with an imaginary person who actually holds the position he is advocating, and may get to like such a person and, hence, that person's attitudes.

PROJECT FOR ADVANCED STUDENTS

Prepare a research design that will test the various explanations of the phenomenon—self-generated thoughts, various kinds of dissonance, identification with an imaginary person, etc. Examine some of the arguments presented by Janis (1968) in his recent theoretical statement on this topic. Consider what the effect of having different audiences (similar or different from the subject), or of looking at the task differently (for example trying to persuade the audience versus trying to be effective and smooth in delivering the speech) might be on the amount of attitude change that will be observed if these various explanations are correct.

Some Other Experiments

A controversial formulation derived from dissonance theory resulted in numerous experiments in which a student was first asked to participate in an extremely dull experiment. He was then induced to tell another student (actually a confederate of the experimenters) that the experiment was "interesting," "fun," "enjoyable," etc. Here the inconsistency is clear. On the one hand, the subject knows that the experiment is dull and, on the other hand, he knows that he told the other student that it is interesting. The theory would predict considerable dissonance, particularly if the student does not have any justification for lying. Dissonance could be reduced by becoming less negative about the experiment. The more justified he is for lying, the less dissonance there should be. Thus, if he received a large monetary reward for his cooperation, he should experience less dissonance. An experiment by Festinger and Carlsmith (1959) showed, as expected from dissonance theory, that the greater the reward ($20 instead of $1) the less did the subjects change their attitude toward the experiment.

This experiment has been the focus of much criticism and many replications. Rosenberg (1965a), for example, has argued that subjects in psychological experiments experience an "evaluative apprehension," that is an intensive concern that they make a good impression or, at least, not make a bad impression. It is plausible, therefore, that the subjects in the $20 condition will reason as follows: "they probably want to see whether getting paid so much will affect my attitude, whether it will influence me, whether I am the kind of person whose views can be changed by buying him off" (p. 29). Such subjects, in an attempt to show how incorruptible they really are, may change their attitudes less. On the other hand, the subjects in the $1 condition will be less likely to formulate this hypothesis, concerning the purpose of the experiment and, hence, will show more attitude change. An additional possibility, according to Rosenberg, is that the $20 payment will make the subjects suspect that there is a deception; hence, they will become angry and will refuse to change their attitudes in order to show their hostility.

Rosenberg's arguments are similar to the ones suggested by Nuttin (1966) who showed that, even when the subject is induced to do something *consistent* with his attitudes, the large payment produces less attitude change than the low payment. Nuttin argued that the subjects in the high-payment condition become embarassed by the size of the reward and try to justify the large reward by telling themselves that this was, indeed, an unpleasant task that deserved a large recompense. Nuttin's study showed that it is not necessary to have inconsistency (dissonance) in order to obtain the results of Festinger and Carlsmith.

Kiesler (1968) reviewed a number of his studies and concluded that a broader conceptualization of "forced compliance" is in order. Subjects in Kiesler and Sakumura (1966) advocated a position *consistent* with their attitudes, and were paid $1 or $5. Later, in what was supposed to be a different experiment, the subjects received a countercommunication on the same topic. Kiesler and Sakumura argued that the smaller the inducement to perform some behavior, the greater the commitment to that behavior in response to a countercommunication. The data supported this prediction. Kiesler concludes that the less one is pressured to perform an act, either consistent or inconsistent with his beliefs, the more he is committed to that behavior. The greater the commitment, the more the attitude change. It follows that, when there is an inconsistency between an act and one's attitudes, the greater the commitment to the act, the greater the attitude change towards consistency with the act. In other words, in the low justification condition there will be more change. This is, of course, what Festinger and Carlsmith showed, but they did not spell out the importance of commitment, as did Kiesler. It is also interesting to observe that Kiesler's emphasis on commitment is consistent with Nuttin's results. It will be recalled that in that study the subjects who were induced to do something consistent with their attitudes for a large sum of money (low commitment) changed their attitudes very little, but the subjects who did this for a small sum of money (high commitment) changed their attitudes a lot. Kiesler shows that a number of other studies in his program suggest that the subject's commitment is crucial. For example, a typical finding in social psychology research is that the attractiveness of a group and the degree of the disagreement of the group's members with a position held by the subject directly influence his attitude change. The less attractive the group, the less it can influence its members. However, Kiesler shows that these findings are only true when the subjects do not anticipate future interaction with the group. When there is commitment to continue interaction, and the group is unattractive, the group's influence on the individual is almost as great as when the group is attractive.

Kiesler (1968) has further clarified that there are three different emphases in discussions of the relationship between dissonance and commitment: (a) unless the subject is committed, we cannot make an unequivocal prediction from dissonance theory; (b) unless the subject is committed, there may be no dissonance; (c) the more the subject is committed, the greater the dissonance.

The Festinger and Carlsmith (1959) results can be replicated under certain conditions, but the opposite effect, can be obtained under other conditions. The opposite effect, is expected from *incentive theory*—the greater the reward the greater the attitude change. Carlsmith, Collins, and Helmreich (1966) replicated the Festinger and Carlsmith results for the condition when the subjects had sufficient reason for complying with the demands of the experimenter and when the subject thought that the person to whom he is lying was *unaware* of the conflict between private attitude and behavior. On the other hand, when the experiment involved not a face-to-face situation but one of writing an essay to be read by the experimenter, who, of course, was aware that the subject was not presenting his true thoughts, the opposite effect was obtained, as expected from incentive theory.

Elms and Janis (1965) asked subjects to write essays in favor of sending American students to study "the Soviet system of government and the history of communism" in a Russian university for four years. In one condition the sponsor of the essay writing was said to be the Soviet Embassy, but in the other it was said to be the State Department. The rewards ranged from $0.50 to $10. When the source was positive (the State Department), those who received the high reward showed more attitude change than those who received the low reward; in the negative source condition the reverse effect was observed, although it was not statistically significant. Such results support incentive theory. Elms (1967) reviewed the relevant studies and concluded that incentive theory is more satisfactory than dissonance theory to account for attitude change that is induced through role playing. He believes that the results which appear to support dissonance theory are attributable to artifacts.

Brehm (1965) disagreed with these views and pointed out that in the Elms and Janis study the position of the essay was so distasteful that the subjects may have refused to reduce dissonance by changing their attitudes, and dissipated the dissonance by some other means.However, these arguments can be used any time an experiment does not support one's favorite theory, thus making the theory invulnerable and, hence, useless. Useful theories allow people to go beyond them, in the sense in which Einstein went beyond Newton.

Rosenberg's position has also been criticized in a study which showed that either the incentive theory prediction or the dissonance theory prediction can be obtained depending on how free the subject feels to comply. Linder, Cooper, and Jones (1967) showed that when the subject feels free not to comply, the dissonance prediction will be observed but, when this freedom is reduced, the incentive theory prediction will be obtained. They believe that Rosenberg's study reduced the subject's freedom not to comply. Dissonance theory predictions, then, will be observed only when the subject remains free to decide against compliance after he has been fully informed about the incentives being offered by the experimenter. If the incentive is announced after the person is committed to compliance, a reinforcement effect obtains.

The argument gets quite complex [see Aronson (1966) versus Rosenberg (1966)], and some of the methodological arguments in particular become quite subtle. Helmreich and Collins (1968) have done a study that attempted to take into consideration many of the methodological objections, and they have replicated both the Festinger and Carlsmith and Rosenberg results under different conditions. McGuire (1969a) argues that the dissonance and incentive theories are not opposed but are concerned with what is happening at different points in time. Dissonance theory is concerned with what happens up to the point when the subject commits himself, but before he carries out his commitment. Incentive theory is adequate in describing what happens after the subject carries out the counterattitudinal behavior. McGuire reviews a number of studies that appear to be consistent with this reconciliation, but unfortunately there also are some studies that are not consistent with it.

There is a convergence between McGuire's reconciliation and the arguments advanced by Lindner et al. At any rate, one thing is clear: the original dissonance formulation must be modified, and the conditions under which the dissonance predictions will be observed must be stated. The generality of the dissonance predictions appears limited, at least, as far as this experimental paradigm is concerned. McGuire's reconciliation is sufficiently promising to justify some more research in that direction.

Situational Determinants of Attitude Change

An important point made by Festinger (1964a) which is of relevance to attitude change research is that attitude change will disappear unless the environment is supportive of the behavioral change that accompanied attitude change. He argued that what developed the attitude in the first place continues to act on the subject, and he is likely to go back to his earlier attitude unless there is some real environmental change that sustains his new attitude. Considerable evidence supports this formulation.

Similarly, when a person changes his reference group, is subjected to new behavioral norms or, as a law-abiding citizen, behaves consistently with new laws, there are strains introduced between his behavior and his affect and cognitions. This strain is likely to lead to attitude change. However, once the person is removed from the situations that modified his behavior, he may go back to his earlier attitude, since the latter might be consistent with some of his more fundamental values.

Summary

To summarize our discussion thus far, dissonance theory, as elaborated by Festinger and his students, involves four important variables: (a) the discrepancy between the cognitive elements, (b) the importance of the cognitive elements, (c) the subject's freedom of will (volition), and (d) the subject's commitment. Maximum dissonance occurs when the discrepancy is large, the elements are important, and when the subject has been free to exercise his volition and is committed to the outcome of his behavior.

Brehm and Cohen (1962) reviewed the evidence concerning dissonance theory, as of about the beginning of the 1960s, and pointed out the importance of commitment and volition in specifying the conditions under which dissonance will occur. They also pointed out that dissonance from many sources is implicitly assumed in the theory to be additive. That is, any relevant cognition can serve in either the arousal or reduction of dissonance, and the effect of any given element is added to that of any other element. If a person commits himself to saying something discrepant with his private belief, money for doing so reduces the dissonance; but dissonance can also be reduced by the perception that he was interpersonally obligated, the judgment that he will become a "better man," the judgment that his compliance will help science (or any other good cause), an interpersonal attraction to whomever made the request, a change in his private belief, and so on.

As mentioned previously, the forced compliance experiment is only one kind of paradigm derived from dissonance theory. There are many other formulations derived from this theory, but they cannot be discussed here. The interested reader can find a good discussion in Insko (1967, pp. 206 to 284). Limitations of space will permit only a few more comments on the general validity of the Festinger theory.

First, there is some physiological evidence that can be interpreted as being consistent with Festinger's basic assumptions. Buckhout (1966) points out that, according to Festinger, attitude change will be preceded by dissonance, and dissonance is likely to be reflected in the activation or arousal of the autonomic nervous system. Specifically, there should be increased heart rate, systolic blood pressure, blood sugar, and a lower skin resistance level. After attitude change, there should be a decline in autonomic activity, since dissonance will have dissipated. In a study in which subjects engaged in a structured interview in which they were rewarded for reading aloud statements opposite to their initial attitudes, Buckhout found that those subjects who were initially higher in their base-line heart rate and showed a drop in rate during the interview exhibited attitude change scores consistent with the direction of reinforcement. Those who were anti-conformers, that is, changed their attitudes in the opposite direction, had low initial base-line heart rates, showed slight increases in the mean heart rate during the experiment, and showed less change in heart rate before and after the interview; in other words, they behaved as though they had not experienced dissonance, as compared to the conformers.

Second, in certain research areas, dissonance theory has been reasonably well supported. Among the better supported predictions is the expectation that when the two alternatives in a given decision are both attractive, the subject will experience dissonance. Davidson and Kiesler (1964) had female subjects play the role of a person who had the responsibility of hiring a vice-president for a firm that they owned. They rank ordered 8 qualities, such as leadership and experience, in terms of their importance for people filling this job. They then were given information about two hypothetical persons: Mr. Brown and Mr. Jones. Following this, half of the subjects were asked to choose a candidate and then to rerank the 8 qualities. The other half of the subjects did the reranking before the decision making. There was a significantly greater increase in the ranking of the qualities belonging to the chosen candidate than of the qualities belonging to the rejected candidate in the postdecision measurement condition than in the predecision condition. Making the decision, then, creates dissonance that spreads apart the qualities.

Third, in some research areas the dissonance predictions are usually obtained, but the interpretation of the effects is unclear because other theoretical formulations may be superior. Perhaps, the forced compliance situation, which we have already described, is the most controversial in this respect.

Dissonance theory experiments have been criticized on both methodological grounds and on the basis of superior explanations by other theoretical formulations (Chapanis and Chapanis, 1964; M. J. Rosenberg, 1965a, 1966; Elms, 1967; Bem, 1965, 1967). The counterattack by dissonance theorists (for example, Brehm, 1965; Aronson, 1966; Linder, Cooper, and Jones, 1967) has been equally vigorous.

In this book we cannot do justice to this extensive literature. The interested reader should consult Abelson, Aronson, McGuire, Newcomb, Rosenberg, and Tannenbaum (1968) and Kiesler, Collins, and Miller (1969).

STUDY QUESTIONS

1. Review the major theories that argue for the consistency of the elements within the cognitive component of attitudes.
2. Review the theory of cognitive dissonance and the major arguments about various kinds of cognitive consistency made in this chapter. What are the major common themes?
3. What is Rosenberg's affective-cognitive consistency theory?
4. What happens when people are induced to role play an attitudinal position that is very different from their own position? Why?

FURTHER READINGS

McGuire (1960c); Tannenbaum (1967); Festinger (1964a); Janis and King (1954); Abelson et al. (1968). Kiesler et al. (1969).

Social Judgment Theory

The reaction of a person to information and statements concerning any issue depends on this person's previous experiences with the particular domain of attitudinal statements. The most extreme positions to which the subject has ever been exposed function as two extreme anchors, and the geometric mean of all the positions he has been exposed to function as the neutral point for making judgments about attitude statements. There is considerable evidence in studies of perception that the person's *level of adaptation* (Helson, 1964) must be considered in understanding perceptual phenomena. The level of adaptation is a kind of neutral point that a subject develops and around which he anchors his judgments. The position that is most acceptable to an individual plus other acceptable positions constitute the individual's *latitude of acceptance*. The latitude of acceptance includes the individual's level of adaptation. The position that is most objectionable to an individual plus other objectionable positions define his *latitude of rejection*. The remaining positions define his *latitude of noncommitment*. Statements that are more positive or more negative than his level of adaptation are rejected in proportion to their distance from the level of adaptation because the subject finds them either too positive or too negative. The level of adaptation itself is an average (actually, the geometric mean) of all the "legitimate" attitudinal positions to which the subject has been exposed in the course of his life. Thus, if a subject has grown in an environment in which most of the legitimate positions he has heard were of the "extreme right," he is likely to develop a level of adaptation that will be the average of these positions, hence, much to the right.

The notion of legitimacy presented above must now be clarified. If the subject does not *respect* the person who makes an extremely rightwing statement, this statement would not enter the pool of legitimate statements. On the contrary, under these circumstances the subject's level of adaptation may shift to the left.

Sherif et al. (1965) presented data showing the effects of the level of adaptation as well as the effects of two kinds of cognitive distortions in the judgment of attitudinal statements: assimilation and contrast. *Assimilation* occurs when statements that are rather close to the level of adaptation and to the person's preferred position are perceived as more similar to statements that are close to the person's own position than they really are. *Contrast* occurs when statements that are different from the level of adaptation and the person's preferred position are seen as being more different than they really are.

For example, in 1956 and 1960, the Sherifs studied the attitudes of more than 1000 persons toward the presidential campaigns. Figure 10 is reproduced from one

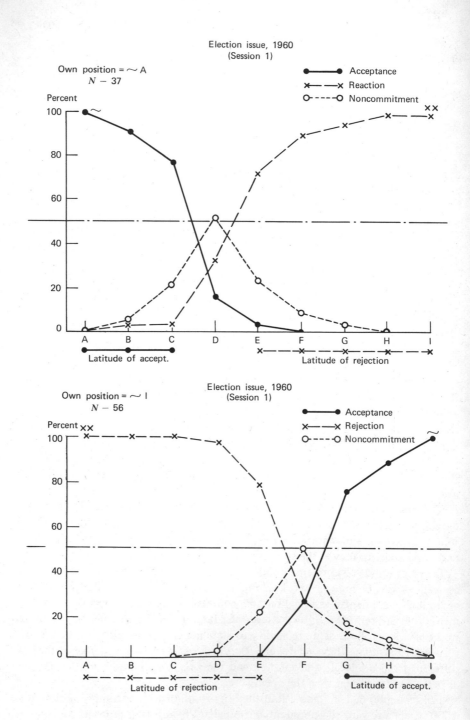

FIGURE 10.   Percentages of persons accepting, rejecting, or noncommital to different attitudinal positions.

of their studies. The solid line on the top figure presents the responses of those persons who selected as their most preferred position the statement: "The election of the Republican presidential and vice-presidential candidates in November is absolutely essential from all angles in the country's interest" (position A). The solid line on the bottom figure (position I) represents the responses of those who agreed with a similarly worded statement that referred to the Democratic candidates. Position B (or H) was that "On the whole the interests of the country will be served best by the election of the Republican (Democratic) candidates. . . ." Position C (or G) was that "It seems that the country's interests would be better served if the . . . candidates of the Republican (Democratic) party were elected in November." The positions D and F were endorsed by less than 30 percent of the extreme Republicans or Democrats, although the wording was as follows: "Although it is hard to decide, it is probable that the country's interests would be better served if the Republican (Democratic) presidential and vice-presidential candidates are elected in November." In other words, the extremist Republicans (or Democrats) assimilated strongly worded statements and rejected moderately worded Republican (or Democratic) statements. The graphs show that the Republicans assimilated statements B and C and showed contrast on statements D to H. The Democrats assimilated statement H and showed contrast for statements B to F.

Another illustration of this phenomenon is provided by Selock (1967). He administered Newcomb's political-economic conservatism scale to a sample of subjects and then asked the subjects to simply judge whether 21 persons or political groups were "conservative" or "radical," using an 11-point scale. He found that extreme conservatives differed from extreme radicals in the way that they judged these attitude objects. For example, the more conservative a person, the more he placed Martin Luther King on the radical side of the 11-point scale; the more radical the person, the more he tended to place the Reverend Dr. King on the conservative side of the 11-point scale. Similarly, the more conservative the subject, the more he tended to see the Ku Klux Klan as a "moderate" organization.

According to Sherif, Sherif, and Nebergall (1965), the more extreme the position of an individual, the smaller is his latitude of noncommitment and the larger his latitude of rejection. However, such results also can be accounted for by other theoretical views.

PROJECT FOR ADVANCED STUDENTS

Dawes (1965, 1970) argues that the results obtained by Sherif are artifacts due to the assumption that the subjects who use equal-appearing interval scales also employ such scales "in reality" when they make subjective judgments. He reviews several studies and his own data, which suggest that the subjective scales used by students have broader categories on the extreme ends, as shown in Fig. 11.

The typical Sherif finding is that subjects who take extreme positions have wider latitudes of rejection than subjects who take moderate positions. Dawes believes

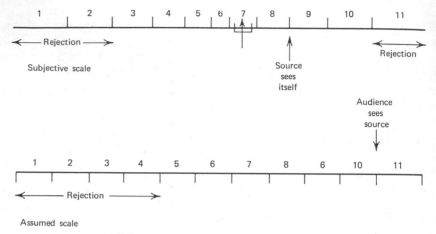

FIGURE 11.   Subjective and assumed scales.

that these findings can be accounted for by the nature of subjective scales. It is not that the latitudes of rejection change, but that the subjective and assumed scales are different. As an illustration, consider a subject who is located in position 7 of the subjective scale and rejects positions 1 and 2 as well as position 11. If you compare his latitude of rejection with the latitude of another subject who is located in position 11 and whose latitude of rejection is of exactly the same size (measured in inches or millimeters), it is clear that his latitude will include 4.2 categories (see the arrows in Fig. 11). Thus, although the moderate subject appears to reject 3 categories, the extremist appears to reject more than 4, but the size (in inches) of the latitude of rejection is the same.

It is unclear at this time whether Dawes' argument is sufficient to account for the Sherif results. Sherif and Sherif (1967) report that the average latitude of rejection in the midpoint is 3.5 and at the ends 5.0, a difference that is too large to be accounted for by the artifact. In the example of Fig. 11, the ratio of the narrowest to the widest category is 3 to 8, but in most data known to this writer it is only 5 to 8. In short, a *part* of Sherif's results may be accounted for by the characteristics of subjective scales, but it is likely that there is also a genuine phenomenon, isolated by Sherif, that goes beyond the artifact mentioned by Dawes. What is your evaluation of this controversy?

Dawes (1965) also makes the interesting point that a source of attitude change will always appear more extreme than it sees itself. For example, a source that endorses positions 7,8,9, and 10 in Fig. 11 will see itself in a position between 8 and 9, the middle of this range. However, the audience will be particularly impressed by the source's argument that fits position 10, since it would "stand out." An audience located in position 1 would have trouble discriminating between position 10 and 11 and, hence, would perceive the source as being located close to position 11 (see Fig. 11). In short, the source sees itself as moderate but the audience views it as extremist.

To sum up, perceptual distortions are particularly important when the source's position is truly ambiguous, when its arguments are unclear, complicated, and difficult to understand, and when the basic values of the source and the audience are quite different and each is making different assumptions about what is important during the communication. Examples of this sort can be found in abundance in nature. Senator Goldwater's famous "extremism in pursuit of freedom" speech can be considered as one such example.

Active Participation Theory

One of the classic studies in social psychology pointed out that attitude change and behavioral change can be obtained by creating conditions of effective group participation. Lewin (1947) performed a series of studies in which group discussion was compared with individual instruction.

In one of these studies the objective was to increase the consumption of beef hearts, sweetbreads, and kidneys during World War II. Each group participated for 45 minutes in either a lecture, linking the problem of nutrition to the war effort, emphasizing the vitamin and mineral value of these meats and distributing recipes, or in a group discussion. Bavelas, who ran these discussions, used a low-keyed presentation, clearly mentioning the problem of the war effort, followed by a general discussion of feelings about these unaccustomed meats. The information and recipes offered to the lecture groups were also given to the discussion groups. A follow-up showed that only 3 percent of the women in the lecture groups served one of these meats, whereas 32 percent of the women in the group discussion served them.

It is clear that a number of factors may account for this difference. First, in the lecture procedure the audience is passive, in the group discussion it is active, and can become more involved. Second, in the lecture the audience does not commit itself to doing anything. In the discussion group there is likely to be some commitment. Third, the lecture reaches the individual via the cognitive component of his attitudes, but the group discussion reaches him both through the cognitive and the behavioral; and we have already learned in Chapter I that group norms affect the behavioral component. The individual can "see" the group's norms changing in front of his eyes as the discussion moves on.

A number of additional studies reported by Lewin showed the same pattern of superiority of the group decision method in changing the behavior of persons.

However, the exact bases of the process of group decision were not explored until Bennett (1955) varied the level of commitment by exposing groups to four conditions—no decision, anonymous decision, partially anonymous, and public decision. In the no decision condition the subjects were dismissed after an influence attempt. In the anonymous decision condition they wrote unsigned statements about their decision. In the partially anonymous they were asked to raise their hand, without giving their name. In the public decision, which represented the maximum commitment, they raised their hand and gave their name which was conspicuously recorded. When a subject indicates that he approves of the position of the source of influence, this does not mean that he in fact will carry out the behavior. But 31 percent of those who said they would do as asked, did actually do it. On the other hand, all of those who said they would not do as asked, did not do so either at that time or later. In other words, the decision is a major factor in the prediction of the behavior. On the other hand, Bennett's data did not show that commitment is a major factor in determining the behavior. In fact, her results showed the opposite trend: 29 percent of those in the anonymous decision group but only 19 percent of those in the public commitment group did what they said they would do. On the other hand, her data show that the mere decision, that is, private commitment, and the perception of the changing group norms are sufficient conditions to make the group discussion method more effective in changing behavior.

Although Bennett's study suggests that public commitment is no more effective than private decision making, the majority of the studies which compared the two indicate that public commitment is more effective [see McGuire (1969a) for review].

The effect of public commitment on opinions is to increase their extremeness. Jellison and Mills (1969) found that just asking students to make a tape recording which would be played publicly of their *own* position on certain issues made them more extreme on those issues, as compared to other issues about which they did not tape record their views. One explanation of this phenomenon is that public commitment motivates the person to think of additional reasons why his position is correct and why the opposing side is wrong. Thinking of such arguments leads to the adoption of a more extreme position.

Lewin's theories, which inspired the studies we have just reviewed, also had important social consequences. For example, mainly under the influence of Lewin and his students, the "participation approach" has become very fashionable in American industry and other organizations. Studies like those of Coch and French (1948), in which it was suggested that participation improves morale in industry, have led to widespread adoption of the group decision procedure, in certain industries. Caution, however, is indicated by studies that show that other variables must also be considered. For example, job attitudes, for instance, job satisfaction, do not depend only on whether or not the supervisor asks for the opinion of the employees and encourages their participation in decisions that affect them. It is important to consider cultural, subcultural, personality, and task variables as well. In certain cultures, participation is viewed as illegitimate; in certain subcultures (for example, the urban versus rural United States) there are expectations about the way a boss should behave that may interfere with participation; persons low on the F scale and high in the need for independence appreciate the opportunity to participate, but persons high on the F scale and low in the need for independence are indifferent to such opportunities (Vroom, 1959); when the task is highly repetitive, very structured, and well understood, and when the leader has much power relative to his subordinates and is well liked by them, participation does not appear to be desirable (Fiedler, 1967a). Nevertheless, the participative behavior of the audience is an important factor which increases the impact of the message under certain conditions.

The finding that participation in the development of a solution to a problem makes the person more favorable toward the solution is consistent with derivations from dissonance theory. The person who participates has "an investment" in the decision; he has expended effort to reach the decision and he is likely to modify whatever cognitive elements are incompatible with the decision, in order to bring them into line with the new solution. In short, participation leads to active, cognitive work that is likely to change attitudes. What we described thus far in this section is active overt participation, but covert participation is also an important phenomenon in attitude change. We now consider some studies that describe these more subtle forms of participation.

When a communication is presented to a person, the process of perception is an active one in which the person attempts to refute the arguments and to restore his cognitive system to balance. This can be seen in a study (Maccoby, Maccoby, Romney, and Adams, 1961) in which women exposed to a communication concerning the proper age for toilet training babies chose to interact with those whose position was in agreement with their attitudes and to engage in conversations that supported these attitudes. People who did not engage in such conversations "backslid" to their original attitudes.

There are many kinds of "self-generating thoughts" that constitute part of this reaction. Internal events also may be part of it. A person may realize that the way he understands a problem does not lead to its solution; he may have a thought that threatens his self-esteem; he may have an insight that leads to new values which must be expressed in terms of new attitudes; he may realize that his present attitudes do not help his adjustment and, instead, may seek new ones that will.

Greenwald (1968a) has worked on these internal factors and has shown that the "recipient generated thoughts" used by subjects are more important in attitude change than the externally originated thoughts, for instance, the ideas contained in the attitude change message. Greenwald argues that when a person receives a message he is faced with the decision to accept or to reject it. He arrives at this decision by relating the message to his already existing knowledge, feelings, and behavioral intentions. In the course of such an evaluation of the message he may change one or more of the components of his attitude.

The basic design of Greenwald's studies includes the presentation of a message to the experimental subjects and to a sample of control subjects. All subjects are asked to list their thoughts concerning the attitude object. The listed thoughts are analyzed by assigning them to three categories: (a) externally originated (included in the message); (b) recipient modified (transformations of the message); and (c) recipient generated (thoughts not traceable to the message). Greenwald's studies suggest that recipient generated thoughts are deeply involved in attitude change.

Greenwald and Albert (1968) also showed that subjects tend to accept and to recall their own improvised arguments more than the comparable arguments improvised by others and that personally improvised arguments are evaluated more highly than the ones of others on a dimension of argument originality. In other words, people have a higher regard for their own arguments.

One of the major considerations in the subject's reactions is the finding of ways to maintain his self-esteem. If he considers it important to have opinions and attitudes that are well-developed and not easily changeable, he will try to bring his attitudes in line with those of the source if he is simply forewarned that he will receive an attitude change attempt from a respected source. By preparing himself for the attitude change attempt in this way, he can tell himself that he had to change very little, if at all, because of the communication. McGuire and Millman (1965) found such an effect. The more the expected message is discrepant from the subject's position, the larger the amount of anticipatory counterargumentation.

Counterarguments can be conceived as the "antibodies" that prepare the organism to resist "an infection." This inoculation analogy was used by McGuire to explain how the organism learns to resist persuasion. In a series of studies, reviewed in McGuire (1964), subjects were exposed to attitude change attempts directed toward widely accepted beliefs, such as "everyone should brush his teeth after every meal if at all possible." Most subjects accept such "cultural truisms" without question. When exposed to attack, these truisms are dramatically modified. However, if the subjects are given the opportunity to develop belief defenses, such dramatic modification of these beliefs does not occur.

McGuire experimented with different kinds of defenses. Some were "supportive" and consisted of giving the subjects various arguments in support of the truism. Others were "refutational" and mentioned several arguments attacking the belief and then proceeded to refute these attacking arguments. Other variations in these experiments included the degree of participation of the subject, that is, whether he simply read or actually produced defensive arguments by writing an essay.

The basic assumptions behind McGuire's formulation is that the subjects are unpracticed in generating counterarguments against the particular truisms and also that they are not motivated to generate them, since they never have to argue in support of such beliefs. The defensive treatments just outlined were designed to make the subjects learn to use counterarguments and to be less complacent about these issues.

Broadly speaking, these studies found considerable "immunization effects." That is, persons who had learned to use counterarguments were better able to resist persuasion attempts than persons who had not learned to do so. The best way to produce resistance to persuasion is to use refutational defenses, with arguments of the same type as the ones used in the attack statements. Passive reading produced more immunization than active reading, and free writing produced more immunization than the restricted writing of essays arguing against the attacking statements.

Practicing production of counterarguments is not the only way to reduce the effectiveness of propaganda. One can derogate the source of the attacking message (Anderson, 1967), refute the arguments, or boost the strength of the existing beliefs (Tannenbaum, 1967). Furthermore, it should be clear that McGuire's results were obtained with cultural truisms and the generality of the findings is unclear. However, they do generalize beyond cultural truisms, as is clear from a study by Schulman (1968) who argued that popular issues are likely to be in the same category as cultural truisms. People who agree with a popular issue have little opportunity to defend their beliefs; hence, they will not develop the necessary defenses against attack. Schulman demonstrated that those holding a popular view showed greater attitude change than those who held an unpopular position on the same issue.

When we reviewed the Janis and King (1954) study we showed that the improvisation of arguments in favor of a particular point of view changes attitudes in the direction of the arguments. Greenwald (1969) suggests that this phenomenon is because of the greater open-mindedness of the counterattitudinal role player. His study showed that subjects who expected to advocate a position opposing their own, evaluated controversial information in an unbiased and open-minded way, which is something they rarely would do under other circumstances.

McGuire and Papageorgis (1961) found that passive reading led to greater attitude change than active improvisation of arguments. It appears that the variable that makes a difference here is whether or not the individual has any arguments to improvise. If he is asked to improvise arguments about a topic on which he has information, he is likely to be quite successful in convincing himself that the position he advocates "makes sense." On the other hand, McGuire's (1964) studies have focused on issues that he called "cultural truisms," such as, "It is a good idea to brush your teeth after every meal, if at all possible." Subjects may have difficulties in finding arguments with which to refute such a position, so that in this kind of situation the passive reception of arguments may produce more attitude change than the active improvisation.

Another reason for preferring active to passive participation is that active participation leads to a longer persistence of the attitude change. In a study by Watts (1967) the persistence was studied under two conditions—active (writing an argument) and passive (reading an argument). After six weeks the active was shown to be superior to the passive. Active participation also resulted in greater involvement, that is, subsequent discussion of or reading about the topic and a superior recall of the topic.

STUDY QUESTIONS

1. Define the latitudes of acceptance, rejection, and noncommitment. According to Sherif, what is the role of these concepts in attitude change?
2. Define assimilation and contrast. Under what conditions can one or the other of these phenomena be observed?
3. What is the central thesis of Kurt Lewin concerning participation and attitude change?

4. What did Bennett find that modified part of Lewin's conception?
5. Is active participation more likely to lead to attitude change than passive participation? Under what conditions?
6. Outline McGuire's theory of immunization to persuasion.

FURTHER READINGS

Sherif et al. (1965). Dawes (1965). Lewin (1947). Bennett (1955). McGuire (1964).

Learning of Attitudes

When a person experiences a rewarding state of affairs in association with an attitude object, his affect toward the object will become more favorable. Conversely, if the experience is punishing, the person will change his affect in a negative direction. A major research program that explored such a theoretical expectation was initiated by Hovland at Yale University. An early summary and a theoretical framework were provided by Hovland, Janis, and Kelley (1953) and Hovland (1954).

You will recall, from your introductory psychology course, the difference between classical conditioning, such as occurs when some reinforcing event is associated with an ordinarily nonreinforcing event, and operant conditioning (instrumental learning) which occurs when some response of the organism is followed by a reinforcing event. Attitudes can be learned according to both of these learning paradigms. Specifically, an attitude object may become associated with a rewarding state of affairs and thus may acquire positive affect, or a person may behave in a way that is frequently followed by reinforcement, and his attitudes may then develop to give justification to his behavior. Let us first look at some examples of the classical conditioning of attitudes.

The rewarding state of affairs can take many forms. There is some evidence in the literature that eating a free lunch, hearing the words "happy" or "good," winning in a debate, hearing desirable information, getting an A on an essay, hearing expressed agreement with one's new opinion, and receiving a compliment can function as rewards that lead to attitude change. A number of experiments will illustrate this process.

Razran (1940) asked his subjects to evaluate a set of slogans, such as "Workers of the World, Unite," to express their personal approval, and to judge their social effectiveness and literary value. He then presented one set of slogans while the subjects were enjoying a free lunch and another set while they were required to inhale unpleasant odors.

After 5 to 8 "conditioning trials" the slogans were reevaluated by the subjects. Razran found that the slogans that were associated with lunch increased in rated personal approval and literary value, but the slogans that were previously associated with unpleasant odors showed a decrease in these qualities. Razran included a number of control slogans not associated with anything and also checked the subjects'

ATTITUDE THEORY/95

recall. The subjects were unable to recall which slogans went with which condition—lunch, odors, or nothing—although they did show a reliable tendency to evaluate more favorably the slogans that were associated with lunch. It would appear that the subjects were not aware that they changed their evaluations as a result of the type of reinforcement condition in which they experienced the various slogans.

McGuire (1957) demonstrated that a communication that presents desirable information before undesirable information is more persuasive than a communication that presents information in the reverse order. McGuire explains this phenomenon, theoretically, by arguing that reward conditions the attention and comprehension responses of the individual so that he continues to attend to the communication even when it becomes less desirable. Conversely, the communication that begins with undesirable information establishes an avoidance response, which has a tendency to continue even after the information becomes desirable.

A related phenomenon concerns audience experience with positive or negative reinforcement in connection with some attitude statements. A series of studies by Rosnow showed that opinions tend to change in the direction of whichever arguments are closer in time to the positive and farther in time from the negative reinforcement. Specifically, in presenting a two-sided communication, the first side of the communication has greater effect if positive reinforcement precedes it, but the second side of the communication has the greater effect if it is followed by positive reinforcement. The reinforcement can be pleasant events, such as increasing the grades of a class of students, or noxious events, such as giving them a surprise examination. (See Chapter VI for a detailed description.)

To illustrate, suppose one of your friends is sipping his favorite brand of *liqueur* or puffing his favorite cigar while you say "this place has a lovely view, but the climate is unpleasant." According to the Rosnow effect, the auditor will acquire a slightly positive affect toward "this place" if he sips or puffs just before your statement, and a slightly negative affect toward the particular place under discussion if he sips or puffs just after your statement. Hence, if you wanted him to acquire a slightly negative affect and you saw him sipping or puffing, you should immediately say: "This place has an unpleasant climate, although the view is lovely!"

We now consider studies that utilized operant conditioning. Golightly and Byrne (1964) employed consonant statements (that is, statements with which the audience strongly agrees) or dissonant statements (that is, statements with which the audience strongly disagrees) as the reinforcement in one study. They showed the reinforcing function of these statements by teaching their subjects a simple discrimination learning task. If the subjects made a correct discrimination response, they were presented with a statement with which they agreed; if they made an incorrect response, they were presented with a statement with which they disagreed. Their learning acquisition curve for the attitude statements was almost as good as the curve that used the words "Right" and "Wrong."

Insko (1965) showed that students who were reinforced by telephone with the word "good" for agreeing or disagreeing with certain opinion statements responded to a questionnaire, a week later, in a manner consistent with the reinforcement. Scott (1957, 1959b) showed that the "winners" in a debate changed significantly in the direction in which they had argued and that the "losers" changed in the opposite direction from which they had argued.

In another study, reported by Staats (1967), a motor response was followed by words such as HOLIDAY, SUPPER, and LAUGHTER; for another group the response was followed by BITTER, UGLY, FAILURE. For a third group it was followed by BOX, WITH, TWELVE. Positive attitudinal words presented in a response-contingent manner strengthened the instrumental response; negative words weakened the response, and neutral words had an in-between effect.

Incidentally, the Staats' (Staats and Staats, 1958) also are widely quoted for studies that supposedly demonstrate the classical conditioning of attitudes. These studies have shown that the evaluation of nationalities (for example, Dutch) or familiar masculine names can be changed by associating these categories with words having a positive (or negative) evaluation.

One of the most recent statements of this approach was presented by Staats (1967). He defined an attitude as an emotional response to a stimulus. In other words, he deals with the affective component of attitudes. He states, "if a new stimulus is paired with a stimulus that elicits an emotional response, the new stimulus will come to do so also" (p. 373). Once a stimulus has come through classical conditioning to elicit an emotional response, it can transfer the response to a new stimulus with which it is paired. In other words, a conditioned stimulus can acquire reinforcing characteristics, as in the Golightly and Byrne study mentioned above. Experts disagree on whether the Staats' have demonstrated the classical conditioning of attitudes or have reinforced particular instrumental responses—but this is a subtle point.

Even subtle influences, such as receiving a compliment or a good grade, may change attitudes. Bostrom, Vlandis, and Rosenbaum (1961) had students write an essay advocating a position that was inconsistent with their own attitudes. Those who received an A, on a chance basis, for this essay showed greater change in their attitudes in the direction of the essay than those who received a D. Calvin (1962) had 24 experimenters at Hollins College reinforce those who wore blue or red with expressions such as "My, that is a nice-looking sweater." The frequency of wearing of the rewarded colors increased in that college during the period of the experiment.

In short, when a category is frequently associated with rewards or positive outcomes, it acquires the characteristic of eliciting pleasant emotions. The affective component of attitudes then can be developed or changed by the kinds of associations between the attitude object and the pleasant or unpleasant states of affairs that the person has experienced. When the subjects have no previous attitudes or do not know much about a particular attitude object, as in the studies by Eisman (1955), Rhine and Silum (1958) and Rhine (1958), the association of the attitude object with other categories becomes the basis for the development of an affective response. When the subject is rewarded for a response his attitudes also may change.

STUDY QUESTIONS

1. What is the Staats' position concerning the learning of attitudes?
2. What kinds of events can act as reinforcers in the learning of attitudes?

FURTHER READING

Eisman (1955); Staats (1967); Staats and Staats (1958); Rhine (1958); Anderson and Fishbein (1965) [all to be found in Fishbein (1967a) where Eisman uses her married name, Lott]; Hovland, Janis, and Kelley, (1953).

PROJECT FOR ADVANCED STUDENTS

Some of the Staats' results have been questioned with respect to whether they represent a change in affect or in "symbolic reference to affect" (Insko and Oakes, 1966). It is also questionable that their procedure involves classical conditioning. What is your assessment of these points of view?

The Functions of Attitudes

In Chapter I, we mentioned the need to tailor attitude change messages to the functions of the particular attitudes in the total "economy of the personality." The most basic assumption of the functional theory of attitude change (Katz and Stotland, 1959) is that the key factors in attitude change are the *relationships* between situational forces and information on the one hand, with the individual's pattern of motives and values on the other. In sum, it is the relationship between incoming information and personality characteristics that leads either to the assimilation or to the rejection of this information.

These theorists consider three kinds of motives, in descending order of urgency: (a) biological drives, such as hunger, thirst, etc.; (b) ego and social drives, such as needs to preserve one's self-esteem, to be admired by others, to be close to loved ones, etc.; and (c) curiosity and the need for understanding. Maslow's notion of a hierarchy among these drives which specifies that as motives at one level become satiated the motives at the next level become more powerful is adopted by Katz and Stotland. The principle of consistency among the cognitive, affective, and behavioral elements of attitudes and the motive patterns is always operating, but the authors postulate that inconsistency may be avoided by *compartmentalization*—a defensive weakening of the link between the various elements. New information that is incompatible with the individual's motives or existing attitudes might be rejected or "put in a deep freeze," so to speak, so that it will not disturb the existing integration of attitudes. Motives and behavior are assumed to be more powerful determinants of psychological functioning than cognitions (that is, beliefs, information, etc.), although cognitions can be extremely important in changing certain intellectualized attitudes. Ego-defensive attitudes will be relatively susceptible to change through procedures designed to give self-insight and will be resistant to change through procedures that employ information.

A series of experiments, using the "insight procedure," can illustrate this approach. The insight procedure explains to subjects how defense mechanisms operate to repress inconsistent and unacceptable thoughts. It had lasting effects, as measured six weeks later, in changing the attitudes of the subjects, but informational methods of attitude change had little effect in the long run. Furthermore, for some of the subjects, who were particularly ego-defensive, the informational approach did not result in attitude change, but the insight approach did (Katz, Sarnoff, and McClintock, 1956). McClintock (1958) obtained significant attitude change toward Negroes by means of the insight procedure, and Culbertson (1957) found such attitudes changing *only* in the case of persons low in the *F* scale, that is, the less ego-defensive, when a role-playing techinique was used to change attitudes. In sum, certain attitudes cannot be changed by information or by producing inconsistency, but require the person to be aware of the connections of the attitude object to his structure of motives.

Baron (1965) manipulated his subjects' need for cognitive clarity by asking them to focus either on the overall impact and meaning of a message or on the message's individual words and sentences in judging whether a letter would be too difficult for a 12 year old. He varied the ambiguity of the persuasive communication and selected his subjects to be high in differentiation (use many cognitive categories) or low in this trait. He predicted from functional theory and found (only for males) that those who had a strong need for cognitive clarity and had few categories showed less attitude change for the ambiguous communication than those who had many cognitive categories. However, the same persons showed much change when the communication was clear. The derivation of this prediction argues that those high in the need for cognitive clarity, who have few categories, become frustrated by the ambiguous message, but if the message is clear they change a great deal.

Functional Bases of Attitudes and the Effects of Personality on Persuasion. A message can give a person better understanding of the world, or can help him make better decisions. It is obvious that some attitudes have such "knowledge functions," and it is possible to show that audiences expose themselves to information and change their attitudes much more readily when they need the information than when they do not. A clear example comes from a study by Maccoby, Romney, Adams, and Maccoby (1962). These authors selected three samples of mothers. One sample consisted of mothers who had only one child between 3 and 12 months old. This was the critical sample. Another sample consisted of women of a similar age who did not yet have a child, and still another of women whose youngest child was a first grader. The authors sent a letter on Stanford University stationery to these mothers offering to them a pamphlet on toilet training. The mothers of the critical group asked for the pamphlet much more frequently (71 percent of the time) than the mothers in the other groups, who asked for it half as often. The authors, then, sent the pamphlet to all the mothers, regardless of how they answered, and finally interviewed them to see whether they had read it. Again, the mothers in the critical group showed more interest; 88 percent had read it, although only slightly more than one half as many of the other mothers bothered to read it. The pamphlet advocated late toilet training (child should be older than 24 months), and most women indicated they expected to train before 18 months. Thus, there was some room for attitude change. Six months later the mothers were reinterviewed and opinion change was studied. The mothers in the critical group showed more opinion change (by about 2 months) than the mothers in the other groups. One half of these mothers changed their attitudes in the direction advocated by the pamphlet.

The particular needs of the audience enhance the acceptance of a message. Weiss and Fine (1955) showed that two personality characteristics, (a) extrapunitiveness (blaming others when something goes wrong) and (b) aggressiveness, correlated with the degree of acceptance of a message arguing that juvenile delinquents should be punished most severely. Weiss and Fine (1956) insulted their subjects and made them fail in a task and then presented communications concerning severe or lenient punishment of juvenile delinquents. Those subjects who were thus "aggressively aroused" responded more to the punitive and less to the lenient communications. McClintock (1958) showed that the defensiveness and other directive aspects of the personality of subjects predicted how they would respond to a message that argued about the "superiority of Western White culture and the innate superiority of Whites."

There are many studies which show that the person's membership and reference groups influence the way he accepts information. For example, ardent Boy Scouts are least influenced by anti-scout messages (Kelley and Volkart, 1952).

Finally, the value expressive functions of the message are likely to have an effect, as demonstrated in a study by Di Vesta and Bossart (1958). The message in this study was a description of a marginally unethical situation, involving a father with a low income, living in a housing development that did not allow persons with incomes greater than $2900 per year. The father wanted to send his son to college and took additional jobs to earn the required money, but he did not report the additional income so that he could continue living in the housing development. The subjects were asked to indicate whether they opposed or favored the father's action. Three different sets were evoked, each with a different value. The "ethical issue," the "social issue," and the "problem of managing one's money" were mentioned to different groups of subjects. The results showed that those given the ethical set approved of the father's action much less than those who were given the other sets; women tended to disapprove and men tended to approve of the action. This study suggests that when the values of a particular audience are included in the perceptual framework of a judgment, the meaning of a message can be modified.

STUDY QUESTIONS

1. What is the functional theory of attitude change? What empirical support can you cite for this theory?

FURTHER READINGS

Katz and Stotland (1959).

A Final Note

This introduction presented the major theoretical positions in this field. There are several more recent and less well-developed positions that should be studied by those who are more interested in this topic. A good introduction to additional positions can be found in Feldman (1966) and in Greenwald, Brock, and Ostrom (1968).

IV

Introduction
to Attitude Formation

Attitudes are learned. The problem of the present chapter is to explore how they are acquired and how they develop. The analysis will follow the structure of previous chapters by focusing on the development of the cognitive, affective, and behavioral components first, and then on the development of the interrelationships between these components. It will further analyze a number of theories that have been proposed in order to account for the presence of certain attitudes rather than other attitudes in particular groups of people.

In the first chapter we mentioned stereotyping as one of the most characteristic aspects of the cognitive component of attitudes.

Why do stereotypes develop?

Why do people experience negative affect in the presence of certain groups of people?

There is much evidence of discriminatory behavior that sometimes involves very subtle cues. Allport (1954b) reports a study by S. L. Wax in which he mailed two letters to 100 resort hotels advertising in the Toronto, Canada newspapers. The letters were identical, except that one was signed "Mr. Greenberg" and the other "Mr. Lockwood." The Mr. Greenberg letter led to offers of accommodations from only 36 percent of the hotels, although the Mr. Lockwood letters resulted in accommodations in 93 percent of the hotels. How were the attitudes formed that led to this difference in behavior?

In seeking to answer these questions, we must return to our discussion of the functional approach to the analysis of attitudes (Chapter I). According to this analysis, we form and develop attitudes in order to understand the world around us, to protect our self-esteem, to adjust in a complex world, and to express our fundamental values. To understand the world, we need concepts that summarize the complex information that impinges on us from our environment. We need to know how to evaluate different concepts and how to behave correctly in relation to various objects found in the environment. Much of this information is acquired from other people. Allport (1954b) has suggested that the majority of attitudes held by a person are acquired from talking with his family and friends. Although

101

these attitudes are not particularly intense, other people are nevertheless the sources of information for so many of our attitudes that this is an extremely important aspect of attitude formation. Furthermore, we join different kinds of groups and we would like to join other groups. The attitudes of the members of the groups we belong to, or would like to belong to, become guides for the development of our own attitudes. For example, a young couple who wants to join the local country club, but has not yet been admitted, might be very sensitive about the attitudes of existing members of the country club, as reported in newspapers or by others. Such attitudes may be used as guides in the development of the couple's own attitudes about the same issues.

We also learn attitudes through direct exposure to the attitude object. These attitudes are more intense, but only a small proportion of our attitudes are developed from direct experience. Finally, we may develop attitudes through a "traumatic experience" with the attitude object. A person who is robbed by a Negro, for instance, may generalize his dislike for the particular Negro who robbed him to all Negroes in the world. Attitudes developed through "traumatic experiences" are rare but, if they occur, they are extremely intense.

Some attitudes develop in order to protect our self-esteem. For example, some people are prejudiced toward Negoes because they like to feel superior to another group. Feeling superior bolsters their self-esteem. Finally, some people hold attitudes in order to express fundamental values, for instance, people who have experienced harsh and punitive child training, who may feel very negative toward people in general. Disliking certain groups of people makes these pathological cases "feel good."

The Formation of the Cognitive Component

Categorization

Why do we develop categories? Our environment presents us with millions of events every day. If we think of them at all, we type them. That is, we behave in response to many similar events as though they were identical. We do this because it is impossible for the human brain to employ all the information present in man's environment. Furthermore, there is a natural tendency to simplify our problems and to solve them as easily as possible. A "pet formula" such as "Mexicans are lazy" makes it possible for an Anglo employer to eliminate much of his mental effort by simply not considering Mexicans for jobs in his firm. If he were to check on each applicant and to understand the causes of his behavior he would have to work much harder. Furthermore, categorization helps perception. When somebody tells us, "Careful, a drunken driver!" our driving instantly becomes more defensive. The category "drunken" implies many behaviors on the part of the other driver, and we adjust to them quickly and usefully.

But categorization also has a penalty. The broader the categories, the more inaccurate they are likely to be. The more they help us, in that they allow us to simplify our problems, the more likely they are to cause us to perceive the world incorrectly.

PROJECT FOR ADVANCED STUDENTS

One of the categories of the greatest importance, for any individual, is his SELF. It is probably the most central concept, in any conceptual structure. How does it develop?
Consult a series of excellent studies by M. Rosenberg (1967).

STUDY QUESTIONS

1. What are the major ways in which attitudes are learned?
2. What are the major influences on the formation of the cognitive component of attitudes?

FURTHER READINGS

Allport (1954b); Rosenberg (1967).

The Formation of Political Concepts

Adelson and O'Neil (1966) studied the development of political concepts in 11, 13, 15, and 18 year olds. They found that before age 13 concepts are concrete and unstructured. The functions of government are perceived as coercive (for example, so that things "will not get out of hand," "so everything won't go wrong"), there is no time perspective, and the subjects are unable to envision long-range social consequences. A substantial change occurs at age 13, and at 15 there is a good deal of formal thought, information, and abstract thinking. The subjects were asked: "Should men over 45 be required to have a yearly medical checkup?" All of the 11 year olds answered "Yes." The "No" option, "because of infringement on liberties" was chosen by 13 percent, 27 percent, and 37 percent of the 13, 15, and 18 year olds, respectively. Perhaps the younger subjects, who submit to much discipline in the home, find no reason why government should not also be coercive.

Sociotypes and Stereotypes

A human characteristic of great generality is the tendency to "type" other people and groups, which is a natural consequence of the process of categorization. Once a category is established, for example, JEWS, there is a tendency to associate this category with a variety of characteristics, such as SHREWD. Some of these characteristics are, in fact, accurately assigned to a group of people. For example, the characteristic "Democrats" is accurately assigned to the category "Northern

Negroes," in the sense that there is a considerable tendency for Northern Negroes to vote Democratic. Northern Negroes, of course, have not always voted Democratic. Up to 1930 they voted for the party of Lincoln, but in 1936 President Roosevelt's New Deal, with its welfare proposals, caused a dramatic realignment of the Negro vote. In one Michigan metropolitan area the 1930 Negro vote was only 19.5 percent Democratic, but by 1936 it had jumped up to 63.6 percent, and since then the majority of Northern Negroes have voted Democratic. In 1964, 97 percent of them voted Democratic in the presidential election (Campbell, 1968). Hence, to characterize Northern Negroes as Democratic would generally be accurate. Accurate characterizations of social groups define *sociotypes*. What people believe about another group of people defines their *stereotype*. Stereotypes overlap with sociotypes only imperfectly.

Stereotypes. When we think of people about whom we know very little, for example the Chinese who live in Peking in 1970, we tend to adopt the beliefs of other people—for example, journalists, authors, and other elite. On the other hand, when we think of persons we know very well, for example, our close relatives, we rely mostly on our own experience. When we consider our relatives, for instance, we are likely to perceive dozens of characteristics; but when we consider remote groups of people, we tend to think in simple terms and to assume that most of them have a few characteristics. Intermediate between the remote and the close people are people we know something about—for example, Blacks, Jews, Catholics, and so on. Here whether we adopt the views of others or rely on our own perceptions depends to some extent on personality characteristics. In sum, we stereotype more and more those we know less and less; in some cases, the degree of stereotyping depends on personality characteristics which we shall discuss in the next chapter.

Stereotypes tend to be more rigid and less open to experience than the beliefs that we develop on our own. To reject a stereotype that we learned from our parents is a little like rejecting them. For this reason, we pay less attention to information that is inconsistent with our stereotypes. In other words, the greater the degree of stereotyping of a particular group, the less likely it is that new information will change our stereotypes.

Some stereotypes are modified through direct experience. In a series of studies on the American stereotypes of Greeks, Triandis and Vassiliou (1967) and Vassiliou, Triandis, Vassiliou, and McGuire (1968) found that Americans view Greeks as *unsystematic, lazy, inefficient,* and so forth regardless of the amount of contact that they have had with Greeks. On the other hand, certain stereotypes change with contact. For example, Americans complain that Greeks "pry into their personal affairs." This is a veridical perception. Greeks prefer much more intimacy in their interpersonal relationships; they like to "get close" to people. Their relationships with their friends are more warm, close, and supportive than is the case for Americans (Triandis, Vassiliou, and Nassiakou, 1968). Americans find such closeness in interpersonal relationships most uncomfortable. Hence, the greater the amount of contact they have with Greeks the more they complain that Greeks pry into their personal affairs. At the same time, however, the greater the contact, the more they see the Greeks as "witty," "charming," and "obliging." In other words, the stereotypes do not always become more negative. Instead, with increased contact, they become more differentiated and more ambivalent (containing both good and bad characteristics).

Persistence and Change. Stereotypes tend to persist over time. The Katz and Braly (1933) study, which was done at Princeton, was repeated by Gilbert (1951) at the same university. The stereotypes of 10 national groups were quite similar over the 20-year period, but there was also a "fading effect"—the stereotypes became weaker. The fading may be related to a disappearance of stereotyping from the entertainment media, a greater degree of sophistication, and a greater knowledge of other cultures by American college students of the 1950s as opposed to the 1930s.

An additional study of Princeton students, by Karlins, Coffman, and Walters (1969), however, showed that there was an increase in stereotyping between the early 1950s and the late 1960s. The only exception was the stereotype of Negroes which did show continuous fading (less agreement among the students on which traits should be used to characterize blacks). The mean favorableness of traits comprising the American stereotype dropped from .99 (in 1933) to .86 (in 1951) to .49 (in 1967). The Negro stereotype improved, from −.70 to .07, as did the stereotype of Jews (.24 to .66). The Japanese showed fluctuations, associated with their participation in war, from .66 (in 1933) to −.14 (in 1951) to .84 (in 1967), and a similar trend can be seen for the Germans. The English had a steady positive stereotype (around .60), and the Turks a steady negative (−.98; −1.03; −.62). The Irish and Italian stereotypes deteriorated, and the Chinese improved over time. In assessing the meaning of these fluctuations, it is clear that we must take into account historical events. On the other hand, it also is necessary to consider norms permitting expression of disapproval of an ethnic group. In 1922, white students probably experienced few pressures against the use of derogatory terms concerning blacks; this has now changed. In short, both historical events and norms allowing or opposing the expression of derogations of ethnic groups may influence stereotyping.

That stereotypes tend to change with historical events is further shown in a study of Prothro and Melikian (1955), who used an adjective checklist to obtain the way Arab students perceive various nationalities before and after a visit of the Seventh Fleet in Lebanese waters. Although stereotypes of other groups remained unchanged, the American stereotype changed by addition of the characteristics sociable, jolly, superficial, and simple. Sinha and Upadhyaya (1960) showed that the stereotypes of the Chinese, as perceived by Indian students, were markedly changed in an unfavorable direction as a result of the Sino-Indian border dispute of 1959 to 1960.

Vassiliou, Triandis, Vassiliou, and McGuire (1968) distinguish between "normative" stereotypes and stereotypes without a normative component. Normative stereotypes are beliefs held by groups of people concerning "the appropriate" and "correct" way of thinking about another group of people. Americans have normative stereotypes about Russians; Greeks have normative stereotypes about Americans. The major characteristic of a normative stereotype is that it is rich and definite, despite a total lack of personal contact with the group that is being stereotyped. Nonnormative stereotypes are vague and undefined stereotypes concerning people about whom one does not know very much, such as many American stereotypes about Greeks.

When a person knows little about a friendly foreign group, he tends to assume that this group is more or less the way he is. On the other hand, if the foreign group is characterized as hostile, then he tends to think that it is extremely different. Figure 12 presents the changes in stereotyping that occur for normative and nonnormative stereotypes as a result of contact. It is assumed that nonnormative stereotypes exist only in the case of friendly outgroups.

Line *CD* shows how the autostereotype of A changes; line *EF* shows how the nonnormative stereotype of A concerning group B changes; line *GH* shows how the normative stereotypes of A concerning group B change as a result of contact. Notice that as a result of contact both the normative and the nonnormative stereotypes of group A concerning group B approach the sociotype of B, that is they become more accurate. It is assumed that the difference between the two sociotypes is substantial, so that group A tends to exaggerate it (contrast effects)

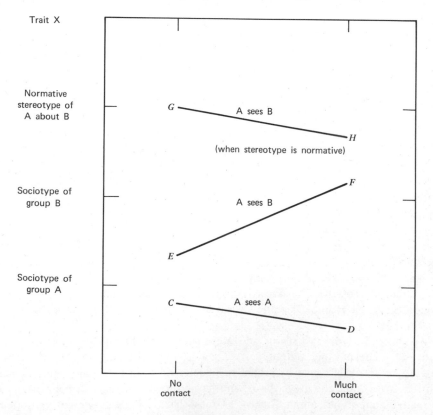

FIGURE 12.   Changes in stereotypes as a result of contact.

when it is in frequent contact with group B. This is why the autostereotype of group A changes in the direction away from the sociotype of group B. The two central points of the diagram are that the stereotypes become more accurate with contact (they approach the sociotypes) and that the difference between the values of the two sociotypes on trait X is reflected in the heterostereotype.

According to an extensive investigation of stereotypes conducted by Buchanan and Cantril (1953), friendliness toward other nations appears to depend on factors such as (a) the place of the subject's nation in the bipolar world of Russia-USA, (b) the place of the subject's nation and the nation's being stereotyped during World War II, (c) common boundaries, (d) common language, and (e) neutrality in war of the nation being stereotyped. Thus, political alignments are major determinants of stereotyping.

The Kernel of Truth Hypothesis. The shifts of stereotypes with political events suggest how people use them as explanations of what is going on in their environment. The accuracy of stereotypes is quite poor, and they are inferior judgmental processes. However, they probably do contain a kernel of truth; two lines of argument support this hypothesis.

One is that autostereotypes (the way a group of people looks at itself) are strikingly similar to heterostereotypes (the way one group looks at another) (Campbell, 1967). For example, Fischer and Trier (1962) used a semantic differential (see Chapter II) to obtain the autostereotypes and heterostereotypes of French- and German-speaking Swiss. They found with impressive regularity that the German-Swiss view themselves as angular, dry, and conservative. The French-Swiss also view the German-Swiss as angular, dry, and conservative—only more so. Furthermore, the stereotypes of the German-Swiss and the Germans and the stereotypes of the French-Swiss and the French are quite similar. An analysis of the kinds of words that were most closely associated in meaning with the concept German-Swiss showed the words "manly," "work," "father," and "authority" as being quite closely related. The meaning of French-Swiss, on the other hand, was close to the concepts of "love," "friend," "mother," and "female." In a study by Triandis and Vassiliou (1967) on the stereotypes of Americans and Greeks, a similar set of results appeared. Both groups saw Greeks as unsystematic, suspicious, competitive, etc., and also viewed Americans as systematic, efficient, naive, etc. On the other hand, there are several characteristics on which the autostereotypes differed from the heterostereotypes—for example, the Greeks regarded the Americans as dull, but the Americans considered themselves as witty.

Such similarities in stereotyping can be explained either by the kernel of truth hypothesis or by the hypothesis that each group of people learns the stereotypes that others have of it and then develops its autostereotypes to match. The latter explanation seems unlikely, but there is support for it in the case of American Negroes. The differential status of whites and Negroes in American society has sometimes made Negroes adopt the views of themselves held by prestigeful whites.

Another line of argument also could explain the similarity of auto- and heterostereotypes. Suppose that two groups of people have a characteristic that is clearly different. Americans, for instance, have a higher standard of living than most Asians; hence, they differ on the characteristic "wealthy." Each characteristic is "naturally" correlated with many others. In fact, people have "implicit theories of personality," that is, ways of thinking that relate characteristics to each other. There is not very much known, as yet, about the extent to which people from different cultures have similar or different implicit personality theories, but it is probable that the implicit personality theories of culturally similar peoples will be rather similar. If this happens, then given a particular objective difference in a particular characteristic, there will be *similar* differences in a host of other (correlated) characteristics. For example, assume that everyone has the theory that "efficient people are wealthy." Then, Americans looking at a group of Asians may reason: "they are poor, therefore they are inefficient." The Asians, looking at themselves, may reason: "we are poor, therefore we are inefficient." Thus, starting from the objective characteristic *poor,* both groups arrive at an agreement on the nonobjective characteristic *inefficient,* because they share a theory that links these characteristics.

Our knowledge of stereotyping is insufficient to enable us to choose among these various explanations of the similarity between auto- and heterostereotypes. Clearly, however, the majority of the explanations suggest that there is a "kernel of truth" in stereotyping, and that the process may begin from an observation of real differences on some trait, as the case of the hypothetical Americans and Asians mentioned above.

Another line of support for the kernel of truth hypothesis comes from direct attempts to validate stereotypes. In an interesting study by Schuman (1966) the regional stereotypes held in East Pakistan were obtained from college students. The students were asked to choose from a list of 50 adjectives the four that best described the people in each of 12 districts of East Pakistan.

The validation data were obtained from a stratified random sample of urban industrial workers of rural origin from the various districts. Specifically, the most frequently mentioned characteristic of the people from the Noakhali region was *pious*. Workers from that and other regions were asked questions concerning the frequency of their prayers. The Noakhali workers reported five prayers daily 87 percent of the time, but only about 50 percent of the workers from other regions mentioned such a high frequency. In answering a large number of different questions, it was clear that workers from the Noakhali region were more religious than workers from the other districts. Here, then, is an example of a stereotype that has some validity.

On the other hand, it is well to remember that different traits have either very narrow or very wide distributions in a given population. For example, the characteristic *pious* may show little variability from person to person in certain Moslem populations, and show a great deal of variability in populations of Scandinavians. Thus, it is easier to make a valid statement about this characteristic concerning Moslems than it is to make a valid statement concerning Scandinavians.

Furthermore, for a characteristic to have validity, the group being stereotyped should not be changing very much, otherwise the stereotypes will be out of date.

If the "kernel of truth" hypothesis is valid, what is the most likely basis for the development of stereotypes? Campbell (1967) argues that when two populations have various traits, some of which have different values, the greater the difference in the mean value of a trait, the more likely it is that the trait will become part of the stereotype. This proposition has an important implication: stereotypes are not only a function of the group being stereotyped but also of the group doing the stereotyping, since the *difference* in the mean value of a trait is the determinant of the stereotype.

The implication of this point is important and needs to be illustrated with an example. Suppose that we consider the number of times per day that people in all cultures of the world wash their hands. Let us say that the average for all cultures is five times per day. Now suppose that the members of culture A wash their hands 15 times per day and that the members of culture B wash only 10 times per day. When the members of culture A stereotype the members of culture B, they are perfectly justified to call them filthy. Moreover they do not know what is average around the world, and why should they consider the average anyway? What they do know is what is "standard" in their own culture and, with respect to their own culture, members of culture B wash only two thirds as frequently as is "proper." Hence, they are filthy. Of course, from a worldwide perspective, members of culture B would be considered very clean and members of culture A "compulsively clean."

Granted that stereotypes have a kernel of truth and *can* be valid, they also can be demonstrated to be patently false . In a classic study LaPiere (1936) showed that, when checked, the stereotype held in Fresno, California about the local Armenian minority was point-by-point in error. Furthermore, the stereotypes held by certain people with personality disorders can be completely unrelated to reality.

Stereotypes lead to poor judgment for several reasons that have been brilliantly analyzed by Campbell (1967). First, there is a sense of absolutism in the stereotype. If a group of people is said to have a characteristic it is assumed that all of them have it. There is also no awareness of the selective distortion involved in stereotyping. Moreover, there is no awareness of the extent to which our own personality and needs distort reality to make the stereotypes fit our desires.

Second, people tend to perceive great similarity among members of their ingroup and great differences between them and members of their outgroup. In fact, however, all evidence shows tremendous overlaps between any groups of humans and any other group of humans on most ability tests and most personality traits.

Third, there is a confusion of causes. There is a tendency to think that group X has a particular characteristic because of its race, religion, or nationality. Actually, the characteristic is most likely explicable by an analysis of the environment and history of this group of people. There is evidence, for example, that Negroes in the United States score less well on intelligence tests than do whites. There is a strong tendency to attribute this difference to race; in fact, it is most likely the result of environment. In the few cases where the Negroes had had superior educational environments to those of whites (for example, some Northern Negroes versus some Southern whites) the difference in intelligence scores was reversed.

Another confusion involves the fusion of characteristics, for instance, race with social class. In America there is a tendency for Negroes to be lower class with the result that the stereotype of Negroes tends to be similar to the stereotype of the lower class. Bayton, McAllister, and Heimer (1956) found that when subjects judge stimuli such as Lower-Class Negroes, or Upper-Class Whites, their stereotypes vary more as a function of the social class than as a function of race. Triandis and Triandis (1960) pointed out that simple stimuli like "Negroes" should not be used in stereotype research because of this strong association with social class. They employed stimuli that varied simultaneously in several characteristics such as race, religion, occupation, and nationality. By using this technique, it is possible to isolate the racial stereotype from its associations with social class, religion, and nationality stereotypes.

Fourth, there is a relationship between hostility toward a group and stereotyping of that group. Avigdor (1953) and Sherif et al (1954) have shown that groups that are in conflict develop negative stereotypes; the same people in cooperative situations develop positive stereotypes of each other. In other words, conflict leads to hostility, and hostility leads to the negative stereotypes. Yet, there is a tendency for people to reverse this sequence, to say that "because this outgroup has several undesirable characteristics, we feel hostility toward members of this outgroup."

When two groups are in conflict, they assume that they are more different from each other than they really are. In other words, there are contrast effects (see Chapter III). Conversely, when two groups are similar (for example, the Americans and the British), they tend to assume that they are more similar than they really are—assimilation effects. This point can be illustrated by an experiment performed by Jahoda (1966), who presented the results of an opinion survey conducted in Poland to students in a Scottish university. The students were asked to inspect the opinion poll results in detail and to guess where the poll had been taken. A list of eleven countries, including the United Kingdom and Poland, was presented to the students. Only 1.4 percent of the students guessed correctly. Fifty percent guessed that the poll was taken in the United Kingdom; substantial percentages guessed Belgium, Denmark, West Germany, or France, but only negligible percentages guessed that the results were obtained in a communist country. Thus, we tend to exaggerate the cognitive differences between ourselves and the groups with whom we are in conflict.

Campbell and LeVine (1965) examined a variety of theories relevant to the problem of ethnocentrism—that is, the tendency for a group of people to put itself in the center of most judgmental scales and to think of itself as good, moral, and virtuous while considering outgroups as bad, immoral, and threatening. Their most stimulating review included a number of propositions about stereotypes, which were further elaborated by Campbell (1967). The next section contains a simplified version of some of these propositions.

Some Propositions Concerning the Development of Stereotypes.

1. The more real the contrast between two groups on a given trait, the more likely is that trait to appear in the mutual stereotypes each has of the other.

2. The more opportunities for observation, and the longer the exposure to the outgroup, the larger the role of real differences in the stereotype. This implies that nearer groups will be more accurately stereotyped. Therefore, the more remote and less well known the outgroup, the more purely projective the content of the stereotype and the less accurate it is.

3. The trait differences involved in intergroup interaction will be most strongly represented and also most accurately represented in mutual stereotypes.

4. Among trait differences of approximately equal contrast, those that are relevant to the needs and desires of a group of people are most apt to be noticed and represented in stereotype imagery.

5. Once a stereotype difference or perception of difference is established, less real difference is required to maintain or to re-evoke it.

6. Those traits that have well-established rejection responses associated with them, for within-ingroup usage, will be most apt to be perceived in outgroup stereotypes.

The evidence in favor of these propositions is rather strong. For example, in Africa those who have two rainy seasons are seen as "active" and those having one are seen as "lazy." Groups with a high degree of acculturation to Western standards are seen as "progressive" and "clean"; those with less acculturation are seen as "stupid." In fact, the causes of acculturation may well be accidental, having to do with the development of the railway. Groups specializing in physical labor are stereotypes as strong, stupid, pleasure-loving, and improvident. Groups specializing in trade as grasping, deceitful, industrious, and aggressive. Campbell's paper presents several additional examples and a good deal of evidence that supports the above-mentioned propositions.

Avigdor's (1953) theory of stereotype development is in some respects complementary to Campbell's. She argues that when there is hostility between the two groups, the difference in the unfavorable traits becomes accentuated and the difference in the favorable traits is eliminated. On the other hand, when there is cooperation between the two groups, the reverse process takes place. Hence, stereotypes begin by reflecting the differences between two human groups and become distorted in a favorable direction if two groups are friendly and cooperative, and in an unfavorable direction if they are in conflict.

Of course, cooperation or competition is often determined by economic, political, or other environmental factors. But the point of Avigdor's theory is that once the stage is set for cooperation or conflict, it is possible to predict which characteristics will become salient and which characteristics will not be included in the stereotype. Avigdor tested her hypotheses with ten-year-old girls in a settlement house. Regular competitive games constituted the conflict situation. Cooperation of two or more groups in the production of a musical comedy show provided the cooperative condition. A 32-adjective checklist was employed to test the stereotypes of the children after they worked in the two conditions. In addition, six psychologists rated the various groups, in an effort to establish whether any of the groups actually had the particular characteristics. The results of this study showed that (a) the stereotypes in the cooperative condition were much more favorable than the stereotypes in the conflict condition; (b) for those items that according to the psychologists were the "real" characteristics of the groups, there were more unfavorable judgments than favorable judgments in the conflict situation; (c) on the other hand, in the cooperative situation there was no greater number of favorable judgments on the "real" characteristics. In other words, in conflict situations, stereotypes are greatly aided by "real" undesirable characteristics which tend to increase the conflict. We can conclude that Avigdor's hypothesis that differences in unfavorable traits become accentuated in conflict situations is supported. On the other hand, there is no evidence for the reverse process, that is, differences in favorable characteristics do not become accentuated in cooperative conditions.

PROJECT FOR ADVANCED STUDENTS

Prepare a report on Ehrlich's (1967) five components of ethnic stereotypes.

The Development of National Stereotypes. Lambert and Klineberg (1967), in an ambitious study of 3300 children from eleven countries, examined the stereotypes of 6, 10, and 14 year olds. In most countries the children did *not* give their nationality when they were asked the simple questions: "What are you?" . . . . "What else are you?" The typical response was for the child to give his or her sex. Only the Bantu and the Lebanese children deviated from this pattern: the former mentioned their race; the latter their religion. Reference to nationality increased with age, but it seldom was mentioned by more than 10 percent of the children. Younger children tended to characterize foreign people in terms of physical-racial descriptions and descriptions of clothing and customs. Older children noted more personality descriptions, political and religious characteristics, and material possessions.

The development of the cognitive component proceeds through four stages:

(a) The child learns the category—most children cannot utilize categories such as Negroes or Jews until they are three years old. The majority of four year olds are able to discriminate between Negroes and whites when forced to do so, but they do not normally distinguish between two groups of people. Thus, although perceptual discrimination (that is, the ability to discriminate) comes early, the actual use of the categories comes later.

(b) The child learns to associate the categories with other categories—once the child has categorized attitude objects in certain categories, it begins to learn the connections between the categories and other categories. In the case of the Negro category, certain connections are more likely than others. For example, the association of Negro and Dirty can occur because the child perceives a physical similarity in the stimuli classified in these two categories. Usually, by age five most children have associated the racial categories with other categories, that is, have racial stereotypes.

(c) The child learns to evaluate—the associations mentioned above lead the child to experience a positive or negative emotion in relation to the category. By the age of five most children have a definite affective response to stimuli such as Negroes.

(d) Judgments about attitude objects become more differentiated with age. Jaspers et al. (1965) found that Dutch children in grades 2, 3, 4, 5, and 6 steadily improved their discriminations among countries. In grade 2 there was little differentiation; it gradually increased. In the later grades countries were organized along a dimension of evaluation (good: Netherlands and England; bad: Germany and Russia) and a dimension of power (powerful: America and Russia; weak: Netherlands).

STUDY QUESTIONS

1. Describe the development of categories and stereotypes.
2. Are stereotypes stable?
3. What is the "kernel of truth" hypothesis? What line of evidence supports it?
4. Why are stereotypes inferior judgmental processes?
5. What variables affect the development of stereotypes?
6. Summarize the development of the cognitive component of attitudes.

SUGGESTED FURTHER READING

Allport (1954) Chapters 1, 2, 3, 10, 11, 12, and 18. Campbell (1967); Vassiliou et al. (1968); Sherif et al. (1954).

The Formation of the Affective Component

The affective component of attitudes is characterized by the presence of positive or negative emotion. Physiologically, emotion involves mainly a state of arousal; it becomes positive or negative when it is cognitively "interpreted." In a series of experiments reviewed by Schacter (1964), it has been shown that a physiological state of arousal is "labeled" by the individual in terms of his available cognitions. If he experiences arousal with a sufficient explanation (for example, he knows he received an injection of adrenaline), he does not experience emotions such as fear. If he experiences the cognitions, but not the physiological arousal (for example, he knows he is in danger, but has taken a drug that prevents physiological arousals), then he again will not experience an emotion. Only when both the arousal and the cognition are present will he experience the emotion.

The effect of reward on attitude change is illustrated in a study by Scott (1957). Seventy-two subjects were induced to engage in debates on three different issues, taking sides opposite to those which they had indicated as their own in an opinion pretest. One half the subjects were rewarded, in predetermined order, by a purported vote that proclaimed them the better debators. The other one half were punished for presumably losing the debate. Posttests showed a tendency of the "winners" to change their opinions in the direction of their debates, although the "losers" did not change significantly. A control group of nondebators also did not change their attitudes. Thus, the ones who were rewarded did change their attitude. The social reward for expressing a new opinion tends to reinforce the new attitude.

Frequency of Exposure and Affect

In an interesting review of a large body of evidence, Zajonc (1968) has argued that the pleasantness of a stimulus is a function of its familiarity. The pleasantness may be measured through judgments on the evaluative factor of the semantic differential (see pp. 47-48, Chapter II). The frequency of exposure of the person to the stimulus may be manipulated experimentally, or we might examine the frequency of the stimulus in the everyday environment. Zajonc assembled an impressive array of facts to support his argument. He presented 154 pairs of antonyms (for example, able-unable, good-bad, high-low, likely-unlikely, on-off, together-apart, yes-no, near-far, play-work) to college students and asked them to indicate which they preferred. He also observed the frequency of occurrence of these words in printed English texts. In 82 percent of the cases the preferred word had a higher frequency in English texts than the nonpreferred word. Or, to take another example, the frequencies of 555 adjectives that may be used to describe a person were compared with their likeability judgments obtained by asking "how much you yourself would like the person described by that word." The correlation between the likeability ratings and the logarithm of the frequency counts was .83 (very high and extremely significant).

There is excellent evidence that frequent words are short, and it may be that we have here a phenomenon that can be explained by the the principle of least effort. However, this explanation is unsatisfactory in view of other data presented by Zajonc. He showed that nonsense words, or Chinese characters exposed a few times, elicit less positive affect than nonsense words or Chinese characters presented frequently. Similarly, photographs presented frequently elicited more affect than photographs presented less frequently.

Further evidence consistent with Zajonc's arguments can be found in a study by Jaspers, Van de Geer, Tajfel, and Johnson (1965). Dutch children judged pictures according to whether they were "Dutch" or "not-Dutch." They also rated the pictures on a dislike-like dimension. There was a tendency for those pictures that were perceived as being Dutch by a large proportion of the children to be rated as more liked, and for those pictures seen as Dutch by small proportions of children to be rated as less liked. This tendency was present in all the data, regardless of the age, sex, religion, or socioeconomic level of the child.

The Formation of the Behavioral Component

In our discussion of the formation of the cognitive component of attitudes, we emphasized the importance of cognitive factors, such as categorization, selectivity in perception, associations between categories, and the accentuation of certain traits. In our discussion of the affective component's development we mention conditioning and familiarity. In the present section we discuss the formation of the behavioral component and our emphasis is on social norms.

Social norms are ideas held by a group of people concerning what is correct or incorrect behavior.

Children are told by their parents how to behave. In fact, a good deal of the interaction between parents and children consists of "don't do that" or "do that." The explanations given by the parents are of various kinds. Some are authoritarian, for example, "do that because I say so." Other explanations are in terms of cognitive arguments, for example, "do not play with Negroes because they are likely to be dirty." Still other explanations are in terms of social norms, for example, "do not do that because people will talk." The latter kind of explanation implies that the child already knows what people consider "good" or "bad" behavior, and the parent simply reminds the child of the existing social norms.

It is particularly important to realize that social norms are of different kinds. Some norms are very strict (for example, murder of an ingroup member); some very vague and deviation is almost permissible (for example, preferring an outgroup instead of an ingroup member in a political election). Some arouse great emotion (for example, marrying a member of the outgroup) and other norms are of little consequence (for example, expressing admiration for the ideas of a member of the outgroup). In general, those behaviors that are most intimate and that define the existence and nature of the ingroup (marriage, death, birth, etc.) are associated with the most clear and emotion producing norms.

There is overwhelming evidence that different cultural groups have different norms about appropriate behavior with outgroups. Triandis and Triandis (1965) reviewed a number of studies which indicate that Americans exclude other people on racial grounds more readily than for other reasons; Greeks exclude people more readily on religious grounds; Germans and Japanese exclude people more readily on social-class and on racial grounds. Thus, the ingroups are determined by different criteria in different cultures. Furthermore, there may be several levels of ingroups. Marriage defines the most intimate; friendship the next, work collaboration another, and so on. Some people show their prejudice only at the core (marital rejection), others show it both at the marital and the friendship levels, and others at all levels.

What is intimate is usually defined by culture. This is particularly clear in a study by Mahar (1960). Members of different Indian castes were asked whether they would allow members of other castes to behave in certain ways. The most intimate behaviors used in this study were (a) "can touch our earthenware vessels," and (b) "can come into our cooking area." Mahar found that only Brahmans were allowed to engage in intimate behaviors of this kind with other Brahmans. Brahmans allowed some of the "higher" castes to engage in less intimate behaviors, such as "smoke our pipe" or "touch our brass vessels" with them, but most other castes were excluded from these intimacies. The shoemakers, agricultural laborers, and sweepers were excluded from even such nonintimate behaviors as "can touch me." Thus, in India there was in the mid-1950s a "ritual pollution scale" that corresponded to the ranking of the Hindu castes. As behaviors became more intimate, more and more people were excluded from them, until one reached behaviors that were allowed only with members of one's own caste, or with a higher caste.

Why do such norms for behavior toward outgroups develop? Triandis and Triandis (1960) have argued that economic conditions place one group in a position of advantage over another. To maintain this advantage, it is necessary to keep the two groups from merging. Norms of social distance are developed to prevent such merging and loss of the economic advantages. Even after the economic differences are no longer relevant, there may be a tradition of social distance that continues the attractiveness of these norms. Specifically, Dollard (1957) has detailed the economic, sexual, and prestige gains of whites in relation to Negroes. The disparity in wages and average annual incomes of the two races is becoming larger, in spite of the recent civil rights protests. Whites have more access to Negro women than is the case for the reverse. Lower class whites feel more satisfied when there is at least one group that they can consider as lower in the social status scale.

If the distinctions between the races were to be eliminated, all these gains would disappear. Thus some whites tell their children not to mix with Negroes. Depending on how strongly they feel about the desirability of separating the two race groups, they will insist on different degrees of social distance. But, at any rate, they do teach their children that it is wrong to be friendly with Negroes, and they do punish them for behavior that they regard as too friendly. Under these circumstances the behavioral component of attitudes toward Negroes becomes formed to reflect the existing social norms.

When a group is discriminated against, it reacts by developing self-hatred, apathy, or by asserting itself. In many studies, Negroes have been found to be low in self-esteem. Other studies have emphasized their apathy and lack of self-improvement. However, some Negroes have taken the path of self-assertion, as is found in in the black power movement. All three reactions can readily be observed in the same group of people.

Self-assertion is likely to be found in groups that have developed a considerable body of distinguishing cultural elements. For example, Jews, generally, have not adopted apathy in reacting to discrimination. Although there is evidence of anti-Semitism among Jews (that is, self-hatred), the pattern in general has been one of assertion. The same is true for various national groups when they have had important unifying cultural characteristics which could set them apart from the dominant group. The French Canadians have reacted to discrimination by asserting their rights and threatening separation from the rest of Canada.

Reactions, such as self-hatred or self-assertion, can develop social norms of their own. The leadership of the group being discriminated against may instruct its members to retaliate, to avoid friendly relations, and so forth. Although in most studies of social distance nationality plays a relatively insignificant role, Shim and Dole (1967) found that the parents of first- and second-generation Japanese in Hawaii gave nationality a large weight in determining their social distance. On the other hand, their children gave nationality a very small weight. In this case, the leadership of the group was trying to keep the group's identity, but the followers were hoping to merge into the broad current of American society.

One important point concerning intergroup relations is that most of the norms that are effective in controlling the behavior of people are proscriptive rather than prescriptive. Ehrlich and Tubergen (1967) replicated and extended the work of Triandis on the structure of the behavioral component of attitudes and pointed out that proscriptive norms of interpersonal and intergroup behavior determine behavior more definitely than prescriptive norms. For example, when parents say "you will *not* marry a Negro" they are likely to impose the norm, but when they say "you will marry a professional" they are less likely to be successful in imposing the norm.

Summary

When two groups of people meet they will differ on a number of traits. The greater the difference on a given trait, the more likely it is that this trait will appear in the stereotypes that each has about the other. People bring to the process of stereotyping implicit theories of the human personality. Thus, traits are assumed to be correlated. Given that two groups are different on a particular trait, the stereotype is likely to reflect several other traits, which correlated with the "true trait" but which do not have much validity. In general, then, stereotypes have a kernel of truth and a body of invalid judgments. When two groups are in conflict, or when one group is obtaining an economic advantage by its separation from another, then norms of interpersonal behavior that sanction discrimination, avoidance, and social distance are likely to develop. The reaction of those being discriminated against will be one of self-hatred, apathy, or self-assertion. Depending on the kind of reaction, they will develop appropriate norms of interpersonal behavior. Finally, in the process of interaction the two groups are likely to reinforce each other, or to punish each other. The greater the reinforcement, the greater the likelihood of positive affect developing in connection with the other group; the greater the punishment, the greater the negative affect that is likely to develop. When two groups are in conflict, the probability of negative affect developing is very high. By contrast, when two groups are in cooperation, they are very likely to develop positive affect.

In sum, the development of intergroup attitudes depends on the traits of each group, the kind of reinforcements that each will experience during the interaction, and the kinds of social norms about interaction that will develop. Direct experience with the attitude object is most likely to increase the kernel of truth in the stereotype, but it will also have effects on the affective component. The kinds of effects are largely dependent on the cooperativeness or hostility of the relationship.

The Development of the Interrelations
Between the Components of Attitude

There is evidence that as children become older the three components of attitude become more and more consistent (Horowitz, 1936). There also is evidence that the three components do not have identical growth curves. Horowitz (1936) presented the theoretical curves of Fig. 13 to show the growth of prejudice. Prejudice was determined by a child's differential liking for pictures of 12 boys—four white and eight Negro. The more he tended to prefer the white to the Negro pictures the higher was his prejudice score. Such liking probably reflects the affective component.

Horowitz also used a "social situation test" which had photographic prints of social groups. Some were all white and others had one white child substituted by a Negro child. The situations included playing marbles, choosing sides for baseball, hand-wrestling, playing the piano, being in an ice cream parlor, etc. The child was asked: "Do you want to join in with them and do what they are doing?" These

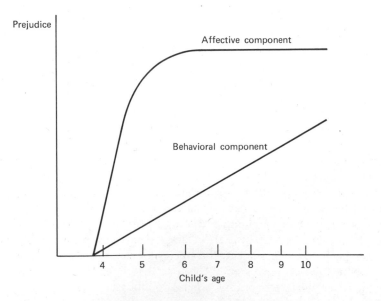

FIGURE 13.   The probable growth of prejudice (adopted from Horowitz, 1936).

situations and the particular question asked are probably more relevant to the behavioral component. As can be observed in Fig. 13, the two components do not develop in identical fashion, although there is a tendency for them to become consistent when the children are older.

Summary Comment on the Development of the Three Components

The major point of the preceding discussion is that each of the three components of attitude develops under the influence of somewhat different variables. We learn our attitudes either from direct experience or from other people. Direct experience is most relevant to the development of the cognitive and the affective components; other people (family and friends) are most relevant to the behavioral component. Of course, direct experience can have some implications for the behavioral component, because the three components interact and there is a tendency for them to become as consistent as possible. Conversely, other people can tell us not only how we should behave, thus influencing our behavioral component, but also how we should think and how we should feel about various attitude objects. On the other hand, they cannot impose their views; although our parents make an attempt to tell us how to think and feel, we often develop our own ways of thinking and feeling. Nevertheless, when they tell us how to behave they can also provide sanctions that will discourage us from deviating from these norms. It is for this reason that the behavioral component of attitudes is much more rigidly related to social norms than is the case with other components.

STUDY QUESTIONS

1. Explain how emotion is related to cognition according to the work reviewed by Schachter (1964).
2. Explain how conditioning is involved in the development of the affective component of attitudes.
3. What is the evidence that pleasantness of a stimulus is a function of its familiarity?
4. How do social norms affect the development of the behavioral component of attitudes?

SUGGESTED FURTHER READING

Allport (1954b) Chapters 17, 19; Staats (1967); and Triandis and Triandis (1965) in Fishbein (1967a); Proshansky (1966).

V

Societal and Personality Determinants of Attitudes

In the previous Chapters we examined certain determinants of the formation and development of attitudes. The focus was on the determinants that are particularly relevant in the formation of each of the components of attitude. In this Chapter, we ignore the distinctions among the three components and examine a broad range of theories that deal with the development of attitudes but that do not discriminate among the components. In other words, in the present Chapter we assume that the three components are highly interrelated. In examining the various theories that discuss the formation of attitudes we shall focus on (a) the individual, (b) interpersonal relations, (c) groups, and (d) intergroup relations. Under each of these headings we shall examine a number of theoretical points of view.

Focus on the Individual

The kinds of child-training experienced by a person determines the kind of personality that he develops. People with different personalities are likely to have different attitudes.

One of the most significant studies in social psychology was presented in a book called the *Authoritarian Personality* (Adorno et al, 1950). The main argument in that book can be summarized as follows: People who had aloof, stern, and punitive fathers, whose parents administered a good deal of physical punishment, or threat of physical punishment, and who grew up in families organized along hierarchical lines, with a feared father as the most powerful figure, developed a particular kind of personality called *authoritarian.*

Authoritarians tend to employ a particular cognitive style. Specifically, they avoid introspection, reflection, speculation, and imaginative fantasy; they believe in mystical determinants of individual fate. They also have characteristic attitudes concerning a variety of attitude objects. Thus, they accept ingroup authority figures without questioning them; they desire powerful leaders; they approve of obedience and respect for authority, particularly for children; they approve of severe punishment of deviants, particularly sexual deviants, they perceive others as deviant and mankind as anarchic; they have a preoccupation with power viewing human relations in terms of dominance and submission; they admire military men, athletes, and financiers. By contrast, those low in authoritarianism view authority figures as being sometimes correct and sometimes incorrect; they prefer equalitarian leaders; they emphasize warmth and love in interpersonal relationships; they are tolerant of deviance; they admire scientists, artists and social reformers.

The central theoretical thesis of the authors of the authoritarian personality is that prejudiced and hostile attitudes are expressions of inner needs or impulses created as a result of certain child-rearing experiences; the inner needs are manifested not only in prejudiced attitudes but also in a variety of perceptual, conceptual, and behavioral styles.

The *Authoritarian Personality* generated a good deal of research. Only six years after its publication, Christie and Cook (1958) were able to review 230 papers dealing with aspects of the theory. The output during the last decade was almost as great. Kirscht and Dillehay (1967) refer to approximately as many publications that appeared in the next decade (1956 to 1966).

One reason for the popularity of this research is that the authors of the *Authoritarian Personality* developed a scale, called the *F* scale (*F* stands for Fascism), which is very easy to administer and which is supposed to measure the extent of authoritarianism of a given individual. The scale consists of about forty Likert-type attitude items. Table 5 presents seven items. We suggest that the reader "answer" this scale and obtain his own score. The scale is related systematically to ethnocentrism, anti-Semitism, and a variety of prejudiced attitudes. However, critics of this scale pointed out that a subject gets a high score by simply agreeing with each item. Thus, a person with an "acquiescence response set," that is, a tendency to answer "Yes" to *any* question, will automatically get a high *F* scale score, regardless of whether or not he agrees with the fascist content of the scale. In order to take care of this objection, a number of psychologists developed scales containing so-called reversed *F* scale items. However, the reversed items appear to measure something different from the original items. It has been difficult to successfully reverse the original *F* scale items and to develop scales that control for the acquiescence response set. Nevertheless, some success in obtaining these balanced scales has been reported by Berkowitz and Wolkon (1964) and Lee and Warr (1967).

Much of the argument concerning the *F* scale's response set is too technical to review here. Suffice it to say that although the critics of the *F* scale insist that it measures mostly acquiescence response tendencies, the supporters have argued that these tendencies are typical of authoritarians. Other critics have argued that the *F* scale is mostly a measure of the extent to which a person has had wide or limited experiences (Kelman and Barclay, 1963). The high *F* scale scorers are relatively unsophisticated; the low scorers have had a wider range of experiences and a broader perspective than the high scorers.

The important point, as far as the study of attitudes is concerned, is that people

Table 5 **Some Items From the *F* Scale**

Instructions. We would like to have your personal opinion concerning some statements about which people have different opinions. Please place an "X" in the box that best describes your opinion. If you strongly agree, mark the +3 box; if you slightly agree mark the +1 box; if you strongly disagree mark the −3 box; if you slightly disagree, the −1 box. Please be sure to make a response to each statement.

	Agree			Disagree		
	+3 Strong	+2 Moderate	+1 Slight	−1 Slight	−2 Moderate	−3 Strong
An insult to our honor should always be punished.			X			
A person who has bad manners, habits and breeding can hardly expect to get along with decent people.						X
Obedience and respect for authority are the most important virtues children should learn.					X	
No sane, normal, decent person could ever think of hurting a close relative or friend.						X
Science has its place, but there are many important things that can never possibly be understood by the human mind.			X			
What youth needs most is strict discipline, rugged determination, and the will to work and fight for family and country.					X	
In my opinion, patriotism and loyalty are the first requirements of a good citizen.						X

−|0

How to Score. Sum the scores, taking into account the −3 to +3 values marked above. The minimum possible score is −21; the maximum is +21. Most college students would average close to −5. Hence, if your score is higher than −5 you are relatively high on this scale.

You also should know that there is a negative correlation between *F* scale score and intelligence. This means that people who are more intelligent tend to get negative scores on the *F* scale.

Since the original scale had 40 items, the score you obtain by answering only seven is much less reliable than the score you would obtain by answering the original scale. The important point here is simply for you to get an impression of what kinds of items are involved in this scale.

who report certain kinds of child-training experiences are high on the *F* scale, and these people have a distinctive set of attitudes concerning political and social issues. For example, authoritarianism of the right seems related to nationalism and to anti-world mindedness, and to hostility toward foreigners who are not completely pro-American.

Sociological studies of attitudes have generally found support for these results. Martin and Westie (1959), for instance, interviewed a representative sample of 429 persons in Indianapolis and selected 41 tolerant and 59 highly prejudiced interviewees. They found the tolerant to be less nationalistic; for example, they saw little danger from foreign ideas and agitators. On the other hand, the prejudiced tended to be intolerant of ambiguity; for example, they agreed with the statement that there "are two kinds of women—the pure and the bad." In addition, the prejudiced were high on the F scale, stressed obedience, harsh discipline, and physical punishment in child-rearing, and felt threatened and economically deprived; finally, they were fundamentalist in religious matters.

Rokeach (1960) has stressed that the F scale measures right-wing authoritarianism instead of the more general authoritarian syndrome that he identifies as dogmatism. The characteristic of the dogmatic is not so much *what* attitudes he holds but *how* he holds them. Thus, the dogmatic tends to be intolerant of ambiguity, to look at the world in terms of black and white instead of in terms of shades of grey, and to rely on authority and the sharp categorical rejection of beliefs that are not consonant with his established values. The dogmatic is anxious, rigid, and a poor problem solver.

The argument that cognitive style is associated with extreme social attitudes, regardless of the actual content of these attitudes, is supported by a number of investigations. For example, Taylor (1960) found that extreme liberals and extreme conservatives behaved similarly with respect to a variety of perceptual tasks, but moderates acted quite differently. Harvey, Hunt, and Schroder (1961) considered the degree to which an individual is concrete versus abstract in his cognitive functioning. They found some low but consistent relationships between the degree of concreteness and authoritarianism. They also provided an interesting typology of cognitive development, which they related to a theory of child training. According to Harvey et al., parents raise their children by (a) rewarding and punishing them either consistently or inconsistently, and when they do punish them they (b) either provide or do not provide an explanation. This leads to four kinds of child-training patterns: consistent without, inconsistent without, consistent with, and inconsistent with explanation. These four types (see Fig. 14) lead to four levels of cognitive functioning. Type I is the most concrete; Type IV the most abstract. When parents provide no explanation, for example, they answer the child's questions with a "because I say so," they are making the child pay very much attention to their own demands, wishes, and expectations. The child thus becomes 'tuned" to obeying authority figures. When the parents provide an explanation, they force the child to understand the complexities of the world, to become tuned to the situation, to other people, and so on. Thus, Types III and IV are more abstract than Types I and II.

Harvey (1967) has reviewed a large body of evidence concerning the relationship of these personality systems to attitude change. First, he summarizes a number of studies that provide descriptions of what is implied by concreteness (Type I or Type II) versus abstractness (Type IV). The concrete thinkers tend to (a) make few differentiations among categories that are concerned with issues that are central or

Parents reward or punish

Parents give	consistently	inconsistently
No explanation	Type I	Type II
Explanation	Type III	Type IV

FIGURE 14.   The four levels of cognitive functioning (after Harvey, Hunt, and Schroder, 1961).

ego-involving to them; (b) tend to judge in an extreme, black and white manner; (c) depend on the status and authority aspects of the sources of messages; (d) form quick judgments in ambiguous situations; (e) have a greater need for cognitive consistency; (f) have difficulties in changing sets and in behaving flexibly; (g) have trouble solving problems that require different ways of looking at situations; (h) are more insensitive to subtle cues; (i) have a smaller capacity to act "as if" and to take the role of others; (j) are more sure of their opinions; and (k) tend to follow the rules.

Since the Type II children have experienced unreliable rewards, they tend to reject authority figures, by contrast the Type I people tend to accept authority figures strongly. Hence, the reaction of Type I and Type II people to high-status sources is likely to be one of compliance, as long as the source controls reinforcements, but if the source has power and does *not* seem to want to use it, there can be a difference in the reactions of these two types, with Type I complying and with Type II showing counterconformity (if you tell me to do X, I will do the opposite). Such an interpretation of the Harvey (1964) study seems reasonable.

Although the F scale discriminates Type I people from others, it is not an adequate measure of concreteness, according to Harvey's analysis. A slightly better approach is to employ both the F scale and the D scale (which measures Dogmatism, Rokeach, 1960) and to consider those who are high on both, as Type I; those who are low F and high D, Type II; those who are high F and low D, Type III; and those who are low on both scales, Type IV. However, Harvey (1967, pp. 210 to 212) reviews a number of other measures, which he considers superior.

PROJECT FOR ADVANCED STUDENTS

Examine the original papers quoted by Harvey (1967) and write a paper on the reasons why you believe *one* of the several measures that he reviews is superior to the other measures.

Evidence for General Susceptibility to Persuasion

There is a fair amount of evidence suggesting that persuasibility is a general trait (Janis and Field, 1959; Abelson and Lesser, 1959a). This was the point of view that prevailed in the book edited by Hovland and Janis (1959). Abelson and Lesser (1959b) proposed a theory of persuasibility which they supported with a number of empirical findings. We can only present a brief description of this theory, which consists of almost a dozen propositions. Basically, the authors argue that the greater the reward experienced for agreement with others, or the greater the punishment for disagreement, the greater the individual's general persuasibility. Firm and frequent parental control correlates with persuasibility, because they will be rewarding agreement with them and will punish disagreement. The more the parents accept the child the greater will be its persuasibility.

SPECIAL PROJECT FOR ADVANCED STUDENTS

Deduce the propositions of the Abelson and Lesser theory of persuasibility from your knowledge of learning theory. If you need to refresh your mind about learning theory, examine a standard text in experimental psychology (for example, Osgood, 1953) or learning theory (for example, Hilgard and Bower, 1966).

Other Personality Variables

Related to the various types of cognitive functioning, as discussed by Schroder, Harvey, and others, is the form of control of behavior that people develop and use.

Children can learn to avoid "naughtiness" in order to avoid punishment by their parents (external control), or they may develop internal controls (conscience). There is a good deal of evidence that when the mother is the chief socializer and uses psychological techniqes of disciplining, for example, withdrawal of love, the child develops internal controls. On the other hand, when the father is the chief socializer and uses physical punishment, this leads to weak internal controls. The reasons for these relationships may be as follows. The mother is the main source of nurture for the child. When she punishes the child by withdrawing her love, the experience is devastating. Nothing in the world is worth the loss of his mother's love, and the child learns to control his own behavior in order to avoid this devastating punishment. If socialization is carried out by the father, who is not the main source of nurture, the child feels less threatened than when it is carried out by the mother. Furthermore, physical punishment, although disagreeable, is not nearly as devastating as loss of love. In fact, there are some behaviors that are "so much fun" that they are "worth a good spanking." Thus, the child does not learn to control himself.

People who learn to use internal controls are more likely as adults to act according to their own standards. Those who are under the influence of external controls are more likely to act according to the norms of their ingroup and authority figures in that ingroup. When ingroup values include prejudice and discrimination, those who depend on external controls are likely to adopt them. Support for this theoretical analysis was provided by Triandis and Triandis (1962) who found that people who were raised by their fathers, or who reported that they had been subjected to physical punishment, were more prejudiced than people who had been raised mostly by their mothers and reported that they had experienced mostly psychological techniques of discipline.

The kind of child training experienced by different individuals results in different conceptualizations of the nature of interpersonal relationships. Some people develop a conceptualization that stresses that people are good, strong, and humanistic; others develop the opposite conceptualization, that is, that people are bad and weak. The more positive conceptualization of man leads to a greater tendency to advocate negotiation in international conflicts, to accept international controls, and to support economic aid to other nations, as well as to lower ethnocentrism and authoritarianism (Worchel, 1967). People who experience highly punitive child-training practices are likely to develop very negative views of human relations. In sum, these kinds of studies suggest that the kind of child training experienced by different people will lead to different kinds of attitudes.

Related studies show that those who are very anxious are often very conservative. For example, Lawson and Stagner (1957) found higher levels of Galvanic Skin Response among conservative than among liberal individuals. The authors also found that highly anxious subjects were more susceptible to social pressures and tended to bring their opinions "in line" with those of the majority, no matter whether the majority opinions were consistent or inconsistent with their own.

Triandis and Triandis (1960) analyzed differences in prejudice by means of three constructs: *conformity, cognitive dissonance,* and *insecurity. Conformity* refers to the adoption of the norms and values of the ingroup. *Dissonance* theory was applied to prejudice by pointing out that economic competition, and the socioeconomic inequalities that result from it, are important factors in prejudice. Dollard (1957) has described not only economic, but also sexual and prestige gains that white Americans derived from racial prejudice. These gains, derived from economic exploitation, are inconsistent with the American creed ("all men are created equal...") and the prevailing religious ethic. The result has been the so-called "American dilemma"(Myrdal, 1944). The dissonance caused by this contradiction may be reduced by regarding the exploited group as so inferior that the democratic ideal is not relevant, that is, cannot be applied to it. In short, when one group establishes an economic advantage over another, it justifies the continuation of the unfair advantage by arguing that the other group deserves to lose because it is inferior. The third construct, *insecurity*, refers to a personality characteristic that causes a person to be intolerant of ambiguity. Such a person may adopt either an extreme version of the equalitarian ideal (for example, communism) or the exploitative-*status quo* position (for example, the KKK). This occurs because to be able to "live with" the gap among his cognitions is too threatening to the insecure person, that is, such a person is unable to tolerate this gap. By adopting one or the other of these two positions, the insecure person reduces his dissonance, since there is only one clear, "correct" position to which he must adhere. This position suggests that the left-wing fanatic and the prejudiced have a common psychological basis for their attitudes—insecurity.

Triandis and Triandis (1962) followed up on this research by hypothesizing that in any culture the more insecure the individual the more prejudiced he will be. Additionally, certain kinds of child-training practices will lead to insecurity. They tested both Greeks, who showed very little prejudice toward Negroes but a good deal of anti-Semitism, and Americans, who showed the reverse pattern of prejudices, that is, a good deal of anti-Negro prejudice and a little anti-Semitism. In both cultural groups the more insecure individuals were more prejudiced. In both cultures the highly prejudiced subjects also reported that their parents punished them inconsistently and without explanation, a condition which is bound to cause confusion in a child.

Insecurity is not only caused by the kinds of child training that a person has experienced but also by loss of status. For example, a person whose parents belong to the upper class, and who is unable to hold a middle-class job, loses status. This person is likely to be more prejudiced than a person whose social class is the same as the social class of his parents. This phenomenon was shown 20 years ago by Bettelheim and Janowitz (1950) and has since been confirmed and reconfirmed. More recently, Kaufman (1957) measured "status concern" with items such as: "Ambition is the most important factor determining success in life," "One should always try to live in a highly respectable residential area," "Raising one's social position is the most important goal in life." He found a substantial correlation (.66) between his status-concern scale and anti-Semitism.

Insecurity can occur not only if one loses status but also if one gains it. The person who has gained status may feel uncertain about the proper way to behave and the best way to preserve his status. Thus, Bettelheim and Janowitz point out that it is the *change* in status that is related to insecurity and insecurity is related to prejudice.

If insecurity is related to prejudice, one should be able to reduce prejudice by increasing the self-acceptance of an individual. Rubin (1967) has shown that this can be done. He measured prejudice before and after a person participated in a group in which mutual trust and openness were encouraged. He showed that such a group increased the individual's self-acceptance and decreased his prejudice. There was a significant relationship between changes in self-acceptance and prejudice.

In addition to differences in the child-training practices experienced by a given individual, which lead to different attitudes, the individual is exposed to a variety of other influences. Some of them are physiological, for instance, the influences associated with aging. It stands to reason that as a person becomes older he is less adaptable to environmental changes, hence, less willing to face novel situations. As a result his attitudes toward social objects that involve social change become less and less enthusiastic. A young person may welcome change; but an old person will generally reject it and, for this reason, his sociopolitical attitudes will be more conservative.

Some support for the expectation that older people will have more conservative attitudes is obtained from Freedman's (1961) study of Vassar alumnae who graduated between 1904 and 1956. He found that the F and E scale respones of the older women were much higher. However, interpretation of such results is difficult, since these women differed not only in age but also in the kinds of experiences that they had when they grew up. A longitudinal study of attitudes is needed to determine the effects of chronological age on attitudes.

The evidence suggests that influencibility increases with age up to age 8 or 9, after which it declines and reaches a plateau in adolescence. McGuire (1969a) reviews a number of studies that fall into this pattern.

Other demographic characteristics, such as sex, show influences on attitude change.

Several studies found that women are more susceptible to influence than men. McGuire (1969a) suggests that this is due to the more effective reception of the message by women rather than to greater yielding. Another clear finding is that most of the correlations between personality variables and influencibility have been found with male samples and almost none with female samples (for example, Janis and Field, 1959; Abelson and Lesser, 1959a). Hovland and Janis took the position that this was because of American cultural influences which require girls to conform to a greater extent than boys. Since boys may or may not conform, there is variability on this characteristic, and it is possible for it to correlate with other characteristics.

At this time there is not enough evidence to make any of these conclusions dependable. For example, Leventhal, Jones, and Trembly (1966) presented communications concerning the need to take tetanus shots to both males and females. Females reported higher levels of fear than did males. Women who had not been previously inoculated felt more vulnerable to tetanus and were more favorable to shots. However, there was no evidence that women actually took more shots. In other words, the female sample appears to have received the message more effectively (showed fear) without yielding to it. The results of this study show many interactions, and Leventhal et al, speculate that, perhaps, men experience a greater feeling of imposition, and reduction in their freedom of choice (an idea that reminds us of reactance, as described by Brehm, 1966) than do women. This notion, then, would be consistent with the generalization that men oppose influence, although the previous generalization was that women are more influencible. Chu (1967) presented several communications to Chinese boys and girls and factor analyzed the change scores. He found different factors in the two samples. Although men showed "general persuasibility" and attitude changes that followed particular ideological commitments, women showed rather different factors, for instance, one which was interpreted as resentment against male authority. This suggests that the nature of the influence process may be different for the two sexes, at least, in traditional Chinese society.

STUDY QUESTIONS

1. What are the major points of the theory of authoritarianism?
2. In what way do child-training practices determine the kinds of attitudes that a person is likely to have?

FURTHER READING

Kirscht and Dillehay (1967); Triandis and Triandis (1962); Campbell and LeVine (1968).

A Partial Summary

Personality is a very complex field. In the previous sections we suggested some determinants of personality characteristics that have relevance for attitude formation and change. We pointed out the importance of socialization, particularly the use of physical punishment, consistent versus inconsistent explanations, and firm and frequent parental control on the development of personality characteristics that have relevance to attitude change.

Personality variables typically interact with other variables when attitudes change. In other words, some kinds of people react to certain kinds of messages, which reach them through certain media, and which are produced by certain sources of messages, differently from other kinds of people. This kind of complexity requires that we postpone further consideration of the personality variables until we have time to review some of the simpler aspects of attitude change.

Focus on Interpersonal Relations

One person can influence another to the extent that he is (a) trustworthy, (b) attractive, and (c) powerful. In Chapter VII we shall review a number of experiments that demonstrate the importance of these variables in attitude change. Suffice it to say here that at the point in time that is most critical in the formation of attitudes, a child's parents have all three of these characteristics and are, therefore, the chief agents of attitude formation. Later in life the teenager's peers may be most attractive and, at that point, they may become the chief influences on attitude formation. Still later, the mass media may be very important and, at times, teachers have such an effect. In general, we learn few of our attitudes from direct experiences with the attitude object and many through other people. This is illustrated by Doob's (1940) study in which students who had shown a real attitude change over a ten-week period attributed this change to personal experiences or to actual observations only 29 percent of the time. These students mentioned as the cause of change (a) a college course 26 percent of the time, (b) the mass media, or reading, 31 percent of the time, and (c) conversations with other people 8 percent of the time. In other words, at that age, about three quarters of the incidents of attitude change were traceable directly or indirectly to social influences.

One of the most important characteristics of an interpersonal ralationship is the attitudinal similarity between the two people. When two people are attitudinally similar and have an opportunity to interact, they reward each other because it is generally rewarding to hear another person agree with one's opinions. This is particulary true when the other person is a stranger. When a person is rewarded, he seeks to repeat the rewarding experiences, which in this case means that he seeks to interact more frequently with the person with whom he agrees. As the two discuss matters, they tend to increase their cognitive similarity so that gradually they converge in their attitudes even more than they did previously (see Fig. 15). This completes the cycle, which is likely to continue, unless the opportunity for interaction becomes small (for example, one of the two leaves town), or a person is placed in a new social environment (for example, college) where a new set of attitudes prevail and his attitudes change to become similar with the ones of his new environment, thus, becoming cognitively dissimilar from his previous friend.

The theoretical relationships suggested in Fig. 15 were tested by Triandis (1959a) in a study in which the cognitive similarity of foremen and workers in industry was measured with the Kelly (1955) and Osgood et al. (1957) procedures (see Chapter II). It was found that workers who are cognitively similar to their supervisors like their supervisors significantly more than workers who are dissimilar to their supervisors. The theoretical context of such studies can be derived from both Heider's and Newcomb's theories, which we discussed in Chapter III (under consistency theories).

Rokeach, Smith, and Evans (1960) extended this thinking by arguing that belief

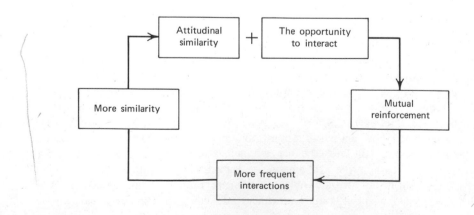

FIGURE 15.   The relationship between cognitive similarity and the frequency of interaction.

dissimilarity is the most important determinant of prejudice. To test this idea, they asked their subjects to rate, on 9-point scales, stimulus persons differing from themselves in race, religion, and belief. The ends of the scales were defined by the statements: "I *can't* see myself being friends with such a person," and "I can *very easily* see myself being friends with such a person." Friendship preferences were found to be determined primarily by congruence in beliefs rather than by race or religion.

Triandis (1961) accepted these findings on the friendship variable, but argued that prejudice involves more than nonacceptance as a friend; it involves negative behaviors as well, such as excluding someone from one's neighborhood. He showed that race, rather than belief dissimilarity, determines the rejection of hypothetical stimulus persons from intimate social situations.

Stein, Hardyck, and Smith (1967) presented a study designed to reconcile these differences. They asked 44 white ninth-graders to complete a teenage social distance scale in which the subjects indicated how friendly they felt toward white and Negro teenagers who were like or unlike them in values. Stein et al. obtained a strong effect due to belief congruence and a lesser race effect. They concluded that both race and belief are important determinants of prejudice.

The inconsistency found in the above studies is in part because of the fact that most authors assume that attitudes are unidimensional constructs. In Chapter II of this book we showed that this is an oversimplification. There are differences not only among the results we obtain with the measurement of the three components of attitude, but the behavioral component is itself multidimensional. Rokeach et al. used *only* friendship rejection in their test of the importance of belief congruence and race.

In a study that is too complex for complete review in this book, Triandis and Davis (1965) showed that people give different weights to belief dissimilarity and race dissimilarity depending on the kind of behavioral intentions [measured by the behavioral differential (see Chapter II)] under investigation. Specifically, on social behaviors that are quite intimate, such as marital rejection and rejection from the neighborhood, all subjects reject on the basis of race and not on the basis of belief dissimilarity. For behaviors intermediate in intimacy, such as eating with another person, both race and belief are important. For behaviors that are quite formal, such as respecting or evaluating the moral character of another person, belief dissimilarity was the important determinant of rejection. These general trends, however, depend on the kind of people who respond to the behavioral differential. Some people are particularly sensitive to race (they are "race" or "conventionally prejudiced"), but others are particularly sensitive to belief dissimilarity ("belief prejudiced"). The racially prejudiced show greater prejudice in situations of intermediate intimacy, and they give some importance to race in formal (nonintimate) situations. On the other hand, the belief prejudiced respond only to belief dissimilarity in nonintimate social situations. Thus, both the kind of individual and the nature of the social situation determine the relative importance of belief dissimilarity versus race in the determination of prejudice. Insko and Robinson (1967) replicated the most important aspects of this study.

In spite of the note of caution suggested by Triandis and Davis, it is clear that Rokeach is correct when he argues that belief dissimilarity is important for friendship choices. Stein (1966) has obtained a good deal of support for Rokeach's position, as have several others. Rokeach and Mezei (1966) reported three experiments that examined the effects of race and belief on discrimination in actual social situations. In two of these experiments the experimental session involved a group discussion among four stooges and one naive subject. By prearrangement the naive subject was always elected chairman of the group. Two of the stooges (one Negro, one white) agreed with the subject, but the other two (one Negro, one white) disagreed with him. At the conclusion of the discussion the naive subject was asked, as chairman, to select two persons with whom to go for coffee, while the experimenter supposedly interviewed the other two.

In the field study, a similar design was used. The subjects were applicants for various jobs at two mental hospitals. The stooges played the role of applicants who were also waiting to be interviewed. The stooges engaged in a "spontaneous" discussion that was arranged so that two (one Negro, one white) agreed with the subject's opinions, and the other two (one Negro, one white) disagreed with the subject. After twelve minutes the experimenter returned and asked the applicants to write down the names of the two persons in the group with whom they would most prefer to work. Rokeach and Mezei found that across all three experiments there was a tendency for the subjects to choose the white and Negro stooges who agreed with them more than any other combination of stooges. In other words, there was no tendency to choose the white stooges but, instead, the choice was on the basis of belief similarity.

However, Dawes (1966) points out that there is a definite interaction in Rokeach and Mezei's data: there were many cases in which the Negro who agreed and the white who disagreed were chosen, or the white who agreed and the Negro who disagreed were chosen. In other words, there was a significant tendency to form mixed pairs. Dawes interprets this result as being due to a norm that applies in liberal circles in the North, according to which it is impolite to form racially homogenous groups whenever there is a clear possibility of forming mixed groups. The Rokeach data, then, are limited to a very special condition that is applicable to liberal Northern social circles. There is much doubt that these results would be replicated in the South. Nevertheless, the importance of belief dissimilarity, as a determinant of some responses that may be described as prejudice, is not here in dispute.

On the other hand, the generality of the belief similarity effect is not unlimited. Novak and Lerner (1968) had subjects participate in an "impression formation" experiment in which they evaluated a partner who was presented as either similar or dissimilar to themselves, and who was further presented as either normal or emotionally disturbed. When the partner was believed to be normal, the subjects expressed a greater desire to interact with him when he was similar than when he was dissimilar. However, when the partner was perceived as disturbed, the subjects preferred a dissimilar to a similar partner.

To summarize, both race and belief are important determinants of interpersonal attitudes. For certain kinds of people, one is more important than the other. For intimate interpersonal behaviors, race is more important than belief; for formal behaviors, belief is more important than race. For behaviors intermediate in intimacy, such as friendship, both factors are important, and the relative importance is largely because of differences in subculture and personality.

Focus on the Group

A person belongs to certain groups, called membership groups, and aspires to belong to other groups, called reference groups. A person's attitudes depend on both his membership and his reference groups. This was demonstrated in a study by Siegel and Siegel (1957). Women students, during their freshmen year, were asked to indicate their preferences for living in different kinds of housing.

At the particular campus, preference for "Row houses " (in Fraternity Row) was indicative of high authoritarianism, as measured by the F scale and a related E (ethnocentrism) scale. Now those who had a high preference for living in Row houses were randomly assigned to two conditions: one group (let us call it group 1) was assigned to Row houses during their sophomore year, and the other was assigned to non-Row houses. The latter group was further divided, according to whether or not they chose to move to Row houses at the end of their sophomore year, after spending a year in non-Row houses. Let us call those who moved group 2 and those who stayed group 3.

Since authoritarian attitudes are consistent with living in Row houses, we can predict that the girls who moved at the end of their freshman year (group 1) and, hence, had maximum exposure to that environment, would be the most authoritarian; those who wanted to move after a year in non-Row houses (group 2) would be intermediate; and those who changed their minds and decided not to move to Row houses (group 3) would be the least authoritarian. These predictions were made by the Siegels, and they were confirmed. Thus this study demonstrates that both membership groups (comparison of the girls in group 1 with those in groups 2 and 3) and reference groups (comparison of groups 1 and 2 with group 3) are important in the determination of attitudes (in this case measures of ethnocentrism).

Since a person's attitudes are anchored in his membership and reference group, one way in which to change these attitudes is to modify one or the other. Newcomb's (1943) classic study demonstrated that college attendance can have a significant effect on one's attitudes. The study was conducted in Bennington College during 1932 to 1935. At that time, the college community was small, consisting of 250 girls and about 50 faculty members. The atmosphere was one of great interaction between faculty and students. There were no extracurricular clubs, as such, but there was much discussion, common dining, workshops, and study-labs. There were no classrooms, in the ordinary sense of the word, because all the studying was done informally. The girls came mostly from wealthy homes and were rather conservative. On the other hand, the faculty was extremely liberal.

The girls, coming from homes from the upper socioeconomic levels, found themselves in a new membership group where liberalism was the norm. Up to the time when they went to college most of the people they knew who had any "intelligence and breeding" were conservative. Suddenly they faced intelligent people who had different attitudes. The result was that their attitudes changed; in fact, each year the girls became more and more liberal. The freshmen had a most conservative score (74.2 on a socioeconomic conservatism scale). The sophomores dropped to 69.4; the juniors to 65.9 and the seniors to 62.4. After leaving college, the more liberal of the girls chose environments that provided reinforcement for liberalism. Newcomb (1963) followed up on as many girls as he could trace and found that 25 years later, as a group, they were conspicuously more liberal than women of the same age and socioeconomic background. They had married men who were more liberal than their socioeconomic background might predict. One of the most dramatic findings of Newcomb's study was that the attitude scores obtained in the 1930s, in college, predicted the way the person voted in the Nixon-Kennedy election of 1960—the more liberal the college scores, the more likely it was that the person would vote for Kennedy.

Capel (1967) found considerable consistency in Thurstone attitude scale measures concerning the concepts Negro, War, Patriotism, Church, Sunday Observance, Law, and Birth Control over a 30-year period in a group of Southern women. There were, however, also shifts in attitudes toward War (toward a more militaristic position) and the Negro (toward less prejudice). Such shifts undoubtedly reflect changes in the social climate between the 1930s and the 1960s.

In sum, children's attitudes are closely related to those of their parents. There is much evidence that children's prejudices are similar to the prejudices of their parents (Epstein and Komorita, 1966). The social class of the family is also related to the kinds of attitudes acquired by children. For example, Haire and Morrison (1957) have shown that children from low socioeconomic groups have very different perceptions of unions, bosses, and other labor-management concepts, than children of high socioeconomic groups. Later in the person's development, the mass media and his peers have a great influence. In some kinds of social systems the peers (same generation) have greater influence than in others. For example, Rettig (1966) showed that in the Israeli kibbutz and moshava, where the kinship system is replaced by an age-group system for the transmission of attitudes, there are large differences in attitudes across three generations of people. In other kinds of societies, for instance, the family-centered cultures of Southern Europe, the attitudes of the children are quite similar to the attitudes of their parents. A child that is exposed to a limited range of attitudes, from a homogeneous social group, such as his relatives, is likely to be quite ethnocentric. On the other hand, a child that has been exposed to a wide range of attitudes, of many social groups, is likely to be liberal and to have a worldwide perspective. Lambert (1967) points out that a bilingual child is more likely to be nonethnocentric, because he has been exposed to two cultures and has learned to appreciate different points of view.

Finally, Manis, Houts, and Blake (1963) examined the beliefs that various people had about "mental illness" and found that these beliefs change as a result of psychiatric hospitalization. The patient's beliefs about mental illness become quite similar to the ones held by the hospital staff. This is an example of a more general phenomenon: people acquire the beliefs of the people with whom they interact. For example, when a Southerner moves to the North he is likely to select his friends so that they have similar beliefs. If this proves difficult, he begins changing his beliefs, and after some time his beliefs are similar to those held by many people in the North.

One of the more dramatic circumstances of attitude change has been described as brainwashing. In a typical brainwashing experience, the person's membership group is dramatically changed. Schein (1956) showed that one of the first things done by the Chinese, when they captured American military personnel during the Korean War, was to modify the social structure of the camp so that the officers reported to the privates. However, these modifications in the membership group were relatively ineffective, except for the case of a few privates who suddenly found themselves in a position of power and grew to like their new place in life. A more intensive kind of brainwashing was described by Lifton (1957) in the case of the thought reform of Chinese intellectuals. Here the new membership group was "the Revolutionary College." The "teachers" in that college were dedicated party members. Lifton divided the "curriculum" into three phases: The Great Togetherness, the Closing in of the Milieu, and Submission and Rebirth.

In the first phase the atmosphere was austere but friendly. They formed small groups of ten and were simply told to get to know each other. Next a series of lectures focused on the old society—it was evil and corrupt—and the new society was presented as morally uplifting, harmonizing, and therapeutic.

The next phase involved a shift from the intellectual and ideological to the personal and the emotional. A pattern of criticism, self-criticism, and confessions was extended to every aspect of daily life. Relationships with the opposite sex were discussed and evaluated solely in terms of their effects on the individual's progress in reform. The small group was employed to extract confessions. As one person confessed, the others felt that they too must confess the evils of their past life. A "confession compulsion" swept the group. Those whose attitudes were not shifting with the group were singled out for special attention.

The last phase involved a final "thought summary" presented by each student to a mass gathering of Communist officials. During this long statement he confessed his past sins, analyzed the evils of his father's and grandfather's lives, and showed that he had mastered the new way of thinking. The final phase was an expression of the individual's rebirth in the Chinese Communist community.

The important elements of this thought-control program are social. They consist of (a) the skillful manipulation of the group environment, so as to provide criticism, harassment, rejection, and public disgrace, until the student shows signs of acceptance of the communist ideology, and (b) the providing of approval, support, and help in the consolidation of the new ideology.

In the case of important Western political prisoners, the Chinese have employed a brainwashing procedure of even greater intensity. First, they attempted to destroy the individual's ideological structure by confusing him as much as possible. He was not allowed to know the time and place and subjected to vague accusations and to capricious changes in the prison regiment. By keeping the person in chains, they were able to establish degrading and regressively infantile procedures for eating and bowel movements. Second, he was deprived of sleep, food, cleanliness, comfort, warmth, etc., and this permitted the prison wardens to reinforce him for "confession" of guilt. As the person confessed, he was made more insecure with threats of torture, hints about the irreversible deterioration of his health, etc. Finally, the third phase consisted of reinforcing the desired new belief systems. The prisoner was first rewarded for superficial and poor self-criticism, confessions and betrayals, and later only for major confessions. During most of this "training," new categories of thought were provided by the interrogators, which were designed to make the prisoner an expert in the use of communist ideology (Lifton, 1956).

A question exists concerning the effectiveness of these procedures. There is little question that they produce compliance. But there seems to be little evidence that they produce an enduring attitude change, *unless* the person remains in the communist environment. In the case of the Western prisoners the Chinese were successful in producing a number of psychiatric breakdowns, and they had little trouble extracting confessions. But there is no evidence that they were able to obtain enduring and important attitude change. In the case of their own intellectuals, on the other hand, they were generally successful, primarily because these intellectuals did not have outside reference groups, as was the case with the Westerners.

A similar comment can be made about T groups, which are widely used in industry to provide "sensitivity" in human relations. Those who participate in these groups enjoy themselves and feel that they "get much out of this experience," but there is little evidence of permanent attitude change. The central message of these groups is that supervisors should be sensitive to their subordinates' needs and point of view. In the context of these groups such nonauthoritarian views are perfectly welcome and widely accepted. However, when the supervisor returns to his job and starts working again in a hierarchical, authoritarian company, most of what he has learned seems irrelevant (Fleishman, 1953). Unless the whole atmosphere of the organization changes, it is not possible to observe any attitude change effects. These findings reinforce our conclusion that the person's group membership is one of the most significant sources of his attitudes.

PROJECT FOR ADVANCED STUDENTS

What is the evidence that T groups change attitudes? Review the evidence by going to some of the original sources reviewed by Dunnette and Campbell (1968).

Focus on Intergroup Relations

There are basically two classes of theories that deal with intergroup relations, particularly intergroup prejudice. One class of theories is mainly psychological; the other emphasizes sociocultural factors. Both kinds of factors are important.

When we focused on the individual, above, we examined the theory of authoritarianism. This is one of the important psychological theories that accounts for individual differences in prejudice. Another is the frustration-aggression hypothesis, which we mentioned only briefly. Frustration is "an interference with the occurrence of an instigated goal response at its proper time in the behavior sequence" (Berkowitz, 1965, p. 305). Aggression is behavior whose goal is the injury of some person or object (Dollard et al., 1939). Frustration leads to anger and anger results in a predisposition to aggression. If proper cues (for example, a disliked person), well-established habits, and a small probability of punishment for aggression are present, the person is likely to aggress. When the probability of punishment is high, the person displaces his aggression to targets that are safe. Again, he selects targets that are disliked. People with whom he is in competition or whom he regards as immoral or particularly different are likely to elicit aggression. Berkowitz clarifies that aggression can take place without frustration, for example, through imitation, and also that frustration does not necessarily produce aggression; it might produce some other reaction, including attitude change. But, in general, the above-mentioned sequence of events is likely to take place. Thus, prejudice is viewed, in part, as a "safe aggression" toward targets that are disliked, because they are very different or because they are in competition with one's own group. Berkowitz reviews a number of studies which illustrate that a disliked person "draws" aggression.

There is evidence, which is consistent with the following proposition: "The more similar an outgroup is in customs, values, beliefs, and general culture, the more liked it will be" (Campbell and LeVine, 1968). One of the studies that supports this generalization is by Mitchell (1956), who found that cultural similarity (matrilineal versus patrilineal organization) was the major factor associated with social distance among workers from 20 tribes in Zambia. If social distance can be conceived as an aggressive response, it follows that tribes that are seen as culturally dissimilar will receive more social distance than tribes that are seen as similar.

Brewer (1968b) found support for the hypothesis that outgroups perceived as similar to an ingroup will be held at less social distance than outgroups perceived as dissimilar. She also found that adjacent outgroups were held in less social distance than nonadjacent ones, presumably because they are culturally more similar. Finally, outgroups that were economically more advanced were held in less social distance than outgroups who were less advanced, supporting reference group theory. The data were obtained from the responses of 30 tribes.

However, similarity obviously cannot account for the unfavorable attitudes of some Americans toward blacks, since those who are more similar in status to that of the average black show more rather than less unfavorable attitudes toward Negroes. Centers (1949), for instance, reports consistently more anti-Negro attitudes in the working class than in the middle class; as many as 76 percent of the rural working class people studied revealed unfavorable attitudes. It is more likely that economic competition and incompatible goals account for these results.

Sherif et al. (1954) showed that it is possible to develop either positive or negative intergroup attitudes by manipulating experimentally the *goals* of groups of white middle-class boys. When the goals were in conflict, extremely negative intergroup attitudes were observed. When *superordinate* goals were established by the experimenters, thus requiring the boys to cooperate, the boys changed their attitudes toward a moderate position. Similar demonstrations have been provided by Blake and Mouton in a number of investigations. These studies show that when groups adopt a "win/lose" point of view, in intergroup conflict, they develop negative stereotypes and distort their perception of reality. When groups are in a "problem-solving mood," they find superordinate goals, consider alternatives, and experience different kinds of intergroup attitudes (Blake, Shepard, and Mouton, 1964).

Although psychological theories such as the theory of authoritarianism and the frustration-aggression hypothesis seem to explain some of the individual differences in prejudice, sociocultural theories are needed to explain the existence of discriminatory norms of behavior toward outgroups by certain groups of people. Pettigrew (1959) showed that the American South is not characterized by unusually high authoritarianism compared to the North. Authoritarianism correlates with prejudice in both regions, but the mean authoritarianism of the two regions is not significantly different. In the South, much prejudice is traceable to cultural norms that urge people to be prejudiced.

In an analysis of the demography of desegregation, Pettigrew and Cramer (1959) found that (a) urbanism, (b) the Negro ratio, and (c) the number of white women in the labor force were exellent predictors of desegregation. Specifically, there is more desegregation in urban than in rural communities; the rural South is more prejudiced, as can be determined from both the desegregation behavior in various counties and from voting patterns. The Negro ratio is inversely related to desegregation; in communities where there are a few Negroes there is more desegregation. Finally, the more traditionalist the community, the less the amount of desegregation. One index of traditionalism employed by the writers was a low percentage of women in the labor force. The three variables, when combined statistically, predicted about one half the variance in desegregation behaviors, by county, in several states.

Behind traditionalism is the economic competition of the two racial groups. A study by Noel and Pinkley (1964) showed that for both white prejudice against Negroes and Negro prejudice against whites "the greater the probability of out-group economic competition, the greater the probability of outgroup prejudice" (p. 621). This is clear from social class data, which shows more anti-Negro prejudice among lower class than among upper class whites. Among Negroes, the most anti-white prejudice is found in the low and the upper levels and the least prejudice among the middle class.

Realistic group conflict theory (Campbell and LeVine, 1965) assumes that group conflicts are rational in the sense that groups do have incompatible goals and are in competition for scarce resources. There is much evidence that real threat causes ingroup solidarity, better morale, and better interpersonal adjustment (Fiedler, 1967b); it also increases ethnocentrism. From such a theory one would predict that a tribe engaged in fishing, surrounded by tribes engaged in agriculture, would be low in ethnocentrism, since there would be little competition between the fishing and the agricultural tribes. This theory would argue that the presence of hostile and competitive outgroup neighbors would lead to ingroup solidarity and outgroup hostility. It makes specific predictions, such as "the weakest group in a cluster of tribes would be the most ethnocentric," and "groups with movable wealth would be more ethnocentric than groups with nonmovable wealth."

Another theory is the social-structural theory of conflict (Campbell and LeVine, 1965). Most individuals belong to more than one ingroup. The ordering of their loyalties to the several ingroups of which they are members has consequences for the solidarity of the total ethnic group. Two basic types of loyalty structure have been described by anthropologists, for instance, by Evans-Pritchard, Fortes, Colson, and Gluckman. These two types are (1) The pyramidal-segmentary type, and (2) the cross-cutting type. In the first one the individual belongs to different "alliances" depending on the "level of conflict." For example, in Bedouin society there may be conflict between brothers, but an alliance of brothers against cousins, an alliance of cousins against more distant relatives, and so on. Conflict occurs between groups that are roughly equal in power. The second type of structure has the characteristic that each male in the society must defend, under conditions of emergency, more than one group. One of these groups is his local group; the other groups might be dispersed over a large territory and are related to him by common descent or age. The important characteristic of the cross-cutting type is that there is no clear ranking of the two types of groups with respect to loyalty. Societies of the first type are likely to be patrilocal, although the ones of the second type are likely to be matrilocal. LeVine (1965) draws a fascinating contrast between the two types and exemplifies it with data from four tribes. Table 6 summarizes his major points.

An examination of Table 6 suggests that the pyramidal-segmentary groups have an unstable internal structure that makes success in fighting with outgroups ex-

Table 6   A Comparison of Two Types of Loyalty Structures

Pyramidal Segmentary	Cross-Cutting
Example from: the Bedouins, the Gusii	Example from: the Mundurucu, the Kipsigis
Hierarchy of male loyalties, endogamy	Cross-cutting loyalties, dispersion
Patrilocal	Matrilocal
Much internal fighting	Little internal fighting
Suspicious, hostile, witchcraft accusations	Sociable, cooperative
Low on sharing	Emphasize sharing
Dominance and obedience	Organized peer groups
Little praise, high fear, in socialization	Use praise frequently, low fear in socialization
Severe aggression training	Mild aggression training
See outgroups as hostile, threatening, powerful	See outgroups as weak, inferior, dishonorable, inviting plunder
In war: defensive, cautious	In war: offensive
Immigration policy: restrictive	Immigration policy: open

tremely unlikely. By contrast, the cross-cutting type structure provides much internal cohesion and a strong probability of success in war. The pyramidal groups resemble Fiedler's (1967b) no-competition groups, although the cross-cutting groups resemble Fiedler's groups that were in intergroup competition and had high morale.

The point of this discussion is that the nature of intergroup attitudes will be quite different in these two types of societies. The images of outgroups are different, the defense-versus-attack dimension of intergroup conflict is viewed from a different perspective, and immigration and, hence, openness to social change and new attitudes will be quite different.

Another theoretical perspective examines cultures from the point of view of cultural evolution. Newcomb (1960) has presented one such perspective, which hypothesizes that there would be less ethnocentrism in food-gathering societies, more ethnocentrism in societies that have slaves and transportable goods, and more ethnocentrism in the more politically organized societies having a high technological level. A number of additional theories are reviewed by Campbell and LeVine (1965); however, they appear less general than the ones summarized above.

In sum, it can be stated that both psychological and societal explanations account for the variance of intergroup attitudes. Each of the explanations takes care of only a small aspect of all the observations; but taken together the various explanations go a long way toward providing an understanding of intergroup attitudes.

STUDY QUESTIONS

1. How do reference and membership groups determine attitudes?
2. Discuss the frustration-aggression hypothesis.

FURTHER READING

Siegel and Siegel (1957); Schein (1957); Lifton (1957); Berkowitz (1965).

VI

Introduction
to Attitude Change

Attitudes can be changed in a variety of ways. A person may receive new information either from other people or through the mass media that could produce changes in the cognitive component of his attitude. Since there is a tendency for consistency among the components of any attitude, changes in the cognitive component will be reflected in changes in the affective and behavioral components. Attitudes also change through direct experience with the attitude object. For example, a person who is prejudiced against Negroes and who meets a pleasant, well-informed, intelligent Negro at the home of one of his friends is likely to feel some dissonance between his cognitions. This will require him to reorganize his thinking about Negroes. Furthermore, a pleasant experience in the presence of a Negro builds up, through conditioning, positive affect toward similar stimuli, such as other Negroes.

Another way to change attitudes is to force a person to behave in a way that is inconsistent with his existing attitudes. This can sometimes be done through legislation. For example, the state may adopt a law prohibiting certain kinds of discrimination. The result is to confront the person with a dissonant state of affairs: on the one hand he has negative affect toward Negroes; on the other hand his law-abiding behavior reflects their acceptance in several social situations. If he is a law-abiding citizen, the law changes his behavioral intentions. The inconsistency between the behavioral and the affective component further changes the total attitude.

Attitudes are also changed by a "fait accompli." In other words, once an event has taken place, attitudes change to become consistent with the implications of the event. For example, consider the attitudes toward Caryl Chessman, who was executed in California in May of 1960. In a study by Cole, Hartry, and Brebner (1962) there is an analysis of the attitudes of students toward Chessman. Chessman's execution was unusual because it followed a legal battle that lasted several years. In February 1960 he had been granted a stay by the Governor of California only hours before his scheduled execution. As a result, the execution attracted widespread public attention, with some of the Chessman sympathizers arguing that

142

he was now a very different person from the one that he had been when he had committed the crime. Cole et al. tested introductory psychology students both before and after the February reprieve and the May execution. Following the execution there was a significant increase in the frequency of endorsement of statements such as "Chessman is probably guilty of the crimes of which he is accused," "A man of his type does not deserve to live in society today," and "Granted that Chessman is ill, society must still be protected from him." There was a significant decrease in the endorsement of "There is still real doubt concerning his guilt." Following the execution there was a tendency for the cognitive component of attitudes to become consistent with the action that had taken place. A similar phenomenon may be observed after an election. The popularity of the president-elect is greater after the election than it was before.

Here the fact that a man is the President of the United States is inconsistent with thoughts that one might have had before the election, for instance, "He is a big crook" or "He is stupid." Such thoughts will drop out, unless of course, they are reinforced by the actions of the new president. In addition, there may be a bandwagon effect—an attempt to identify with the winner and thus obtain vicarious reinforcement, a feeling that one belongs to a winning team, etc.

The ratings of winning candidates become more favorable, after an election, but the ratings of the losing candidates change very little, with most of the change occurring along the "political assertiveness" dimension (Anderson and Bass, 1967). Sears (1965) found that Republicans became less partisan after the assassination of President Kennedy, but Democrats remained unchanged in their degree of partisanship. When President Kennedy was assassinated, the majority of those interviewed by Tomkins, McCarter, and Peebles (1965) reported having more positive attitudes toward him after the assassination than they had had before. It is probable that after the assassination of the president the cognitions that are employed when one is in conflict with another man or group drop out, since they are no longer relevant: the man is no longer an opponent. In the case of a presidential assassination there also are likely to be additional thoughts, such as "He died for our country," which will increase overall favorability.

To summarize, attitude change can occur by first changing the cognitive component (for example, with new information), the affective component (for example, by pleasant or unpleasant experiences in the presence of the attitude object) or the behavioral component (for example, by norm change, or the legal imposition of behavioral changes). It can change also by forcing a person to act or by presenting him with a "fait accompli." When one of the components has changed, the others also are likely to change. One form of change that is most direct and powerful is what is called a "traumatic experience" with the attitude object. In the previous chapter, Allport's suggestion about the frequency and intensity of attitudes formed through this kind of experience was reviewed.

Attitudes also can be changed through psychotherapy by increasing the person's insight into the reasons he holds certain attitudes, by providing positive reinforcement for certain attitudes, by presenting an anxiety-reducing stimulus in the presence of the negative attitude object, and so on. This topic could lead far afield and will not be discussed in the present book.

The various influences on the individual during attitude change begin with the *source* of attitude change. This source can be a person, a group, a newspaper, a radio or television station, or the object of the attitude itself. The source produces a *message* that can be something said or done by a person, a group decision, an item in a newspaper or magazine, a radio or television program, or an experience or incident that a person has had in the presence of the attitude object.

The amount of influence of these two broad categories that were just described depends on the nature of the *audience*. Certain personality characteristics of the audience may increase or may decrease this influence. For example, a person with low self-esteem may be so unsure of himself that he feels he is unable to understand messages produced by the mass media, therefore, he may disregard them. On the other extreme of the continuum, a person with very high self-esteem, who feels that he knows everything, may also ignore the mass media for opposite reasons. Both extremes, then, may ignore the media, and experience no attitude change. Those intermediate in self-esteem may be more easily accessible.

The effect of the two influences described above can take a number of different forms. A person may change his categories (see Chapter I) by classifying a different set of stimuli or situations in some well-established category or he may start using a new category; or he may change the relationships among his categories in some of the ways that are described by Abelson (see Chapter III).

He may change the affect he attaches to one or more categories; or he may change his behavioral intentions. Which of these changes will occur depends on a number of factors. One important consideration is the function (see Chapter I for the discussion of functions) played by the particular attitude in the total "economy of the personality." If the attitude has a knowledge function and helps the individual to understand and to give structure to his universe, he may welcome only those messages that increase his understanding of the universe, and may readily adopt an attitude that fulfills this function better. If the attitude has a value-expressive function, it may be difficult to change it without changing the individual's basic values. If the attitude has an adjustment function, a person may not change it unless the offered alternative attitude can be shown to improve his adjustment. Finally, if the attitude has an ego-defensive function it may be very difficult for a person to change without considerably reorganizing the attitudes he holds toward himself.

In other words, in order to change someone's attitudes, it is a good idea to analyze the functions they play and to adjust your strategy accordingly. Attitude change is a little like medicine—the same therapy is not prescribed for all ailments; nor is the same approach used for every attitude to be changed.

McGuire (1968b, c), following Hovland, Janis, and Kelley (1953), has described a series of steps that characterize the attitude change process: attention, comprehension, yielding, retention, and action. If communication is to have an observable effect, the receiver of a communication must go through each of these steps. When there is a message on television, for instance, there is only a probability, not a certainty, that the audience will pay attention to it. Not all of those who attend to it will understand it. Of those who do, only a small fraction will yield to the message, in the sense that they will tell themselves "that it is a good idea; I'll do that." Of those who yield, only a few will remember it long enough to do anything about it. Finally, of those who remember it, even fewer will actually act. In this example, you can observe that different variables determine whether a person will go from one step to another. Attention may be reduced because of distraction; comprehension may be reduced because of *low* intelligence; yielding may be reduced because of *high* intelligence (for example, the knowledgeable person may know that the frothy looking beer he sees on TV is actually made of soapsuds); retention may be reduced because of the interference of other messages; action may not take place because a person lacks the money to buy what was suggested.

To summarize, in analyzing the attitude-change process we must consider the effect of *who* says *what, how,* to *whom,* and with what *effect.* The who concerns the *source* of a message. The what is the *message* itself. The how is the *channel* in which the message is delivered, the whom is the *audience* to which the message is delivered, and the effect may include changes in attention, comprehension, yielding, retention, or action. In the chapters that follow, we examine the effects of the source, the message, the channel, and the audience on attitude change.

The independent variables (source, channel, message, and audience) often have interactive effects on the dependent variables (such as attention, comprehension, yielding, retention, and action). For example, Hovland and Weiss (1952) presented a message as coming from the chairman of the Atomic Energy Commission to American students. A second equivalent sample of students received the same message, but this time it was attributed to the Soviet newspaper *Pravda.* The topic concerned the practicability of building an atomic-powered submarine about the year, 1950. The results showed that 35 percent of the students changed their attitude in the direction advocated by the Atomic Energy Commission, but none changed in the direction advocated by *Pravda.* When another topic was used, concerning the future of the movies, the difference between the source effects was much smaller. Since the messages were presented in a controlled way, these results must be interpreted as indicating that the same message when produced by one source can have a large effect and when produced by another source may have no effect.

In addition to this source-message interaction, many other kinds of interactions have been observed. For example, some audiences are more susceptible to messages coming from prestigeful sources than to messages coming from ordinary ones, resulting in a source-audience interaction. When a particular audience, (for example, highly authoritarian individuals) is exceedingly susceptible to messages from high prestige sources that are consistent with authoritarian values, there is a source-message-audience triple interaction.

A good way to view the attitude-change field is to consider a system of relationships involving numerous characteristics of the source, channel, message, and audience linked with the several dependent variables mentioned above. Most relationships must be stated with the full conscience that they are operating only with "other things being equal." A change in one variable in this system is likely to interact with many other variables and to have a different effect in one situation than in another. Eventually, we shall have to develop computer programs that will summarize this vast area of knowledge, and in which we shall include the values of the various variables found in the system that correspond to a situation and shall make predictions about the outcome of attitude change attempts that consider all the evidence. When such computer programs result in predictions of subject behavior in attitude change situations this will constitute support for the total theoretical system that guided their writing.

At the present time we can only warn the reader that attitude change is a complex area, where interactive relationships are common, and where change in one variable may have widespread results in many other variables within the system. In spite of the complexity of this system, the tremendous volume of research which has already been generated in this area (not only by psychologists, but also by advertising executives, marketing experts, industrial relations specialists, public opinion surveyors, and others), constitutes the building stones which are suitable for the construction of computer programs. The future is very likely to provide such highly sophisticated computer models of attitude change. The computer programs themselves will then constitute the "theories of attitude change." Until such theories are available, we can only give a rough map of the area. We will begin this discussion by examining some experimental designs which can be used in studying attitude change.

Experimental Designs for Studying Attitude Change

Table 7 presents a design, proposed by Solomon (1949), that controls for many variables and is very useful in studies of attitude change. To use this design, one begins with a sample of subjects and assigns them *randomly* to four groups. Group 1 receives a pretest, let us call it B (for before), then some experimental treatment (X), finally a posttest, let us call it A (for after). Group 2 receives only B and A. Group 3 receives the experimental treatment (X) and the posttest (A). Finally, Group 4 receives only the posttest. The posttest scores are represented by the letter A. We notice that A_1 can conceivably be determined by three kinds of factors: the experimental treatment, the effect of sensitization produced by the pretest, and the interaction of the experimental treatment and the sensitization of the pretest. To illustrate, suppose that the attitudes of people toward various wines is under study. A pretest requires them to evaluate different kinds. They have not seen the names of some of these wines before; hence, they give rather neutral and noncommittal answers. But, soon after they take the pretest, they have a chance to see some information about wines. When they are sensitized to the topic, they feel guilty about their ignorance and quickly learn something about wines. A week later, the

Table 7   The Solomon Design

Groups	1	2	3	4
Pretest	B_1	B_2		
Experimental Treatment	X_1		X_3	
Posttest	A_1	A_2	A_3	A_4

experimenter calls them in and presents to them a communication concerning wines. The subjects who have been sensitized will react to the communication differently than the ones who were never pretested. In this way, it is possible to have a sensitization effect, which changes a person's attitudes toward wines *not* because he has been exposed to a message, but because his curiosity was aroused after being asked his opinion about wines. In such a case, when the message is presented, there may be an interaction, so that the more interested (presensitized people) learn more than the less interested. Finally, the message itself may have an effect.

In group 1, scores A_1 contain all these influences. But the Solomon design permits the determination of the importance of each of these influences. The A_4 scores contain none of these effects, since this group has not been exposed to either the pretest or the experimental treatment. The difference between A_3 and A_4 indicates the effectiveness of the message itself in producing attitude change; the difference between A_2 and A_4 indicates the effect of the sensitization. The difference between A_1 and A_4 contains all three effects. Therefore, if we subtract from it (a) the effect of the experimental treatment, and (b) the effect of the pretest, we can find out (c) the effect of the interaction between pretest and experimental treatment. Thus, this design evaluates all three of the effects. Notice, however, that if we do not care to find out about the effects of the pretest, we simply could use groups 3 and 4 and with these groups alone determine the effect of the message. When sensitization is unlikely to influence the experimental treatment (and this may be the typical condition; see Insko, 1967, p. 5, for a review of relevant studies) and when true randomization of the experimental and the control groups is possible, we recommend the use of only groups 3 and 4 of the Solomon design.

The Solomon design was chosen for detailed discussion here because it is relatively complex and *includes* several other, simpler designs. However, modern attitude studies employ even more complex designs. The illustrative experiment that follows gives some of the flavor of this research.

An Illustrative Experiment

To illustrate the way in which attitude change research is carried out, we give a detailed description of a study by Corrozi and Rosnow (1968). These authors predicted that subjects' opinions should change in the direction of whichever arguments are closer in time to a consonant statement or farther from a dissonant statement. A consonant statement refers to some statement of attitude that the subject will agree with in advance and which is irrelevant to the attitude dimension under study, namely, attitudes toward Picasso. A dissonant statement is one which is counter to the subject's own attitudes. In other words, they predicted that the first statement, of a two-sided communication, will have greater influence on attitude change if the two-sided communication either follows a consonant statement or precedes a dissonant statement. On the other hand, the second statement of a two-sided communication will have the greater influence, if the two-sided communication either precedes a consonant statement or follows a dissonant one.

When the first side of a two-sided communication has the larger effect, this is called *primacy*; when the second side has the larger effect, the phenomenon is called *recency*. In this study, then, Corrozi and Rosnow predicted primacy under two conditions and recency under two other conditions.

The subjects were high school juniors and seniors. First, their instructor administered what he represented as a national high school opinion survey that contained questions about the artist Pablo Picasso. Two weeks later John Corrozi read to eight different groups of subjects a two-sided communication containing positive and negative arguments about Picasso. Four of the groups received the positive arguments first and the other four received the negative arguments first. Corrozi also read to the students either a consonant or a dissonant argument before or after the statements about Picasso. These arguments had no connection with the Picasso statements. This design, then, used eight groups of subjects and varied systematically the time of the positive or negative irrelevant statements (before or after) and the order of presentation. The two-sided communication consisted of 700 words and was half positive and half negative. The consonant or dissonant statements were about 200 words long. The dissonant statements advocated a longer school week (6-to-9-hour days), but the consonant statements took the position that the school week was already long enough. A check of the opinions of similar classes of students had shown that these students strongly agreed with the latter and strongly disagreed with the former statements.

After reading the two-sided communication and the consonant or dissonant statements to the class, Corrozi administered another questionnaire about Picasso. Finally, the subjects were asked to guess the purpose of the study in order to eliminate from the analysis those who had guessed correctly what the experimenter was trying to do.

Let us examine now the nature of the measurements. First, in half the groups, there was a pretest; let's call it (t_1); second, there was a communication that presented first the positive, then the negative argument; finally, there was another measurement, which we can call (t_2). In the other half of the groups the communications were switched, so that the negative argument was presented first, and the positive argument second. To avoid confusion, we shall call these pretest scores

Table 8   Pretest and Posttest Mean Scores and Difference Scores (from Corrozi and Rosnow's Study, 1968)

	Consonant After		Consonant Before		Dissonant After		Dissonant Before	
	Positive First	Negative First	Positive First	Negative First	Positive First	Negative First	Positive First	Negative First
Pre	18.11	16.16	17.16	17.26	17.00	17.05	17.42	15.32
Post	17.63	18.06	17.95	16.53	17.47	16.79	15.47	16.63
Gain	−.48	1.90	.79	−.73	.47	−.26	−1.95	1.31
Obtained Difference	-2.38^b		1.52^a		.73		-3.26^c	
	Recency		Primacy		Primacy		Recency	

Note: primacy and recency were obtained as predicted. All difference scores were tested by one-tailed *t* test.

[a] Means p$<$.10.
[b] Means p $<$.025.
[c] Means p $<$.005.

(t_3), and the posttest scores (t_4). Suppose now that we compute the difference between $(t_4 - t_3)$ and $(t_2 - t_1)$. If there are no order effects (that is, if it makes no difference whether the positive or negative arguments in the two-sided communication are presented first), then the difference between $(t_2 - t_1)$ and $(t_4 - t_3)$ should be zero. It is possible to test the significance of this difference, by a statistic called a *t* test. The particular index just described was worked out by Hovland et al. (1957) to measure the size of order effects. Table 8 reproduces the scores obtained by Corrozi and Rosnow and shows that the predicted primacy and recency effects were obtained, and 3 of the 4 effects were statistically significant.

It should be recalled that the communication concerned Picasso, a topic that is not particularly ego-involving for college students. It is unlikely that much attitude change can be obtained on ego-involving topics through this technique, but nevertheless you may want to play some games and try it on your friends—tell them in close temporal contiguity something with which they strongly agree and something else on which you want to see a change of attitude.

Who Is Doing Attitude Change Research? With What Effect?

A good deal of attitude change research is done in practical settings by organizations such as the armed forces, by the advertising companies, and by some radio and television networks. Most of this research involves field studies. In the greater part of these field studies, the amount of observed attitude change is small. By contrast, most experimental research is done in universities, and the amount of observed change is usually large. Hovland (1959) reviewed the results obtained from studies of the effects of the mass media on political behavior, for instance, voting, and of experimental studies of attitude change and found that there was a large difference in the amount of observed change. More specifically, Lazersfeld, Berelson, and Gaudet (1944) estimated that during an election campaign only about 5 percent of the electorate changes and mainly through personal influence rather than the mass media. On the other hand, Hovland points out that the experimental studies show change in from 35 to 50 percent of the subjects. This difference results from several factors: (1) there is a major difference in the *exposure* to the communication. A message presented through the mass media does not have to be attended to. In most experiments, however, the subjects are students and the source of the message is their professor or a member of the faculty of their university. It is difficult not to pay attention to such a message. (2) When an entire campaign is evaluated, the focus of the communication is rather wide, but in most experiments the communication is very specific and limited. This means that the communication has a greater probability of being understood in the laboratory than in the field, where it is complex, contradictory, and probably confusing. (3) The time interval between the communication and the assessment of the attitude change (posttest) is rather short in the case of experiments but is much longer in field studies. Thus there should be greater retention of the communication in the experimental than in the field setting. (4) The motivation of the subjects is different. In the experiments the subjects are students who are eager to show their intelligence and want to make a good impression on the faculty. In the field situations these factors are of little consequence. (5) The subject's social membership is different. In field studies the message is received while the person is in some natural group, such as his family. In the experimental situation it is received while the subject is isolated from his group. As we mentioned in the previous chapter, group membership influences the attitudes of the subject. When he receives a message that does not agree with the opinions of the majority in his group, he is likely to disregard it. In other words, yielding is less likely when he is in his group than when he is alone. (6) Different populations of people are used. College students are not typical audiences. First, they are brighter than the average member of the public. This means they are more likely to attend, understand, and retain messages than the majority of the general population; but they are also likely to yield less than most. Second, the typical personality of college students is likely to be different. For example, they tend to be more self-confident, which is related to particular reactions to attitude change. (7) The topics of the communication are apt to be more ego-involving and important in the case of the surveys. It is easier to convince a college student that he should like the Prime Minister of Australia than to convince a Democrat to become a Republican.

Some Further Methodological Problems of Attitude Research

Currently there is much concern with the so-called "demand characteristics" of laboratory situations, which might influence data to become consistent with the investigator's hypotheses. There is a definite suspicion that a good deal of the attitude change observed in the laboratory is due to the subjects' attempt to please the experimenter who is often their instructor, or to comply with the task in order to be obliging. After all, when a student is exposed to a message in a laboratory setting, it is reasonable for him to assume that he is "supposed" to change and if he likes the experimenter, or is in the habit of obliging people, he may very well change not so much in response to the message but in response to the social situation. There also is the possibility that subjects might be sophisticated in understanding psychological phenomena and conform to "current theoretical" expectations to show their knowledge of psychology. The following joke, told by anthropologists, is worth repeating here. One of their colleagues visiting a much researched tribe in the American Southwest, sits down with his informant to collect cultural data. He phrases his question in the simplest possible terms to make sure that he is understood. His informant pauses, then asks: "According to whose theoretical framework do you wish to have these data?"

An experiment by Silverman (1968) illustrates some of these points. He found that subjects show more acquiescence to a persuasive message when it is presented in the context of a psychological experiment than when it is not. Furthermore, the context of the study is more important when the subjects who respond are named than when they respond anonymously. Presumably when the subject can be identified he feels that he is particularly likely to gain a favorable assessment by the experimenter and hence, he is more likely to comply.

Studies by Rosnow and Rosenthal (1966), which demonstrate that volunteer subjects show more attitude change than nonvolunteers, are consistent with the previous arguments. However, the opposite effect can also be observed, when the subjects equate acquiescence with "psychological weaknesses"; Rosenberg (1965a) showed that subjects will show less attitude change under these conditions.

How can one deal with these methodological problems? Half the battle is won when the nature and characteristics of this problem are realized. Replications in a variety of settings as well as in different laboratories, and by experimenters who do not "buy" the theory, are likely to lead to a solid understanding. The use of control groups can sometimes appropriately measure context effects; and the use of "unobtrusive" measures is particularly promising (Webb, et al., 1966). This is also true of research strategies that are closer to natural social situations, where the subjects are unaware that they are participating in experiments. These strategies are outlined in recent papers by Weick (1967) and McGuire (1968a), which the serious student of this problem should read.

PROJECT FOR ADVANCED STUDENTS

Examine some of the literature on demand characteristics of experiments and some of the possible solutions suggested above. Write an essay outlining the general nature of this problem and your recommendations concerning the kind of methodology that social psychologists should employ in the future.

STUDY QUESTIONS

1. What kinds of shifts in strategy should a person who is trying to change the attitudes of his audience adopt for different types of attitudes?
2. What are the major advantages and disadvantages of the Solomon design to investigate attitude change?
3. What are some of the reasons attitude change in the laboratory is much greater than in natural situations?
4. What are some of the major methodological problems in attitude research?

FURTHER READINGS

McGuire (1968a); Hovland (1959).

Focus on the Dependent Variables

In the previous section we reviewed the stages of attention, comprehension, yielding, retention, and action. In this section we examine what determines the activation of each of these phases of the attitude change process.

> *Attention—*The Problem of Selective Exposure

Source and Message Factors. In order to change a person's attitudes it is first necessary to expose him to some message. If a person selectively avoids certain sources or messages it is very difficult to change his attitudes. We are constantly bombarded by information—some of it from helpful friends, much of it from the mass media. Since we cannot absorb it all, we avoid most of it. For example, the visitor to a library selects only an infinitesimal fraction of the books available; the viewer of television tunes in to only a small selection of the messages offered.

In short, it is clear that we select information. The problem then is not to document this fact but to specify what variables determine our selection. With respect to our discussion of the functional theory of attitudes, it would follow that we choose those messages that (a) increase our understanding and help us organize the complex input that we receive from the environment, (b) do not attack our self-esteem, and do not reveal unpleasant truths about us, (c) help us adjust in a complex world by making it more likely that we will obtain rewards and avoid punishments, and (d) give us the opportunity to express our values more convincingly to others.

The facts of de facto selectivity in exposure (Freedman and Sears, 1965) are overwhelmingly clear. Republican rallies are mainly attended by Republicans, Baptist services are attended mainly by Baptists, Republican gubernatorial candidates are watched on television by twice as many Republicans as Democrats, and people exposed to mass information campaigns in support of the United Nations are mostly those who already support the United Nations. These facts have suggested the hypothesis that there is a general preference for supportive information and for avoidance of nonsupportive information concerning our attitudes. Analysts of the effectiveness of mass communication such as Klapper (1949, 1960, 1967) have strongly and persistently argued in favor of this principle. For example, Klapper (1967, p. 297) states: "Twenty-odd years of mass communication research have identified some tendencies that are basic and even axiomatic. Perhaps most basic and widely confirmed is the finding that mass communication ordinarily serves as an agent of reinforcement of such attitudes, opinions and behavioral tendencies as the individual audience members already possess." Klapper argues that mass communication creates attitudes, where none exist, but rarely changes the direction of existing attitudes; it modifies existing attitudes, but rarely nullifies them. Klapper describes how selective exposure to the information that is consistent with existing attitudes and its selective retention and recall result in an impact of only the kinds of information that are consistent with existing attitudes.

Festinger (1957) made the principle of selective exposure one of the cornerstones of his theory of cognitive dissonance. Avoidance of dissonance is one of the two basic hypotheses of the theory. He specified curves predicting the relationship between dissonance and information seeking and avoidance (Festinger, 1957, p. 130) Specifically, he described a greater tendency to seek consistent information and to avoid dissonant information as dissonance increases up to a point. At that point, when it becomes unbearable, people will switch from avoidance to seeking more dissonance in order to reorganize their cognition.

Recent reviews of the evidence concerning the selective exposure hypothesis (Freedman and Sears, 1965; McGuire, 1969a), however, cast serious doubt on its validity. It appears that the evidence of de facto selectivity is clear. People avoid situations in which their values will be challenged and flock to hear communications with which they expect to agree. But is this a general principle?

Whenever possible, people tend to select their environment so that it will be compatible with their attitudes (Newcomb, 1967). For example, girls coming from highly conservative homes, after attending Bennington College, became much less so. They then tended to marry liberal husbands, and to continue being more liberal than most of the girls with similar backgrounds. Newcomb also found that the more liberal graduates of Bennington persisted in their liberalism 22 years after they had left college. On the other hand, studies of preference for supportive and avoidance of nonsupportive information do not suggest that this is a *general* psychological preference.

A recent positive study by McGinnies and Rosenbaum (1965) showed that those who attended a televised address by President Johnson previously had expressed greater support for a militant United States policy in Vietnam than those who had not attended. Many of the negative studies did not employ such ego-involving issues. Furthermore, very few studies exposed subjects to several degrees of dissonance as is needed for an adequate test of Festinger's predictions. The issue is further complicated by the fact that a number of additional variables may operate and obscure the relationships. For example, Festinger (1964b) has hypothesized that the subject's choice between avoiding or seeking out opposing information is dependent on how confident he is that his opinion is correct; the less confident he is the more he will avoid dissonant information. Some studies testing this hypothesis have supported it and others have not.

Lowin (1967) presented a theory that explicitly used two variables: actor confidence and ease of message refutation. This theory specifies that, when the message is hard to refute, the subjects will prefer consonant information but, when it is easy to refute, they will prefer dissonant information. A large-scale study supported the model, and an additional study (Lowin, 1969) found further evidence. In addition, subjects were found to have a preference for strong consonant and weak dissonant messages, as opposed to weak consonant or strong dissonant messages. These results might be explained from a theory that postulates preference for complexity among college students (most of Lowin's subjects were in Ivy League universities) or the avoidance of boredom (slightly dissonant messages are less boring). These interpretations are consistent with the findings by Jones and Kohler (1958) that implausible dissonant and plausible consonant statements are remembered better than implausible consonant or plausible dissonant ones. Presumably, the implausible dissonant statements are easy to refute and, hence, amusing (not boring), but the plausible dissonant statements are difficult to refute and painful, hence, forgotten (repressed) more readily. On the other hand, the plausible consonant statements are nice to remember, since they might be used in future discussions, but the implausible consonant statements are useless and, thus, more easily forgotten.

The latter point brings us to the question of what uses there might be for the information. A study by Clarke and James (1967) showed that the uses anticipated for the information determine its selectivity. These authors exposed subjects to three situations. In one situation the subjects received the information by mail; in the second the subjects expected to join a discussion group following exposure to the information; in the third the subjects expected to debate with one another after exposure to the information. The first condition is private; the second is public, but without compulsory participation; the third is not only public but also forces the subjects to participate. The two public situations resulted in higher mean preferences for supportive information than the private situations. Among those in the public situations, support seeking was greater on issues about which subjects felt strongly, but in the private situation there was no relationship between attitude intensity and information choices. In the private situation, the more dogmatic the subjects, the more they sought supportive information, and the less dogmatic, the less they sought such information. In the discussion situation, the greater the self-esteem of the subjects, the more they sought supportive information; but in the debate situation the opposite was observed—the greater the self-esteem, the less there was a tendency to seek supportive information. The authors offer a post hoc interpretation for these findings: in the discussion situation, those with low self-esteem plan to make only minor contributions, hence, they do not care about the nature of the information they have obtained, but those with high self-esteem plan to be active participants and want a store of information to bolster their performance. Both would have to participate in the debate situation, but the low self-esteem persons might plan to defend their own position while the high self-esteem, given that it is a debate, might plan to run down the views of the opposition, which they could do more successfully if they knew its views. Although these are speculations that need to be confirmed by further research, the important point this study makes is that subjects may seek different kinds of information depending on their personalities and on the situation in which they are placed. Such results are clearly supportive of the functional approach to attitude change.

Further support for a functional theory of selective exposure can be found in the data reported by Janis and Rausch (1970). Their study was conducted during a period when draft-age students were undergoing a decisional conflict whether or not to sign a pledge to refuse to be drafted. They divided Yale University undergraduates into four groups: those who were signers of the "We-Won't-Go" pledge, potential signers who were still undecided, formerly conflicted refusers to sign; and prompt (unconflicted) refusers. The subjects were asked how interested they were in seeing four anti-pledge communications. The results were opposite from what might be predicted from the selective exposure hypothesis: the men who refused to sign expressed less interest in reading the articles supporting their position than did the men who were in favor of signing. The authors suggest that draft resisters may have been willing to read information opposed to their own views because of the usefulness of this information when they argue with their parents and others who do not share their views. The more they know about the views of the opposition, the more likely they will be to win these arguments. In addition, draft resisters would be motivated to find out more about the possible unfavorable consequences of their action. In sum, the communications would provide a good deal of useful information to them, and under these conditions the subjects did not refuse to be exposed to the communications.

The functional approach also would predict that if the issue is not ego-involving, the usefulness of the information will be the primary consideration in its selection. In other words, if the information increases understanding, if it increases the chances of adjustment, it will be welcome. Whether it is supportive or nonsupportive to the already existing attitudes is irrelevant. On the other hand, when the issue is ego-involving, and there is a chance that the nonsupportive information will threaten the self-esteem of the audience or will suppress the expression of its values, it will be avoided, suppressed, misperceived, and quickly forgotten. Thus, for ego-involving issues, functional theory will make predictions consistent with the ones of dissonance theory.

A recent study by Rhine (1967) obtained strong support for Festinger's position, that there will be an inverted U relationship between dissonance and information seeking. The subjects were first asked, during the Goldwater-Johnson election, to estimate the conservatism of the two candidates and then were confronted with several degrees of dissonant contradiction concerning the conservatism of these candidates. Finally, they were offered a choice among political pamphlets whose titles differed along the political-economic-conservatism scale. The degree to which various groups of subjects sought or avoided the various kinds of pamphlets was quite consistent with Festinger's theory (see Fig. 16). The analyses were done only on the ego-involved subjects, who had indicated that they favored one candidate strongly over the other. After experiencing the contradiction, it was expected that the subjects would seek pamphlets supporting their candidate and would avoid pamphlets supporting the opposition. The predicted inverted U was obtained (for the total curve), and a statistical check confirmed that the relationship is not linear.

We can summarize the studies reviewed in this section as follows: people in everyday life, in fact, are exposed to disproportionate amounts of supportive information. On the other hand, laboratory results do not support the view that people prefer to be exposed to supportive as opposed to nonsupportive information. Only under certain conditions will they prefer supportive arguments, notably when they are challenged on issues about which they are highly ego-involved, when nonsupportive arguments might threaten their self-esteem, and when the arguments have little utility.

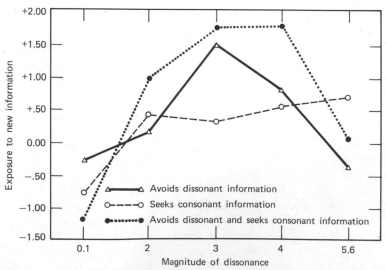

FIGURE 16.   Information seeking and avoiding as a function of dissonance (from Rhine 1967, p. 420).

PROJECT FOR ADVANCED STUDENTS

The evidence above concerning the selective exposure hypothesis has been somewhat oversimplified, in order to include it in the limited space available. Review this evidence more thoroughly by examining, in particular, the papers in Abelson et al. (1969, pp. 769 to 800) by Mills, Sears, and Katz, and McGuire's summing-up. Examine the utility of the theory of Janis and Mann (1968) for the understanding of this problem.

STUDY QUESTIONS

1. What factors may increase a person's tendency to seek supportive information; to avoid supportive information?
2. What factors may increase a person's tendency to seek nonsupportive information; to avoid nonsupportive information?

FURTHER READING

Freedman and Sears (1965); McGuire (1969a).

Channel Factors. Recent studies suggest that television exposes more people to new information than does any other medium. It is the chief source of confirmation of news in moments of crisis, for instance, the assassination of President Kennedy. It gets better ratings of believability than newspapers. On the other hand, its chief function is to change the salience of issues. In short, attention is maximal to television, but yielding, retention, and action follow less readily. Of course, the 20 billion dollars spent on advertising suggest that some action occurs, but most of it concerns nonego-involving attitude objects, for example, different kinds of soap. When the issue is ego-involving, influence follows a two-step process (Katz, 1957). *First,* the media influence the so-called opinion leaders, who *then* influence the masses, through face-to-face contact. It is further suggested that both voting and buying behavior are strongly influenced by face-to-face contacts (Katz and Lazarsfeld, 1955; Berelson et al., 1954). Even among educated audiences such as physicians, face-to-face contact is more important than the formal channels established by the drug manufacturers (Menzel and Katz, 1956). Useful reviews of all these findings are given in Schramm (1963).

Audience Factors. Certain kinds of audiences "ward off" information that is inconsistent with their existing values and attitudes. Although it is not certain whether the warding off occurs at the stage of attention or the later stage of comprehension, the evidence is sufficiently clear that it does occur. Several examples will illustrate this point.

Harvey (1965) had 40 subjects—10 representing each of the four systems of abstraction reviewed in Chapter V—argue in opposition to their own beliefs about philosophy. In one condition they were told that their arguments would never be heard by anyone other than themselves (private), although in another condition they believed that their arguments would be heard by a university curriculum committee (public). There was more attitude change in the case of the concrete than in the case of abstract subjects; there was also an interaction, with the concrete subjects changing more in the public and the abstract subjects changing more in the private condition. Elms (1966) found that people who were high in the ability to put themselves in other people's positions (empathic fantasy ability) changed more in an emotional role-playing situation, such as the one of Janis and Mann, described in the previous chapter. Such people should be more abstract, yet they changed more in this situation.

Kleck and Wheaton (1967), found that highly dogmatic subjects tend to recall less inconsistent information, in other words, they showed some of the warding-off effect, mentioned above, and Steiner and Johnson (1963) found that high F scale scorers are more reluctant to believe that "good people" have both good and bad traits.

Concrete subjects also tend to pay more attention to the credibility of the source of attitude change and to agree with it, when it is of high status. Johnson and Torcivia (1968) found that highly acquiescent subjects (who tend to be concrete) showed a large amount of attitude change when the source was credible, but an unusually small amount of change when it was low in credibility. Low acquiescent subjects did not show as much difference in their attitude change as a result of the high versus low credibility of the source. Vidulich and Kaiman (1961) found that highly dogmatic subjects agreed significantly more with a high-status than with a low-status source, but subjects low in dogmatism showed the reverse pattern.

In other words, the more concrete subjects tend to reject messages or information that is inconsistent with their own beliefs, that is, they attend and comprehend the message poorly. However, they yield more readily to the message, if they understand it (Johnson et al., 1968).

There is also evidence that subjects change their attitudes more when they expect new arguments than when they expect familiar arguments. Sears and Freedman (1965), for example, held the actual novelty of arguments constant, but advertised them as containing new or, in another condition, familiar arguments. They found that the expectation of novelty resulted in greater opinion change. Presumably, the novelty of the arguments increased the attention.

Epilogue. Attention to a message depends on many other factors that have not been discussed particularly widely in the literature but that deserve intensive research. It seems highly probable that people attend to messages emitted by unusual, exotic, loud, and prestigeful sources, and to messages containing controversial, interesting, and surprising elements. The distractability and defensiveness of the audience undoubtedly reduce attention. The evidence (for example, Haaland

and Venkatesen, 1968) suggests that distraction decreases attitude change, when it reduces the likelihood of attention.

Comprehension—The Problem of Understanding

According to McGuire's analysis, which we reviewed in the beginning of this chapter, attention to the message precedes comprehension. Comprehension further depends on a number of additional factors.

Source Factors. If the source knows the audience, it is likely to produce messages that will be of maximum effectiveness.

Message Factors. The message must be understandable to the particular audience. A message that fits into the audience's frame of reference, that is clear, cogent, easy to understand, and does not make the audience defensive is most likely to be comprehended.

Channel Factors. Channels that allow the audience to proceed at its own pace, as in reading, asking questions and obtaining clarification, and in face-to-face encounters, are most likely to maximize comprehension. It is obvious that the more difficult the material, the more important it is to have these channels.

Audience. The defensiveness of the audience is a primary factor that might inhibit comprehension. In a classic study by Cooper and Jahoda (1947) and a study by Kendall and Wolf (1949), Mr. Biggot cartoons were used with subjects who were either very prejudiced or not at all prejudiced. The cartoons were designed to satirize bigots. The researchers found that highly prejudiced subjects simply did not understand the cartoons.

Yielding—The Problem of Conformity

A series of studies by Kelman (1958) suggests the need for a number of distinctions. Kelman distinguishes compliance from identification and internalization. *Compliance* occurs when an individual accepts influence because he hopes to achieve a favorable reaction from another person or group. He adopts the induced behavior not because he believes in its content but because he expects to gain specific rewards and avoid specific punishments. *Identification* occurs when an individual accepts influence because he wants to establish or maintain a satisfying relationship between himself and another person, or group. Identification provides satisfaction through the very act of conforming, not through rewards or punishments. *Internalization* can be said to occur when an individual accepts influence because the content of the induced behavior is intrinsically rewarding. The behavior is congruent with his value system or increases his understanding of the world. The content of the new behavior is the individual's source of satisfaction.

Three basic influences cause an audience to yield to a message: (a) the perceived power of the source, that is, the perceived reward-punishment effects of yielding, (b) the attractiveness of the source, and (c) the extent to which the influence fits with the existing values and cognitions of the audience. It follows from these distinctions that three characteristics of the source of a message will maximize different kinds of dependent variables. Specifically, the power of the source would be most likely to lead to compliance; its attractiveness would be most likely to lead to identification, and its credibility would be most likely to lead to internalization.

Kelman tested this analysis in a study in which the characteristics of the source were manipulated. His subjects were Negro college freshmen. The message, which was presented before the 1954 Supreme Court decision on desegregation, argued in favor of maintaining private Negro colleges as all-Negro institutions in order to preserve Negro culture. Pretests had shown that most subjects opposed this message. The message was presented as a recording of a radio program which the experimenter wanted to have evaluated. Table 9 shows the experimental design and predictions.

The manipulations involved descriptions of the source. In the high-power condition the source was described as the president of the National Foundation for Negro Colleges, one of the most important sources of funds for the college in which the study was being conducted. It was pointed out that the president was the kind of person who would not hesitate to use his power in order to achieve conformity. In the high-attraction condition the source was presented as the president of the student council in a leading Negro university. His message was presented not only as his opinion, but also as representing the overwhelming consensus of opinion of Negro college students. The source of the high-credibility condition was presented as a professor of history in one of the country's leading universities, a top expert on the problems of minority groups who was profoundly concerned with the welfare of the American Negro community. The fourth condition presented the source as "an ordinary citizen." His credibility was undermined by portraying him as a white Southerner. The subjects were randomly assigned to one of the four experimental conditions and heard the identical message. They then answered a questionnaire that measured their agreement with the message.

Three kinds of questionnaires were used, and they were completed under different conditions of salience and surveillance. Questionnaire I was administered immediately after the communication. It was made clear that this was being done at

Table 9   Experimental Design and Predictions in Kelman's Study

	Questionnaire I Surveillance Salience	Questionnaire II Nonsurveillance Salience	Questionnaire III Nonsurveillance Nonsalience
High power	*H*	*L*	*L*
High attraction	*H*	*H*	*L*
High credibility	*H*	*H*	*H*
Ordinary citizen	*L*	*L*	*L*

H signifies high probability that the attitude will be expressed (yielding).
L signifies low probability that the attitude will be expressed (yielding).

the request of the communicator who would see each subject's answers. The subjects had to sign the questionnaire and to identify themselves. It was clear that the communicator had power and would be in a position to use it. Questionnaire II was administered immediately after the communication but was anonymous. Questionnaire III was completed under conditions of nonsalience (two weeks after the communication) and nonsurveillance (anonymous). The results showed that the predictions of Table 9 were confirmed.

Message Factors. Although source factors can produce differences in the kind of attitude change obtained, as described in the previous section, it is probable that comparable differences can be obtained with different messages. For example, a message that makes it clear that there will be positive reinforcements if a given position is adopted, is likely to lead to compliance; but a message that describes how adoption of a particular point of view will be consisten with the subject's values would maximize internalization.

Channel Factors. There is a good deal of evidence suggesting that face-to-face communications are more effective than communication made via other channels, in maximizing yielding. However, this is not always the case, as McGinnies and Turnage (1968) suggest in a study in which they found that students at National Taiwan University produced more associations to printed than to spoken Chinese words. They conclude that in communications with Chinese audiences, the printed form may be more effective, although for American audiences the spoken word is more effective. Perhaps differential prestige between printed and spoken word in China and America accounts for these differences.

Audience Factors. Certain kinds of audiences are more likely to yield to powerful sources (for example, highly authoritarian subjects), other audiences might be more easily influenced by the attractiveness of the source (for example, persons high in need affiliation), and still others might be more influenced by the nature of the arguments and by the way they are related to their values (for example, those subjects who are cognitively more abstract, and have highly interrelated, logically coherent cognitive structures). These relationships have not yet been researched in sufficient detail to permit much confidence in the conclusions, but the total trend in the studies in this area suggest that they are plausible. A number of cognitive factors, such as the perspective of the audience and its tolerance for inconsistency, seem relevant. Ostrom and Upshaw (1968) showed that those who were exposed to a wider range of attitudinal positions rated their own attitudes as more moderate than those who had limited perspective. Those with narrow perspective will reject positions that are only mildly discrepant from their own. Highly committed persons view communications as occupying more extreme positions (Manis, 1961a, 1961b) and, hence, are less likely to yield to them.

Rosenberg (1965b) suggests that some people are more "bothered" by inconsistency than others. Those who are more bothered will yield more readily when inconsistencies within their cognitive systems are made salient. If the message seems to be inconsistent with many central beliefs, the subject is less likely to yield

(Hardyck, 1966). The more a person is involved with a particular issue the less likely he is to yield.

PROJECT FOR ADVANCED STUDENTS

The generalization that the more a person is involved with a particular issue the less likely he is to yield does not hold true under all conditions. Examine under what conditions it is true and under what conditions it does not hold true. Start by reading Eagly (1967).

When a person is placed in isolation, his need for social approval increases, and he becomes more susceptible to interpersonal manipulation (Stevenson and Odom, 1962).

Suedfeld and Vernon (1966) examined the responses of concrete or abstract persons to a "sensory deprivation" experience that involved staying in the dark in a silent room and being restricted from moving for 24 hours. Previous studies had shown that sensory deprivation increases the persuasibility of subjects. Another plausible explanation for this phenomenon is that the information which is presented to subjects after deprivation has no competitors; hence, it is attended and comprehended in an unusually effective manner. If the message is obviously propagandistic, the abstract person will yield to it less than the concrete, since he will have more ways of restructuring the information.

Suedfeld and Vernon used a procedure developed by Vernon (1963) which "reinforces" subjects in the sensory deprivation condition by giving them propaganda. Their argument was that abstract subjects in the sensory deprivation condition would be particularly starved for information; hence, they would experience even propaganda as a reinforcement. Therefore, they would do what is necessary in order to receive more propaganda, but they would *not* show attitude change. Thus, Suedfeld and Vernon made a complex prediction: abstract subjects in the sensory deprivation condition will show more compliance and less internalization (true attitude change) than abstract subjects in the control conditions or concrete subjects in either condition. The data of the experiment supported this prediction.

> ### Retention—The Problem of Memory of the Attitude Change

Once a communication has been understood and the audience has yielded to it, how long will these effects persist? A number of factors are likely to increase the retention of the communication and to permit a continuing influence on the subject's behavior.

Source Factors. Powerful or attractive sources that are constantly present and reassert their messages are most likely to increase the retention of the message.

If the subject finds himself in an environment in which the reinforcements are similar to those under the control of the source of attitude change, he is likely to maintain his new attitudes.

Message Factors. The more frequently a message is presented, the longer it is likely to be retained. Repetition can even lead to "overlearning," so that the message may be remembered when it is no longer functional.

Channel Factors. Certain channels can maximize the repetition variable. For example, television or radio can often provide more repetition than is possible in face-to-face encounters in which the source might become inhibited about repeating its message.

Audience Factors. Memory is one of the basic factors in human intelligence (Guilford, 1967). There are various kinds of memory abilities, such as memory for numbers, for figures, for words, for behaviors, and so on. Obviously, if a person is high on those aspects of memory that are contained in the message, he is most likely to retain it.

Action—The Problem of the Relationship of Verbal Behavior and Other Behaviors

In Chapter I, we argued that action depends on more than just attitudes. Established habits, expectancies of reinforcement, and group norms are among the other independent variables that determine action.

There are few field studies of action, other than responding to questionnaires, or surveys, because it is difficult to control action in everyday life situations. On the other hand, rural sociology has produced a very large body of literature on the factors that determine the adoption of innovations. These adoptions are clearly acts that can be determined precisely and, therefore, are of great interest to us.

The process of adoption of agricultural innovations has been divided by different investigators into a number of stages. Singh and Pareek (1967) distinguish seven stages: need (the farmer becomes aware of a need), awareness (he becomes aware that there is a new process), interest (the farmer begins to be interested in the new process), deliberation (he thinks about it), trial (he does a small-scale experiment), evaluation (he checks the results of the experiment), and adoption (he changes his methods of doing things). Singh and Pareek (1966) showed that the mass media play a major role during the early stages of adoption only. "Impersonal information sources are most important at the awareness stage, and personal sources are most important at the evaluation stage of the adoption process" (Rogers, 1962, p. 311 to 312). In short, different channels are maximally important at different stages of the adoption process.

Adoption is more likely if the cognitive and affective components of attitude are consistent with it. Thus, Sizer and Porter (1960) and Hobbs (1960) showed that the greater the amount of knowledge about an innovation the more likely was its adoption. The way the innovation is perceived, its cost, convenience, and risk are directly related to adoption (Kivlin and Fliegel, 1967). Moulik, Hrabovzky, and Rao (1966) showed that the affect toward nitrogeneous fertilizers was one of the best predictors of adoption of these fertilizers in northern India.

The reinforcement expectations are predictive of adoption. Thus, "the relative advantage of a new idea, as perceived by members of a social system, affects its rate of adoption" (Rogers, 1962, p. 312).

The norms of the group to which the farmer belongs also are relevant. Rogers (1962), after a review of several studies, concludes that "an individual's innovativeness varies directly with the norms of his social system of innovativeness" (p. 311). When the wife is supportive of the farmer's role there is a higher adoption rate (Straus, 1960).

Of great importance is the farmer's habit of adopting new methods. "The innovativeness of individuals is related to a modern rather than traditional orientation" (Rogers, 1962, p. 311). The farmer's values are also predictors of his innovation behavior (Cohen, 1962). Nonadopters put more value on ease and convenience and have lower aspirations and need for money than high adopters.

An important personality characteristic is need achievement (n-Ach). There is evidence that the adoption of agricultural innovations is related to a high n-Ach (Rogers and Neill, 1966). McClelland (1961), who developed this concept, has presented some evidence that those who produce many achievement-related themes in response to unstructured pictures (the so-called Thematic Apperception Test, or TAT) work harder, choose experts over friends as work partners, are more resistant to social pressures, and are more apt to compete with a standard of excellence than those who produce few of these themes. Rogers and Neill (1966), in a study of the adoption behavior of Colombian farmers, showed that agricultural innovation scores vary directly with achievement motivation scores. There was a tendency for need achievement to be related to more exposure to the mass media, more political knowledge, more openness to external influences, higher levels of literacy, more education, higher aspirations, a more positive attitude toward credit, and less fatalism.

Another personality variable is the tendency to acquiesce, which may be measured by Rokeach's dogmatism scale. Jamias and Troldahl (1965) found that there is no difference in the adoption of new practices recommended by agricultural experts between persons high and low in dogmatism when a group's norms of innovation are favorable. However, when the norms for innovation are not too favorable, the low dogmatism group adopted many more innovations. In other words, there was an interaction between norms and a given characteristic of the audience.

In short, there is much evidence that the adoption of innovations depends on the attitudes, norms, values, habits, and reinforcement expectations of the farmers, and on some interactions among these variables.

STUDY QUESTIONS

1. What factors are most important in increasing comprehension of a message?
2. What factors are most important in yielding to a message?
3. Explain the difference between compliance, identification, and internalization.
4. What factors would maximize the retention of a message?
5. What factors determine whether action will be consistent with attitudes?

FURTHER READING

Kelman (1958); Festinger (1964a); Rogers (1962).

Complex Effects on the Dependent Variables

Some recent theoretical formulations suggest that the effect of certain personality variables on the dependent variables may be quite different. Of particular interest is the relationship between self-esteem and persuasibility. The early studies of this relationship tended to support a simple relationship, namely, that the higher the self-esteem of the audience the less is the attitude change (Asch, 1958; Janis, 1954, and others). Later work (for example, Cox and Bauer, 1964) suggested an inverted U relationship. McGuire (1966, 1969a) suggested that self-esteem has a different influence on attention and comprehension, which he called *reception,* than on yielding. He provided in McGuire (1968b) a mathematical analysis of the effects of self-esteem on attitude change, as well as other individual difference variables, such as intelligence. He also suggested that the difficulty of comprehending the message must be considered.

McGuire's theory (see Fig. 17) states that self-esteem makes little difference in the probability of reception $[P_r(R)]$ of a message when the message is either very easy or very difficult to understand. On the other hand, when the message is of intermediate difficulty, the higher the self-esteem, the greater the probability of its reception. Self-esteem is higher in persons who are intelligent, not distractable, and are involved in the affairs of the world (that is, open to new experiences). On the other hand, yielding $[P_r(Y)]$ has a negative relationship with self-esteem, since high self-esteem persons will be so self-confident that they will refuse to yield to the views of others. It follows that total attitude change which requires attention, comprehension, *and* yielding will show a negative relationship with self-esteem in easy situations (that is, the higher the self-esteem, the less the change), an inverted U relationship in moderately difficult situations (that is, as self-esteem increases there is more change up to an optimal point, and then there is a decrease in the amount of change) and no relationship in extremely difficult situations.

A theory of this kind makes a number of very subtle predictions. For example, as difficulty of reception increases, the level of self-esteem at which maximum persuasion occurs also rises. On the other hand, the more difficult it is to yield to the message, the lower will be the level of self-esteem at which maximum persuasion occurs.

Nisbett and Gordon (1967) tested some of these implications by using two messages: (a) one message was easy to receive and difficult to yield to, which simply stated the position of an authoritative source on an issue, and (b) the other was difficult to receive but easy to yield to. McGuire's theory was strongly supported. It appears, then, that the analysis of Fig. 14 is valid.

McGuire (1968b) had hoped that chronic and induced anxiety might simply be additive, and thus the analysis of Fig. 17 might also apply when the abscissa shows the amount of chronic anxiety plus the amount of anxiety induced in the subjects.

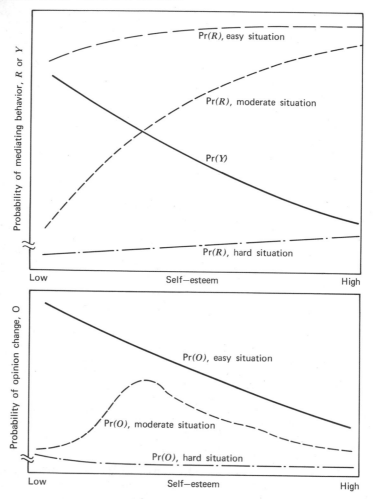

FIGURE 17. McGuire's theory of self-esteem and attitude change (from McGuire, 1968b, p. 1151).

A similar relation was expected with chronic self-esteem. The latter point was checked by Nisbett and Gordon (1967) who also tested this aspect of McGuire's theory but found that the hope for a simple relationship was not supported. They measured the predispositional self-esteem of their subjects and also provided success and failure experiences. Their data suggest that success and failure experienced do not alter the individual's self-esteem, but trigger ego-defensive mechanisms that differ for individuals at different levels of self-esteem. This conclusion is consistent with Cohen's (1959) analysis and Silverman's (1964a, 1964b) studies. Cohen suggested that high self-esteem subjects evaluate themselves more highly after they experience failure than do individuals with low self-esteem; the latter react to such failures by making it even more difficult for themselves to maintain their self-regard. It appears that high self-esteem subjects avoid information about themselves when this information is unfavorable; low self-esteem subjects distort unfavorable information. At any rate, high self-esteem subjects change less when the information is negative about themselves than do low self-esteem subjects. These conclusions also are consistent with Eagly's findings which were reviewed earlier.

Obviously encouraged by these results, McGuire (1968c) has proposed a more general theory of personality and attitude change. He begins by viewing the organism's survival and points out that useful information, guidance from other people, and detailed concepts which are specific to different situations can help in this survival. McGuire's central point is that "any personality characteristic which has a positive relationship to reception, tends to be negatively related to yielding and vice versa" (p. 182). This is an extension of his previous theorizing, which can deal with a large number of personality characteristics, that is, with any characteristic on which people differ. Not only intelligence and self-esteem operate so that there is greater reception and less yielding when these personality characteristics are present in a high degree, but a variety of other personality characteristics may show these relationships. Anxiety shows the reverse pattern, that is, it is negatively related to reception and positively related to yielding.

If this principle is accepted, it follows that a large number of personality characteristics will have inverted U relationships to attitude change. The specific location of the optimal point will depend on specific aspects of the communication situation, for instance, the difficulty of the message. Another variable of importance is the nature of the issue, whether it is a "matter of fact" or a "matter of taste." With the first kind, reception is the critical point, because once a message is received it will be accepted; with the latter, yielding is the critical point, since people feel perfectly free to reject messages with which they disagree if these messages deal with matters of taste. McGuire concludes his paper with a review of several relevant studies that tested aspects of this theory.

PROJECT FOR ADVANCED STUDENTS

Examine the effect of personality variables on attitude change. Begin with a review of some of this literature (Ehrlich and Lee, 1969) and read some of the publications discussed in that review.

VII

The Source

Among the many possible sources of attitude change are the people we know, newspapers, editors, radio announcers, television personalities, authors, and professors. How will the audience (or a listener) respond to a message produced by one kind of source, as opposed to the identical message produced by another source? The answer to this question is complex. It depends on (a) the characteristics of the source, (b) the way these characteristics are perceived by the audience, (c) the nature of the attitude, (d) the channel in which the message appears, and (e) the nature of the audience. Let us examine some of these influences in greater detail.

We have already mentioned some work that analyzed behavioral intentions in terms of five dimensions: *respect, marital acceptance, friendship, acceptance, social distance,* and *subordination* (Triandis, 1964b). The same typology is relevant in analyzing different kinds of sources of attitude change. One reason for this differentiation among the dimensions of social behavior is that each dimension is appropriate for a particular kind of interpersonal relationship. Specifically, we show respect toward people who have knowledge, ability, and skill, that is, people who are *competent* or *expert.* There are people toward whom we feel close, intimate, and with whom we are *familiar.* We usually show friendship toward people we like, because they are rather similar to us and they reward us more frequently than they punish us, that is, they are *attractive* to us. We show social distance toward people with whom we compete or toward whom we are hostile, for whatever reason; that is, some sources are *hostile.* Finally, some sources have *power,* and subordination is a reasonable strategy to minimize punishment and maximize rewards when we interact with them. The traditional literature on source effects has dealt mostly with expertise and credibility, but the present typology suggests that further distinctions will be useful.

To summarize, sources differ in competence, familiarity, attraction, hostility, and power. In general, there is more attitude change when the source is competent, familiar, attractive, and powerful, and less change when it is hostile. However, combinations of these characteristics can limit the generality of these relationships. As an illustration, consider what happens when a powerful source that is unattractive, but competent, convinces a person to do something that is

168

inconsistent with his attitudes. According to dissonance theory, this person's perception of his own actions and his particular attitudes will be inconsistent and will cause him to experience dissonance. The greater the dissonance the greater the attitude change. Under those conditions, the more attractive the source, the less the dissonance, hence, the less the attitude change—a prediction that was supported by a study by Zimbardo et al. (1965), which we review in this chapter. In short, although the common sense notions that competence, familiarity, attraction, and power result in larger amounts of attitude change are generally supported, there also are conditions under which this is not the case.

To return to the typology of different types of sources, what is the evidence that people perceive such dimensions? The dimensions of the perception of sources can be determined empirically. The approach used by a number of investigators is to ask subjects to rate a variety of sources on semantic differentials and factor analyze their ratings (see Chapter II for an explanation of the semantic differential and factor analysis). Andersen (1961) found a factor that he labeled *Evaluation* (honest, moral, fair, sympathetic, reasonable, likable) and a factor that he called *Dynamism* (interesting, strong, fast, aggressive, and active). Lemert (1963) in an extensive study involving several kinds of sources, found three factors: *Safety* (honest, openminded, safe, objective), *Qualification* (trained, experienced, informed, educated), and *Dynamism* (bold, colorful, frank, extroverted). The safety factor concerns the source's *intentions,* and the qualification factor is close to the competence dimension. McCroskey (1966) has provided semantic differential and Likert-type scales (see Chapter II for an explanation) measuring what he called *Authoritativeness* (reliable, informed, qualified, intelligent, valuable, expert), and *Character* (honest, friendly, pleasant, unselfish, nice, virtuous) of a source. These two dimensions appear to correspond to competence and to attraction.

In other words two of the five dimensions of the typology have already been found in other studies. The fact that not all dimensions have been found may be because of the limitations of the particular semantic differential scales which were employed in these studies. For example, if there are no "hostile scales" present in a questionnaire, there can be no hostility factor.

Assuming that these five dimensions of source perception are real, are any of them more important than the others? McGuire (1969a) believes that competence is more important than trustworthiness (character, friendship, attraction). However, the answer to this question is probably complex and depends on the functional bases of various attitudes.

We have already pointed out that attitudes have different functions for an individual. This implies that different sources of messages, designed to create attitude change, can have different degrees of effectiveness, depending on the kinds of functions performed by the particular attitudes.

Some attitudes have a knowledge function. The individual who holds them feels that he is able to understand what is going on in the world somewhat better because of these attitudes. Since *competent* persons can help him understand the world even better they would therefore be quite effective in changing these attitudes. The subjects do not want to be misled, since this would reduce their ability to understand the world and would also threaten their adjustment. The *trustworthiness* of the source, then, is an important factor.

Some attitudes have an adjustment function and help the individual obtain more rewards and fewer punishments from the environment. Agreeing with some sources of attitudes that are *powerful* also means getting more rewards and fewer punishments.

Attitudes can have ego-defensive functions as well. They protect the individual from unpleasant basic truths about himself. It would follow that sources that are regarded as "supportive," "concerned with my welfare," that is, basically *attractive* and *intimate* would be most effective in changing these attitudes.

Finally, attitudes have value expressive functions. When the source is perceived as having *similar values,* it is likely to be regarded as more *attractive* and to be more effective, because the audience will find agreement with the source's views intrinsically satisfying.

The perceived *intentions* of the source may determine its effectiveness. If the audience suspects the source of being insincere, or "having an axe to grind," there may be a reduction in his effectiveness (Mills and Jellison, 1968). However, the problem of suspicion is very complex, since there are many kinds and the contradictory literature makes it unsuitable for inclusion in this volume. Those interested in further reading may consult McGuire (1969b).

Another way to examine those characteristics that make a source effective is to be concerned with the dependent variables. A dynamic source that is overtly arguing for a particular point of view would be more likely to attract attention; a clear source that presents its arguments in a manner consistent with the audience's abilities would be more comprehensible; a repetitious source may be best for the retention of the message; an attractive source may be best for yielding; and a powerful source may be best for ensuring action.

Characteristics of the Source and the Audience

The relationship between the characteristics of the source and the audience is very important, since the characteristics of the audience act as an anchor for perceiving the source. A large number of characteristics may be involved in a process of this kind. We list only the more obvious: (a) the physical attractiveness of the source, (b) the clothes, accent, rate of speech, loudness of voice, and other indicators of its status, (c) the source's demographic characteristics, for example, race, religion, nationality, age, sex, and social status, (d) the source's attitudes, and (e) whether the source's past behavior was generally rewarding to the subject, or mostly indifferent, or punishing.

Exchange theory, such as proposed by Thibaut and Kelley (1959), specifies that when the rewards obtained from another person are greater than the costs, there is a tendency to establish a friendly relationship and to reciprocate. Gouldner (1960) has claimed that reciprocity is a universal norm of behavior. Consequently, if the source has been "nice" to the audience in the past, it would be appropriate for the audience to be "nice" to the source and to accept its message. On the other hand, niceness may also lead to resistance when the audience feels that the source is insincere, intends to persuade, or is likely to remove the audience's freedom of action.

Triandis (1967) has examined how the similarities in the various characteristics of the source and the audience result in different kinds of interpersonal attitudes. Summarizing the studies done in four cultures, he concludes that the various dimensions of the behavioral component of interpersonal attitudes are differentially affected by different kinds of similarity. Specifically, the *Respect* dimension is most sensitive to similarities in beliefs, attitudes, religion, and race, in that order. The higher the status of the source as suggested by elegant dress, fluency in speech, and a high-level occupation, the greater the respect, but the higher the status of the audience, the lower the respect (Triandis, Vassiliou, and Thomanek, 1966). The *Friendship* dimension, which is most relevant to attractiveness, is influenced by similar or higher status, by race, age, and religion.

Many of the demographic indexes mentioned above have definite "status implications" in most societies. For example, in most societies there is a certain rank-order of preferences for males over females, or people who believe in the same instead of a different religion. There are status implications associated with age, race, and many other characteristics.

We have argued above that the greater the similarity of the source and audience, the more attractive is the source likely to be for that particular audience. Similarity in status is particularly important. There is however, a "nonvertical dimension of social status" (Lenski, 1954) which has been called *status crystalization* or *status congruence*, which also is relevant to our analysis. People do not have equal status on all dimensions. For example, a Negro physician and a Southern unskilled worker are clearly of different status on two *different* dimensions, as far as Southern society is concerned. When this happens each person tries to emphasize that characteristic on which he is of higher status. In our example, the black man will emphasize the fact that he is a physician and the unskilled worker will emphasize the fact that he is white. It is clear that when people emphasize different dimensions they will experience conflict. The physician will be insulted; the unskilled worker will be hostile. This example suggests the hypothesis that sources that are low in status crystalization are likely to elicit contradictory reactions and, therefore, be less effective than sources that are status congruent.

Another implication of this analysis is equally interesting: Audiences that consist of persons who are status incongruent will be in a situation of status-tension. That is, people will not respect them as much as they feel they should be respected. These audiences will be dissatisfied with the *status quo* and will feel more sympathetic to sources that advocate a change in the *status quo*. Lenski has shown that radicals are more likely to be status incongruent; for example, they feel that they are more intelligent and less influential than most people.

Thus, status congruence is relevant not only for the analysis of the way the source is perceived by an audience but also for the analysis of audience reactions to different kinds of sources and messages.

What kinds of sources will be most effective for status incongruous audiences? There is no relevant research, but it is probable that the sources should be *similar in status congruence*. For example, in Southern society Negro physicians are status incongruent; however, other Negro physicians are similar to them and would be the best sources of attitude change in spite of the fact that such sources are status incongruent. In sum, status incongruence is not necessarily an undesirable characteristic of the source; it is undesirable only in relation to the type of audience. When the principle of similarity and the principle of congruence are in conflict, for example, when a Negro physician talks to a Negro unskilled laborer versus to a white physician, it is probable, but not certain, that the principle of similarity will be more powerful. Further research is needed on all these points.

Types of Sources and Types of Attitude Change

Although it is unnecessary to repeat Kelman's analysis of attitude change in terms of compliance, identification, and internalization, which we reviewed in the previous chapter, it should be emphasized that each of these attitude-change processes is affected by a different aspect of the source. *Compliance* is generally dependent on the power of the source; *identification* is dependent on its attractiveness, and *internalization* on its competence.

Empirical Studies

Source Credibility

After a review of many studies, Giffin (1967) concludes that interpersonal trust depends on the listener's perceptions of the source's expertise, reliability, intentions, activeness, personal attractiveness, and the majority opinion of the listener's associates. Each of these characteristics may, in turn, be influenced by other characteristics. Expertise may be inferred when the quantity of pertinent information is large, when the ability (for example, intelligence), skill, or good judgment of the source is high. Reliability may depend on the predictability and consistency of the information. The source's commitment to the arguments is likely to lead to greater effectiveness in persuasion. This has been suggested in a study by Sears (1965) which found that material presented by the defense or prosecution lawyer was more effective than material coming from a purportedly neutral lawyer, even though the latter was rated as more trustworthy. The dynamism of the source probably increases the attention and comprehension of the message but reduces the credibility of the source (who looks like a salesman, or propagandist) and, hence, reduces yielding. The attraction of the source is likely to interact with its expertness, reliability, intentions, and dynamism. Finally, when a person thinks that most other people agree with the source, the source is likely to be regarded as more trustworthy.

The various factors just listed should be considered as making independent contributions to the total perceived trustworthiness. In other words, in certain situations, one factor might lead to increased and the other factors to decreased credibility, for example, the source is intelligent, but has "bad intentions."

In analyses of the effects of the source, we must distinguish the effects of the source's perceived characteristics from the effects of what the source says, for example, the message. There is some evidence (McGuire, 1969a) that either high- or low-source credibility may contribute to a corresponding attitude change, although the content of the message is not learned. When the source is of unclear or unspecified credibility, on the other hand, there is greater learning of the message. It would appear that high credibility produces positive reinforcements which condition the affective component of attitudes, as suggested in Chapter I; but these changes in the affective component do not occur through the learning of the source's arguments (for example, changes in the cognitive component). On the other hand, when the credibility of the source is uncertain, its arguments must be considered, hence, there is a change in the cognitive component, first, and possibly later changes in affect.

There is a vast literature which indicates that the intelligence, ability, age, status, etc. of the source influences its effectiveness (for example, Hovland, Janis, and Kelley, 1953). Even irrelevant characteristics of the source's status can have an effect, as was demonstrated in a study by Aronson and Golden (1962). These authors used a speech that extolled the virtues of arithmetic on an audience of sixth graders. The communicators were (a) a white engineer, (b) a Negro engineer, (c) a white dishwasher, or (d) a Negro dishwasher. They found that both the relevant (engineer-dishwasher) and the irrelevant (black-white) characteristics of the source had a significant influence on the effectiveness of the communication. Prejudiced students showed less change when the communicator was black, and unprejudiced students showed more change when he was black.

On the other hand, the common sense notion that the objectivity of the source (not having an axe to grind) would be important has been supported by only a few studies, and the effect shown was insignificant. In fact, there are studies that show the opposite effect, but this is probably because of the differential impact of objectivity on the various dependent variables of attitude change. For example, if you are sure that the source is very objective, you may not pay much attention to the argument, since you know that it would be "OK" or because you do not feel like "arguing with the experts." On the other hand, if the source warns you that it is "out to change your attitudes," you might pay more attention to what it is doing. Therefore, although objectivity may be a favorable factor for yielding, it may not be so favorable for attention or comprehension; hence, it may not help as much in the determination of attitude change as is assumed from common sense notions. McGuire (1969a) reviews several studies that deal with this problem.

One clue to objectivity is whether the source draws its own conclusions from the argument. Although it would appear that a source which lets people make up their own mind would be viewed as biased and, hence, as less effective, the evidence is that drawing his own conclusion makes a source more effective (for example, Hovland and Mandell, 1952; Irwin and Brockhaus, 1963) at least in the short run. On the other hand it is less effective in the long run (Stotland, Katz, and Patchen, 1959.)

By manipulating the credibility of the source, Hovland and Weiss (1952) observed what they called a "sleeper effect." They found a decrease, after a time interval, in the extent to which subjects agreed with the position advocated by the communication when the material was presented by trustworthy sources, but an increase when it was presented by untrustworthy sources. Their explanation was that there was equal learning of the content under the two conditions of trustworthiness, but less acceptance of the arguments of the untrustworthy source. After some time there was a "dissociation of source and content," so that the resistance to the acceptance of the arguments of the untrustworthy source was reduced, and this led to greater acceptance of the message presented by this source. Fig. 18 shows the retention of opinion curves reported in that study.

A sleeper effect also was obtained in several other studies including Kelman and Hovland's (1953) study, which will be described in somewhat greater detail. Identical communications dealing with the treatment of juvenile delinquents were presented to 330 senior high school students. The presentations were transcribed with an "introduction" between "the moderator" and the "guest speaker" that suggested that the source was (a) well informed and fair, (b) neutral, or (c) poorly

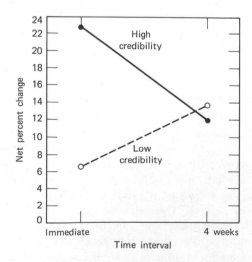

FIGURE 18.   Retention of opinion (from Hovland and Weiss, 1952, p. 646).

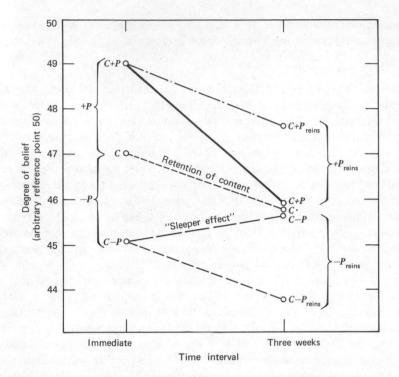

FIGURE 19. Reinstatement of the source (from Keiman and Hovland, 1953, p. 333).

informed and biased. Opinion questionnaires were administered before the communication, immediately afterward, and three weeks later. For one half the subjects, the original transcription in which the speaker was introduced was played back just before the opinion testing on the three-week session. This is called by the authors the "re-instatement of the communicator." Figure 19 shows the obtained results. Observe that if the source is not reinstated, there is a sleeper effect, but if it is reinstated, the reduction in the achieved opinion change is approximately what one would expect from "forgetting curves" and similar to the reduction obtained with the reinstatement of a positive source. In other words, opinion change seems to follow the laws of forgetting, the reinstatement of the source has the effect of improving the memory of the subjects.

PROJECT FOR ADVANCED STUDENTS

The Kelman and Hovland study is one of the classic papers in social psychology. Yet there are some doubts that the effects are anything more than what one might expect from the demand characteristics of the experimental situation. When the audience is reminded of the high prestige guy who delivered the talk, is this not like a suggestion that they better show greater attitude change? Evaluate this argument, by analyzing this classic study from a modern perspective.

The Attractiveness of the Source

In Chapter V (for example, Fig. 15) we examined the relationships between similarity, familiarity, and liking. We pointed out that attitudinal similarity leads to frequent interactions and to interpersonal attraction. There is much evidence that supports the proposition that the greater the perceived similarity between the source and the audience, the greater the effectiveness of the source of attitude change. There also is evidence that persons who are liked are perceived as being more similar than they really are and that those who are disliked are perceived as being more dissimilar. In other words, as suggested in Fig. 15 of Chapter V, there is a circular influence among the similarity, familiarity, and liking variables, and once this circular process starts it is likely to increase or to decrease all three variables. Sources who are high in perceived similarity become familiar and are liked; they also tend to be more effective in changing attitudes.

Although the pattern of findings is, broadly speaking, as described in the previous paragraph, there are also studies that predicted and found quite the opposite results. Since these studies also are inconsistent with common sense expectations, they deserve discussion. Consider, for example, a study by Zimbardo, Weisenberg, and Firestone (1965). Most of the subjects were army reservists and the source was a brigade commander of the ROTC. This source was trained to act according to a particular set of role requirements. In all cases, he was to be seen as conscientious, capable, well organized, concerned with the reactions of the subjects, and industrious. In the "positive source" condition, however, he was *in addition,* polite, informal, considerate, and pleasant. In the "negative source" condition he was *in addition,* snobbish, demanding, tactless, bossy, cold, and formal. These experimental treatments were designed to produce a liked or a disliked source.

During the experiment, the subjects were induced to eat a highly disliked food, fried grasshoppers, and their conformity to the demands of the experimenter as well as their liking for fried grasshoppers were studied before and after the experience. According to predictions of cognitive dissonance theory, if the subject complies with the demands of the experimenter who is disliked, he will be in a dissonant state, since his behavior cannot be justified either by his attitude toward the grasshoppers or toward the source. The way to reduce this dissonance would be to increase his liking for the grasshoppers. This is what Zimbardo et al. observed. Specifically, those who complied with the request from the negative communicator increased their liking for grasshoppers (as a food) significantly more than those who were exposed to the positive communicator. Noncompliance with the demands of the source was associated with boomerang effects, in which grasshoppers became even more disliked. Hence, in this study, as well as in some others (for example, Zimbardo, 1960), attitude change in response to a disliked source was greater than attitude change in response to a liked source for those who complied with the source's demands.

In a similar vein, a number of studies show that praise received by children from friends, or parents, is less effective than praise received from a stranger. Harvey (1962) has shown that, although praise is more effective when it comes from a stranger than from a friend, criticism is more effective when it comes from a friend than from a stranger.

One way to explain these results is to consider the determinants of the attractiveness of the source. Byrne (1961) has presented a theory which argues that the greater the number of reinforcements given by a source, the more attractive it will be. The theory also can be expressed in terms of the proportion of the total acts of the source that are reinforcing with the larger proportions leading to greater attraction. Aronson and Linder (1965) proposed a different mechanism. They suggested that the order in which the reinforcements are received is highly relevant. They allowed subjects to overhear a "personality evaluation" of themselves. In one condition, the first few evaluations were negative, but the remaining ones were positive; in another condition all the evaluations were positive. They showed that the first condition produced more liking for the source than the second, in spite of the fact that the number of positive reinforcements is larger in the second than in the first. Consistent with their theoretical interpretations (see below), the reverse was obtained with conditions in which the subject overheard only negative, or first positive and then negative evaluations. The liking for the source was lower in the positive-negative than in the negative-negative condition.

Sigall and Aronson (1967) did a similar experiment in which the subjects answered the experimenter's questions and were told that they were giving good, bad, or indifferent answers. In the negative-positive condition they were told twice that their answers were bad, and three times that they were good. In the positive-positive condition they were told five times that their answers were good. In the negative-negative condition they were told they were bad five times. In the positive-negative condition they were told that their answers were good twice and, then, bad three times. Following this experience, the experimenter presented a message and the subjects rated their agreement with the message. As predicted, the amount of agreement with the message was highest in the negative-positive condition, next highest in the positive-positive, lowest in the positive-negative condition. In other words, Aronson's theory is that the total amount of reinforcement is less important than the gains or losses in esteem for the subject that can be inferred from the source's actions. If the source shows an increase in esteem, the subject will be particularly predisposed to like it and to agree with it; if the source shows a loss of esteem, the subject will be least apt to like it and to agree with it.

The Power of the Source

McGuire's (1969a) analysis of the perceived power of the source includes three components: first, the subject is concerned with the extent to which the source can administer positive or negative sanctions; second, he estimates whether the source cares about whether or not he conforms; finally, he judges how likely it is that the source will be able to observe whether or not he accepts its position. McGuire reviews several studies which suggest that those who control large rewards also control behavior. Most of the evidence is generally in agreement with McGuire's analysis.

Combined Influences of Several Characteristics of the Source

Sources that are highly respected are likely to be viewed as more dissimilar from the audience than normal sources. Thus, what a source gains in competence, it may lose in attraction. Obviously, it is quite critical to consider the functional bases of the particular attitudes that are to be changed when studying this problem. If the attitude has a knowledge function that is more than an ego-defensive one, the expert who is neutral in attraction may be quite welcome; even the disliked expert may be effective in changing attitudes. Conversely, for ego-defensive attitudes the attractiveness of the source may be more critical than its expertise.

How is a source judged, when it emits contradictory behaviors? In an interesting study by Mehrabian and Wiener (1967) three degrees of attitude (positive, neutral, negative) were communicated with three degrees of tone of voice in all possible combinations. It was found that the tone of voice was the major influence on the way the message was perceived. For example, when a nice thing is said in a hostile manner, the subjects will perceive the communication as hostile.

In a study by Lampel and Anderson (1968) female students rated males characterized by a photograph and two personality adjectives in terms of their desirability as a date. The adjectives had little effect on the judgments when the photographs were less attractive. These authors tested a number of models to determine how the information is integrated, and they concluded that the information is averaged; but a certain shifting occurs in the weights when the photographs are less desirable.

Several of the models reviewed in Chapter III, which deal with the integration of affect, may be applicable in making predictions that involve sources with multiple characteristics.

The Influence of the Source on the Dependent Variables

It has already been stated that one of the characteristics of the source obtained in factor analytic studies (Andersen, 1961; Lemert, 1963) was Dynamism. It would seem reasonable that this variable increases the *attention* of what is said by the source. Also, the more confident the source appears to the audience, the greater the attention. However, it is unlikely that it has much influence on other dependent variables. McGuire (1969a) suggests that the existence of a large "testimonial" industry, in which advertisers ask celebrities to make favorable comments about their products, suggests the belief that such an approach is likely to draw the attention of the audience to the particular products. There is evidence that credible sources are viewed as presenting messages that are judged to be more fair, accurate, well-documented, and so on (Hovland, Janis and Kelley, 1953). An aspect of communication, which has been investigated with both laboratory and field studies, concerns the "cognitive similarity" of the source and message. This similarity is likely to lead to greater comprehension of the message.

Triandis (1959b, 1960a, 1960b) distinguished two kinds of cognitive similarity: (a) the similarity of the attributes used by individuals in categorizing experience; (b) the similarity of the way the attributes were used, that is, in the way stimuli or events were rated on the particular attributes. The first kind of similarity can be measured by presenting triads of concepts, as was suggested by Kelly (1955), and by asking the subjects to judge which one of the three is more different from the other two and, then, to indicate why they think it is more different. For example, given the concepts "my mother," "my wife," and "my sister," a person may be asked to make such a judgment, and may choose his mother and may indicate that the attribute he used to separate her from the other two was *age*. By presenting a large number of these triads to subjects, it is possible to obtain a list of the attributes they employ in thinking about a particular domain of meaning, for example, women, jobs, people, politicians, or whatever. Once a list is obtained from two people, A and B, it can be judged and rated on the relative similarity of the attributes used by A and B. For example, for the domain women, the attributes *intelligent* and *intellectual* would be considered more similar than the attributes *intelligent* and a *good date*. We then can score the degree of similarity of the two lists and can obtain an index of *attribute similarity*.

Once a number of attributes has been obtained, it is possible to construct semantic differentials (see Chapter II) with scales consisting of these attributes. Now we can give to A and B the task of judging a number of concepts, for example, different women that they both know, on the same semantic differential scales. We then can measure the difference in the judgments they make on this task and can obtain another index of cognitive similarity, *rating similarity*.

Triandis' studies were done both in the laboratory and in the field. All studies showed that both attribute and rating similarity are related to (a) actual communication effectiveness, (b) perceived communication effectiveness, and (c) interpersonal attraction. The field studies employed pairs of employees and their bosses.

Triandis (1960a) obtained the attribute similarity of pairs of male students by giving them triads of pictures of emotional expression posed by one actress, and by asking them to judge these pictures by the method just described above. The attribute similarity of the students was thus measured.

The students were then given a communication task. First, they were seated on opposite sides of a table separated by a cardboard, and then they were given two pictures of the same actress. One of the two pictures held by the two students was identical. Their task was to communicate with each other and to find which were the identical pictures. The pictures were labeled A and B for one student and C and D for the other, and if, on a particular trial, pictures B and C were the same, the communication would be considered "successful" if the students were able to say B equals C. They communicated with slips of paper on which they were allowed to write an attribute and a number. For example, one student might write "A is intelligent looking, 5" while the other might write "C looks like a good date, 7."

The study showed that the greater the attribute similarity of the students, as obtained by the method of triads, the better the communication. In addition, judges rated the relative similarity of the attributes used in the actual communications that were exchanged. The ratings of the similarity in these communications correlated .83 with the effectiveness of communication. In other words, if one subject uses *intelligent*, it is helpful for the other to use the same attribute or a related one in describing his pictures. The implication of this study is clear: comprehension is maximized when the source categorizes experience the same way as does the audience. Triandis (1960b) showed that similarity in the ratings also helps; this study was replicated by Shibuya (1962) with Japanese subjects. She employed pictures of applicants at the Tokyo Metropolitan University and had them rated on semantic differential scales. The communication effectiveness was measured as in the previously described study by Triandis (1960a), and her data suggest that both attribute and rating similarity help in communication, that is, in the correct comprehension of the message.

Yielding to the message does not appear to be highly related to characteristics of the source; it appears that the structure of the message and the extent to which it is logical and convincing are more important variables (McGuire, 1969a).

Interaction Effects

The kind of message produced by a source influences the way it is perceived. For example, a study by Feather and Jeffries (1967) showed that a source is judged as less good, less credible, more potent, and more active when it takes an extreme position. In other words, people will attend to it because it is dynamic, but will not necessarily comprehend its message or yield.

A source that takes a more extreme position than the audience on the same side of an issue, will be viewed as more sincere and more competent than one that takes a moderate position; a source that takes an extreme position on the opposite side of an issue, will be perceived as more sincere but less competent than one who takes a moderate position on the opposite side of the issue (Eisinger and Mills, 1968).

Different audiences react differently to various kinds of sources. Steiner (1966) has consistently found sex differences in responses to disagreement with the source. Johnson, Torcivia, and Poprick (1968) found that low F scale scorers (see Chapter IV) are more influenced by differences in the credibility of a source than high F scale scorers.

STUDY QUESTIONS

1. What are the major dimensions that characterize the source which make it (a) more effective; (b) less effective in changing attitudes?

2. Discuss how the functional bases of attitudes determine the relative importance of different source characteristics in attitude change.
3. What determines the perceived attractiveness of a source?
4. What is status congruence? How does status congruence determine the relative effectiveness of a source?
5. What are some of the determinants of perception of source sincerity? Objectivity?
6. What is the sleeper effect? How did Hovland and Weiss explain it?
7. Is it true that under all conditions the greater the attractiveness of a source the greater the attitude change?
8. What does Aronson mean by gains and losses in esteem? How do these gains and losses influence the effectiveness of a source?
9. What is McGuire's analysis of the power of a source?
10. How do different characteristics of the source combine to produce more or less attitude change?
11. How does cognitive similarity influence comprehension of a message?
12. How is an extremist source perceived by the audience?

FURTHER READING

McGuire (1969a). Hovland and Weiss (1952), Zimbardo et al (1965), Aronson and Golden (1962) all in Rosnow and Robinson (1967).

VIII

Focus on the Message
and Channel

Although many kinds of messages exist, we shall distinguish only three major classes of their characteristics: style, structure, and content.

Style refers to connotative characteristics of the message such as whether it is dynamic or subdued, humorous or serious, elegant or clumsy.

Structure refers to the way the elements of the message are organized. Major consideration is given here to whether the first or the second of two messages is likely to be more influential (the primacy-recency discussion presented in Chapter VI). Should the elements be organized so that (a) the more pleasant come first or last; (b) the best arguments are presented earlier or later in the message (climax versus anticlimax); (c) the full amount of attitude change will be advocated at once, or there will be a gradual increase in the demands made on the audience for attitude change. Also, with respect to this situation, (d) are conclusions to be drawn and at what point? (e) Should the arguments of the opposition be refuted or be ignored? (f) Is it better to discuss both sides of an issue or simply to present one's own side?

The content of the message refers to matters such as the relationship between attitude change and (a) the discrepancy between the position advocated by the source and the position of the audience, (b) the creation of anxiety via the message, (c) the presentation of warnings, and (d) the urging of action.

The Style of the Message

Hovland, Lumsdaine and Sheffield (1949) found no difference either in attitude change or in perceived intent to persuade between a dynamic documentary style presentation and a subdued narrator style. It is conceivable that while the dynamic style increases attention, it also increases suspicion that the source is biased. Lull (1940) found that the addition of humor to a speech on a serious topic had no effect on attitude change. Gruner (1965) found that satirical speeches are not persuasive. In general, there are few differences resulting from the elegance of the presentation, although Miller and Hewgill (1964) found that pauses did produce a lower perceived competence but did not affect the perceived trustworthiness of the source.

The issue of the style of the message and its presentation has been central ever since the ancient Greeks started training people in "rhetoric." However, the effects appear to be rather subtle and involve interactions among several variables, hence, progress has been slow. In modern times this topic has been the focus of attention in speech or communication departments, and has received less attention in psychology or sociology departments. For this reason it will not be further discussed in this book.

The Structure of the Message

In Chapter VI we presented a discussion on primacy-recency in persuasion. This was done in connection with Rosnow's work, which concerns the timing of reinforcements and their relationship to the effectiveness of different parts of the message. This discussion only introduced this topic, which is actually rather complex. We turn then to a more detailed consideration of primacy-recency phenomena.

We must first distinguish between the situation when the same source presents two messages and the one in which two sources present two messages. The latter is of greater relevance to real-life situations.

Two theoretical orientations have made contributions to this question. The first was derived from learning theory and is represented in the papers by Hovland and Mandell (1952) and Miller and Campbell (1959). This analysis argues that the learning of the first side's arguments inhibits the learning of the arguments of the second side (technically this is called proactive inhibition). On the other hand, what is learned is also forgotten, and the last side to present an argument has an important advantage.

Miller and Campbell (1959) suggested that the relative size of recency or primacy depends on (a) the interval between the two communications, (b) the timing of the measurements, and (c) the rate of decay of the memory of the communications. Let us look at Fig. 20, which was adapted from their paper. There are two communications, A and B, which have been presented with an interval time d. The rate of decay is here assumed to be the same for both communications and, hence, if we measure the strength of the association or the amount retained from a given communication (the ordinate of Fig. 20) at time $t3$, we should obtain a large recency effect because the elements of the communication B are very vivid, since it has just been presented, but the elements of communication A are rather weak, since it has already decayed. Now consider what happens if we make the interval d very small, that is, if we have communication B', which is shown as decaying at the usual rate, as a dotted line. It is clear from the figure that at t_1 we would have more of a recency effect than at t_2. Furthermore, suppose that we do an experiment in which one group receives the communication B' immediately after the communication A, and another group receives B an interval d after communication A. B and B'

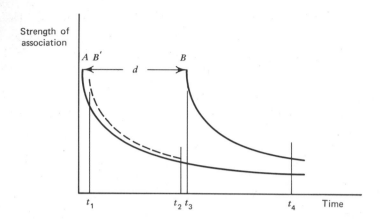

FIGURE 20.   Miller and Campbell's analysis of primacy and recency (adapted from their Figure 1, see text for explanation).

are, of course, identical communications, presented at different times. The curves would predict that the recency effect at t_4 would be much larger than at t_2. According to this model, it also is possible to get a primacy effect; one way to obtain a primacy effect is to assume that the first communication has a larger impact on the subject than the second and, hence, point A is higher than point B. Another way to obtain a primacy effect is to assume that the first communication has a smaller rate of decay than the second communication. This assumption is realistic and can be derived from the work on verbal learning that goes back to the 19th century. Recall, from your introductory psychology course, the Ebbinghaus forgetting curves. From these curves, Jost derived his so-called second law—of two associations equally strong at the moment, the older will decay less rapidly. This is well established and would tend to produce a primacy effect. However, since the primacy or recency effects depend on the simultaneous influence of several parameters, there are many conditions under which this primacy effect may be masked. It should be clear from this discussion that the Miller and Campbell analysis predicts a number of relationships. Their data largely support, although not in every detail, their theory, as do replications by Insko (1964), Wilson and Miller (1968), and others.

The second important theoretical orientation that deals with recency-primacy phenomena is derived from perceptual theory, including adaptation level theory (see Chapter III). This theory predicts primacy because it assumes that the second message will be distorted to fit the subject's perception which was formed and determined by the first message. The first message creates a set that modifies the second (Luchins, 1957). This kind of prediction is often supported by data. But learning theory also predicts primacy, both, because of the so-called "proactive inhibition" and if the rate of decay of the first message is smaller than the rate of decay of the second. Furthermore, in the Miller and Campbell system of curves, it is easy to obtain primacy by making the effect of communication A larger than the effect of communication B. Such an interpretation of primacy agrees with a series of careful studies by Anderson (for example, Anderson and Norman, 1964) and seems to be the best explanation we have to date.

The early work on primacy-recency was done mostly with the instructor acting as the experimenter. Typically, the instructor would present two sides of an argument and test his students. Almost all of these studies showed a primacy effect, leading Lund (1925) to proclaim his "Law of Primacy." It is understandable that when the instructor presents an argument he will have a larger chance of getting it accepted than if a less authoritative or learned person does. However, once the instructor started presenting the contrary argument (communication B) the students would become aware that the issues are not so clear cut, and would be less impressed with the second argument. Hence, it is most likely that when the instructor presents both communications A and B, the effect of A will be large, the effect of B will be small, and assuming that they decay at the same rate, at some point A will catch up and surpass B, and measurements made at t_4 will show primacy. Notice also that in Lund's experiments the same person presented both communications, but in the experiments that tended to find recency two people presented the communications.

PROJECT FOR ADVANCED STUDENTS

Write a paper on Anderson's (1959) mathematical model of opinion change which was applied by Anderson and Hovland (1957) to the primacy-recency problem. Explain the model and review the empirical support for it, including the paper by Anderson (1959).

Anderson (1959) hypothesized that opinion has two components: one which is relatively superficial, and another which is formed during the middle arguments and which is largely resistant to change. This analysis seems quite reasonable. It agrees, for example, with studies of opinion formation in the employment interview. As the interview continues, the interviewer is trying to form an opinion about whether to hire or not to hire the interviewee. Once he decides to do one or the other (which incidentally occurs within a few minutes after the interview starts), new information has relatively little influence. The correlation between the interviewer's decision at a time a few minutes after the start of the interview and at the end of the interview is very high (Webster, 1964). Data like these suggest that in real-life situations Lund's Law of Primacy may well be operating!

The work with employment interviews also suggests that negative information is more important than positive information in forming the final decision. In other words, it is not so important when the information is presented, but what the

186/ATTITUDE AND ATTITUDE CHANGE

information is. This is also in agreement with a study by Richey, McClelland, and Shimkunas (1967) which showed that originally positive impressions can be changed by subsequent negative information, leading to the final result of a negative impression. Originally, negative impressions can be changed by positive information, but nine days later the negative information is remembered and, again, the final impression is negative. Perhaps, the reason for the greater importance of negative information about others is that we generally know only good things about most of the people we know, and when we hear something negative, it makes an unusually strong and lasting impression. Once we learn this mechanism we use it even in the case of strangers.

Although we have covered most of the important points concerning primacy and recency, there is much more information on this topic. The interested student should read the reviews of the problem by Lana (1964) and Rosnow (1966). There he will find a discussion of a number of interaction effects. For example, positive, nonsalient, authoritative communications on controversial topics, or on interesting subjects, or on familiar topics tend to produce primacy effects. Communications that have the opposite characteristics tend to produce recency. It would appear that when the message is "attention-getting," either because it is pleasant, controversial, interesting, or because it is familiar, the first communication produces a large effect. When the message is dull, what was said at the end is all that is remembered.

We now consider other aspects of the structure of the message.

Pleasant Communications First

There is evidence (McGuire, 1957) that it is more effective to present pleasant arguments first and unpleasant ones later. The strategy of presenting criticism by first praising the other person is supported by McGuire's analysis and data. His basic argument is that if the first part of the message contains agreeable elements, the other person is reinforced for listening and tends to pay more attention to the subsequent items.

Climax-Anticlimax

There is no clear-cut evidence concerning the effectiveness of the presentation of the strongest arguments last or first (climax versus anticlimax). This is not surprising if we employ McGuire's analysis of persuasion, since the anticlimax procedure would start with strong arguments and, hence, would create attention which then may decrease, so that at the very point at which the audience is tired and may need something strong, the source has already exhausted its best arguments.

Gradual versus Absolute Approach

Should one start by taking a position that is very different from the one of the audience, or start at a less extreme point? The social judgment theory of Hovland and Sherif (reviewed in Chapter I) predicts that it is better to start at a less extreme point. The presentation of a communication that is well outside the audience's range of acceptance leads to "contrast effects," so that the communication is seen as even more different from the audience's position than it really is, and it is very likely to be rejected. A communication that is approximately at the audience's range of indifference could become assimilated. This assimilation would "stretch" the range of acceptance and would even modify the perception of the extent to which the message is "moderate." In other words, by ordering the elements of the message so that moderate demands are followed by larger demands, one has a better chance of the acceptance of the larger demands than he has if he presents his larger demands at once. Harvey and Rutherford (1958) found that for strong (ego-involving) opinions this set of results was obtained.

A different strategy might be used, however, if one has two communicators. In such a case, one communicator may present a most extreme message that is bound to be rejected but that increases the perspective of the audience. Once the audience's perspective has been "stretched," a moderately extreme communication will be regarded as quite moderate (Ostrom and Upshaw, 1968). This is quite consistent with everyday experiences. As long as the NAACP was the only civil rights organization making demands, its position was regarded as quite extreme by many whites. After the more militant black organizations came into being, the NAACP became a "moderate" organization. Actually, the NAACP has not changed; what has changed is the perspective of the audience.

One or Two Sides of the Issue

Should we present both sides of an argument, or only our own side? There is no direct answer, except that it depends on factors such as the intelligence of the audience, and on whether the audience is in favor of the position to be advocated or against the position to be advocated. In general, if the audience is against the position to be advocated and quite intelligent, it is more effective to present both sides of the argument; if the audience is in favor of the position to be advocated and not too intelligent, it is better to present only one side (Lumsdaine and Janis, 1953; Hovland, Janis and Kelley, 1953; McGinnies, 1966).

If the audience does not know much about the issue and is relatively intelligent, it will seek to learn the arguments of the other side before forming an opinion (Sears, 1966), so it is just as well for the communicator to present both sides of the argument.

To Draw Conclusions?

Should the message contain the conclusions or leave the conclusions up to the audience? McGuire (1969a) reviews a large number of studies which suggest that drawing conclusions increases the effectiveness of the message. It seems that most audiences have trouble understanding the message unless the conclusions are clearly drawn. However, it was found in some studies that if a considerable delay is allowed, giving the audience time to attend and to think about the issue, then letting the audience come to its own conclusion is more effective. For example, in psychotherapy, it usually is better for the therapist to let the client come to his own conclusions, but this obviously requires much time and is not a typical communication situation.

Conclusion early or late in Message

Should the conclusions be drawn early or late in the message? It appears that this depends on the culture of the audience, as suggested by Glenn (1968). The Anglo-Saxons prefer to be given a lot of evidence from which they can draw conclusions, but the continental Europeans, South Americans, and possibly others, seem to prefer to hear the general "theory" and conclusions first and then to be told about several incidents to which the theory applies. Important implications about Russian-American negotiations may be drawn from this view.

Refutation before or after Presentation of Own Position

Given that one is to refute the arguments of the other side, as required for an effective two-sided communication, should this be done before or after the presentation of the arguments that support his position? This again depends on the situation. There is little evidence on this point, but our expectations are as follows: if the audience is not familiar with the issue, it is best to present one's own arguments first to "familiarize" them with it. Once this is done, it is possible to present and to refute the arguments of the opposition. On the other hand, if the audience is already familiar with the issue, and particularly if it disagrees with the communicator, it is best for him to begin by refuting the arguments of the opposition, and then to present his own side.

Message Content

What is included in the message is very critical. Even minute details, for instance, the kinds of verbs that are used, may influence the way in which the message is perceived and accepted.

Verbs and Levels of Abstraction

In studies by Abelson and Kanouse (1966) and Kanouse and Abelson (1967), it was shown that the wording of the message can be important. The basic dimension used in these papers was the induction-deduction dimension of the message.

In these studies various messages were constructed, and audiences reacted to them, so that measures of message credibility were obtained. One dimension of importance that was investigated in these studies is the level of abstraction of elements of the message. This can vary from very abstract (for example, music) to moderately abstract (for example, choral music) to relatively concrete (for example, opera). Inductive arguments are arguments in which the elements increase in level of abstraction. For example, the argument "Candidates buy operas; therefore, candidates buy choral music" is inductive. On the other hand, deductive arguments go in the opposite direction. For instance, "Candidates buy music; therefore, candidates buy choral music" is a deductive argument. Abelson and Kanouse showed that certain verbs produce more credible messages when they are presented in inductive arguments and other verbs are more effective in deductive arguments. For example, the verb *to buy* is more effective in inductive and the verb *to avoid* is more effective in deductive arguments.

The issue is exceptionally important, since it shows that a skillful propagandist might construct effective messages by the mere correct selection of his verbs and levels of abstraction.

Hedonic and Personal Content

Another set of specific content variables was investigated by Rosenberg (1965b), who examined two dimensions of situations: hedonic-antihedonic and personal-general. He hypothesized that subjects would be bothered by the inconsistencies in the cognitive content of a message much more when the message is antihedonic than hedonic, and general instead of personal. First, however, we must explain what Rosenberg means by hedonic. This word denotes a cognition that reports or forecasts *gain*. His hypothesis is that statements that are inconsistent but hedonic will not bother the subjects very much. For example:

My hated antagonist (−) supports (+) my favorite plan for reorganizing the department (+).

The sentence is inconsistent, but this should not bother the subject too much. By contrast consider this antihedonic statement:

The distinguished firm of Schlag and Sons (+) has put on the market (+) a completely worthless sphygmomanometer (−).

This is also an inconsistent statement, but it is antihedonic. Rosenberg presented four types of inconsistent situations to subjects and asked them to rate the extent to which "the illogical and confusing nature of the situation" bothered them.

The situations varied in all possible combinations of the characteristics hedonic-antihedonic and personal-general. For example, one of the situations used in the hedonic, personal category was the following:

G.L. is a fellow student (same sex as you) toward whom you have long felt extreme dislike. You learn on reliable authority that G.L. feels strong and sincere admiration and respect for you.

An example of an antihedonic, general situation follows:

You have a great liking for the president of a certain Latin American country. You read a highly reliable series of articles showing that this same president since being elected has consistently opposed and blocked programs which would have vastly improved the standard of living of his country.

The analyses of the data showed that both the hedonic, and the personal dimensions reduced the degree to which the subjects were bothered by inconsistency, and there was an interaction which indicated that inconsistency was least bothersome when the situations were both hedonic and personal.

Studies of this kind have interesting implications for propaganda. It means that propaganda appeals worded in a personal, hedonic fashion (what *you* will gain by supporting me) can contain cognitive inconsistencies that will not bother the audience.

Warning

We now discuss a third example of the effects of specific types of content of the message. Consider the inclusion in the message of a *warning* (for example, you will hear a message advocating the recognition of mainland China's regime by the United States) or a *persuasion context* (for example, we intend to change your attitudes.) What effects will the inclusion of these elements have on attitude change? This is a complex topic, which recently has been reviewed by Papageorgis (1968), who suggests the importance of drawing a distinction between warning and persuasion context. There is evidence (for example, Apsler and Sears, 1968) that when the subjects are (a) ego-involved concerning a particular topic and (b) warned, they tend to resist the attempted influence; but when they are (c) not personally involved and/or (d) not warned, they are more likely to change their attitudes in the direction of the communication. There also is evidence that warning and persuasion context modify the beliefs of the subjects in the direction to be advocated by the source, probably as a defensive maneuver to protect their self-esteem and to make them appear less gullible, by claiming that they agreed with the source even before hearing his communication (McGuire and Millman, 1965); or in order to reduce dissonance ahead of time, hoping that the impact of the communication will be less unpleasant. The latter interpretation seems consistent with a study by Papageorgis (1967).

To summarize, when the subjects are personally involved, and the issue is important to them, warning has the effect of reducing attitude change.

The persuasion context often has little effect on attitude change, but when it does, it tends to nullify the impact of the communication. Nevertheless, in a minority of studies the persuasion context increased the impact, probably because in those studies some other variable was operating (Papageorgis, 1968).

STUDY QUESTIONS

1. What aspects of the style of a message are likely to influence attitude change?
2. What are the major considerations that determine whether primacy or recency will be observed in attitude change?
3. What is Anderson's model of opinion change? What does it predict about primacy or recency and why?
4. How should one structure a message with respect to the positioning of (a) pleasant elements, (b) strong arguments, (c) gradual shifts in the discrepancy between the positions of the message and the audience?
5. When should one present both sides of an argument?

6. When should one draw conclusions? At what point within the message? Before or after presentations of his own position?
7. What did Abelson and his associates find about the content of messages?
8. What did Rosenberg find about hedonic and personal messages?
9. Under what conditions is forewarning likely to inhibit attitude change?

FURTHER READING

McGuire (1969a); Miller and Campbell (1959) also reproduced in Steiner and Fishbein (1965) and Rosnow and Robinson (1967); Hovland, Lumsdaine and Sheffield (1949), and Anderson (1959), both of which are also reproduced in Rosnow and Robinson (1967).

Fear Appeals

There is an extensive literature on the question of whether it helps, in an attitude-change situation, to scare the audience by presenting messages that produce fear. Two contradictory, theoretically derived predictions can be made concerning the effects of fear. On the one hand, fear is a drive and, therefore, will tend to multiply the tendency to comply with the recommendations of the message. On the other hand, fear is also a cue that elicits avoidance of the source or the message.

The first study, which became a classic in social psychology, was by Janis and Feshbach (1953), who found that the greater the amount of fear introduced, the less effective is the message in changing the behavior of subjects. In other words, the second of the two mechanisms seems to have dominated their results.

However, it appears that a result of this kind is obtained under special conditions and, in fact, the relationship between fear and attitude change is an inverted U curve. At low levels of fear the audience is not particularly interested in the message, does not attend to it, and may not even receive it. As the fear increases, however, reception is likely to be good, and fear will have the additional advantage of increasing yielding. Thus, until the degree of fear is relatively high, we should expect a relationship in which the larger the fear, the greater the amount of change. At rather high levels of fear, however, the reception of the message will decrease, since the subject will start defending himself from such noxious stimuli, and without reception there can be no yielding; hence, there will be a sharp decrease in attitude change. This analysis, which was presented by McGuire (1968b, c), seems to be well supported by recent evidence.

An extensive program of research by Leventhal (1965) with a variety of issues and appeals, generally indicates that the greater the fear appeal the greater the attitude change. For example, Leventhal, Singer, and Jones (1965) found that 60 percent of those receiving a high-fear communication concerning the importance of tetanus shots indicated a strong intention of taking these shots. The low-fear communication resulted in only 31 percent of the subjects having these intentions, and only 18 percent of those in the control group (no fear) indicated that they would take such shots. The study also reports on whether the subjects did, in fact, take the shots. None of the subjects in the control group took the shots. Of the subjects in the two experimental groups with the two levels of fear, only 3 percent took the shots when the message included a nonspecific recommendation about taking the shots. On the other hand, when a specific recommendation was made, which included a map of the campus, on which the student health service was clearly circled, and several practical suggestions about how to schedule an appointment also were included, 28 percent of the students in the experimental group took the shots.

Janis (1967; 1969) has reviewed the whole problem and has presented his own theory, which like McGuire's also predicts an inverted U relationship between fear and attitude change.

Janis argues that by introducing special procedures that will reduce the defenses of the subjects, it will be possible to produce more attitude change. Janis and Mann (1965) arranged a role-playing situation in which subjects played the role of medical patients beginning to suffer from the harmful consequences of cigarette smoking. All of the subjects were young women who had expressed no intention of cutting down on their smoking. In the experimental group each subject was told that in playing the role of the patient she should express her spontaneous personal reactions. The experimenter in the role of the physician wore a white coat and used various props, for instance, X-ray photographs of the lungs. Five different scenes were played, including one in which the patient waits for the physician to arrange for her hospitalization in the surgical ward. This procedure was exceptionally effective in arousing emotion. The results show that there was marked attitude change in the experimental group and even changes in smoking habits. Mann and Janis (1968) asked the subjects to report on their cigarette smoking 18 months later and found that the subjects in the experimental group were consuming fewer cigarettes than those who were in a control group which had only listened to a tape recording of an authentic session that had been conducted by one of the subjects in the experimental group. Figure 21 shows these results and also the effect of the Surgeon General's report on the smoking behavior of these subjects.

Mann (1967) compared three procedures: the regular fear-arousing procedure just described, a cognitive procedure, which required the subject to role play a debater arguing against smoking, and a shame-arousing procedure in which the subject took the role of a helpless smoking addict. The fear-arousing procedure was by far the most effective in changing attitudes.

It would seem, then, that fear can increase the effectiveness of a message, up to a point, but at extremely high levels of fear there is a drop in the amount of attitude change. Exactly at what point the curve will turn depends on other parameters. For example, McGuire (1966) argues that the higher the chronic level of anxiety of the subjects, the greater their concern with the issue and the more complex the message that is presented to them, the less fear may be optimal. If there is more fear than the amount corresponding to this optimal point, there will be less attitude change.

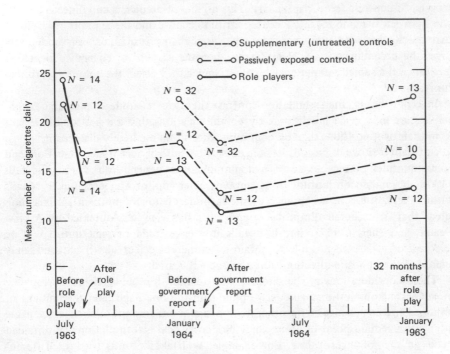

FIGURE 21.   The effects of role playing on cigarette smoking (after Mann and Janis, 1968, p. 340).

Effects of the Discrepancy between Advocated Attitude and the Audience's Attitude

In Chapter III we summarized work by Sherif, Sherif, and Nebergall (1965) that describes attitudes as dependent on the person's level of adaptation. At this point, this section should be reviewed. Notice that the level of adaptation is the weighted geometric mean of all stimuli that have influenced the individual in making a judgment. Those stimuli that are more recent, that have appeared more frequently, and that were more intense receive larger weights. When the stimuli are attitude statements, those statements made by competent, attractive, and powerful sources of information receive more weight than the ones made by incompetent, unattractive, or weak sources of information.

The subject employs his own attitude as an anchor to judge other attitudinal positions. When a communicator presents a position that is similar to that of the subject, his statements are assimilated; when they are different, the subjects may experience contrast (see Chapter III). This argument predicts a curvilinear relationship between the amount of advocated attitude change and the amount of obtained attitude change: when the amount of advocated change is small or even moderately large, the communication is assimilated, when the amount of change advocated is very large, the subjects experience contrast; hence they reject the communication as "unreasonable."

In other words, the assimilation-contrast theory of attitude change argues that persons are influenced much more by communications that are not too discrepant from their own positions than by communications that are highly discrepant.

In Chapter II, we discussed the concepts of latitude of acceptance, rejection, and noncommitment. Acceptance of a communication depends on whether it falls within the audience's latitude of acceptance, rejection, or noncommital. If it falls within the latitude of acceptance or the latitude of noncommitment, it is assimilated, that is, accepted. Empirical support for this view was obtained by Atkins, Deaux, and Bieri (1967). But if it falls in the latitude of rejection, it will be rejected; or, it is even possible to obtain a boomerang effect, and the attitude may change in the opposite direction from the one advocated.

These considerations predict a curvilinear relationship between the discrepancy of advocated opinion and audience opinion on the one hand, and the amount of obtained attitude change on the other, with a maximum amount of change occurring at an intermediate point of discrepancy. Support for this formulation was obtained by a number of investigators. For example, Whittaker (1963) used 12 different issues and eight degrees of communicator discrepancy. For one half the issues the amount of obtained change increased up to the point that involved six steps of discrepancy, and then the amount of obtained change decreased; for four issues a maximum was observed at seven steps of discrepancy; the remaining two issues showed a linear relationship, with a maximum of eight discrepancy steps (the maximum possible in that study).

Closer examination of these data suggest that the degree of the audience involvement with the issue determines where the maximum point will occur. The less the involvement, the larger the discrepancy that results in maximum change. In Whittaker's study the two issues that showed a linear relationship were concerned with the "continuation of the support to the United Nations" and with "prohibiting foreign aid to communist governments"; the issues that showed curvilinear changes involved "abolishing sororities and fraternities," "federal aid to universities," and "curfews for male students"—issues that might be considered more involving for the student subjects. To summarize these and other results, Whittaker (1967) theorized that involvement is a critical variable. He reviewed other studies which showed that low involvement gives a linear and high involvement a curvilinear relationship [for example, Freedman's (1964) study] and suggests that this is the result of different sizes in the latitude of rejection—the more ego-involved people reject more positions and hence, will show the downtrend of the curvilinear relationship earlier than the less involved.

Another variable that determines the position of the maximum on the discrepancy-attitude change curve is the credibility of the source of the communication. The more credible the source, the larger the discrepancy that can be optimal in changing attitudes.

An example can be found in a study by Aronson, Turner, and Carlsmith (1963), who asked female volunteers to rank nine stanzas of obscure poems. The communication referred to the stanza that was ranked eighth by the subjects. For one third of the subjects the communication argued that this stanza was superior to all other stanzas, for another third of the subjects it argued that it was superior to all but two of the nine stanzas, and for the last third it argued that it was average. Thus, the amount of discrepancy between the subjects' position and the communication was 3, 5, or 7 steps. The subjects were told that the communication was written by T. S. Eliot (highly credible source) or by an English major at Mississippi State Teachers College. The amount of obtained change was linear for T. S. Eliot, that is, the more change advocated the more was obtained, and curvilinear for the English major, that is, the maximum change was obtained when the discrepancy was 5 steps, and less change was obtained for steps 3 and 7.

Similar results were obtained by Bochner and Insko (1966), who presented a written communication in the context of a reading comprehension test, which advocated either 8, 7, 6, 5, 4, 3, 2, 1, or 0 hours sleep per night. The high credibility communicator was a Nobel prize winning physiologist; the medium credibility communicator was a YMCA director. Again, the physiologist obtained more attitude change when he advocated much change; the YMCA director obtained maximum change when he advocated an intermediate amount of change.

When a subject is confronted with large deviations between his opinions and the opinions advocated by another, he has a number of ways in which "to defend himself." For example, he can under-recall the discrepancy (convincing himself that the source did not really disagree with him), he can reject the source, he can rationalize (convince himself that the source was jesting, was careless, etc.), he can devaluate the issue of disagreement (for example, he can tell himself, "there is an error in the information"), or he can conform. Johnson (1966) employed measures of all these tendencies. He found that as discrepancy increased, under-recall decreased, and the rejection of the source was greater; the amount of rationalization and the devaluation of the issue were also greater. Conformity, on the other hand, showed a curvilinear relationship with discrepancy. Since Johnson employed a highly involving issue (information about self), his results on conformity are consistent with the results discussed earlier.

A theoretical way to explain these findings, following Sherif, is to assume that the latitude of noncommitment is larger in the case of nonego-involved subjects; hence, a large discrepancy will still be within this latitude and will be accepted. Furthermore, the latitude of acceptance may become larger in the case of highly credible communicators, so that the message is accepted. Sherif has shown changes of the latitude of noncommitment with changes in the ego-involvement of the subjects; hence, this explanation may be reasonable. Zimbardo (1960) found larger latitudes of acceptance among subjects whose attitudes changed, thus, supporting this interpretation.

The actual amount of change obtained, computed as a percentage of the amount of change being advocated, is larger when the amount advocated is small, and is much smaller when the amount advocated is large (Hovland and Pritzler, 1957). Hovland and Pritzler used 12 uninvolving issues. A month later, the questionnaire used in the pretest was readministered with the bogus opinions of various authoritative groups included for each item. These opinions were manipulated so that they differed from the subject's own opinions by 1, 2, or 4 steps. The analysis considered and controlled for the degree of polarization of the subject's initial position. The 1-step discrepancies resulted in change that was 88 percent of the amount advocated; the 2-step discrepancies resulted in 62 percent, and the 4-step discrepancies in 58 percent change of the amount advocated.

A note of qualification is necessary. In the discussions of ego-involvement, which we presented above, we dealt with *issue involvement*. Issue involvement occurs when the mere presentation of the issue is sufficient to elicit concern and interest on the part of the audience. With this type of involvement, the highly ego-involved audiences tend to reject extreme communications. However, ego-involvement also can be used in another sense. Zimbardo (1960) *manipulated* ego-involvement by varying the extent to which a given opinion leads to a desired goal. This is possible when experimental conditions are created that link the opinion with reward, approval, recognition, high self-esteem or low punishment. Such a situation was called *response-involvement*. Zimbardo has shown that subjects who are ego-involved, in the response-involvement sense, change their attitudes more when a highly positive source makes an extremely discrepant statement than when this source makes a mildly discrepant statement. The involvement manipulation was accomplished by telling subjects that their judgments would be a good indication of their personality and their basic social values. This is a special definition of involvement.

Figures 22, 23, and 24 summarize the relationships mentioned above. We might summarize these relationships as follows: in general, the greater the amount of change advocated, the greater the amount of change that is obtained. However, when the audience is highly involved with a particular issue, when it is quite sure of its own position on the issue [Koslin, Stoops, and Loh (1967)], when the issue is ambiguous, or when the communicator is only mildly credible, then the advocacy of an extreme amount of change is less effective than the advocacy of a moderate amount of change. Since many of the messages used in the real world are usually ambiguous, and the communicators are only mildly credible, it is probable that in everyday life, the relationship between amount of change advocated and obtained is curvilinear, with moderate amounts of advocated change being optimal for attitude change.

Peterson and Koulack (1969) found that attitude shifts are consistent with assimilation-contrast theory. A communication that falls within the latitude of acceptance is accepted, but results in very little attitude change; a communication

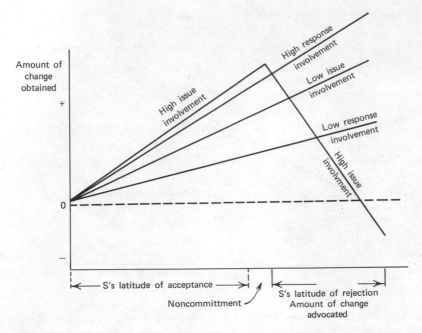

FIGURE 22.   The relationship between the amount of change advocated and obtained under various conditions of ego-involvement.

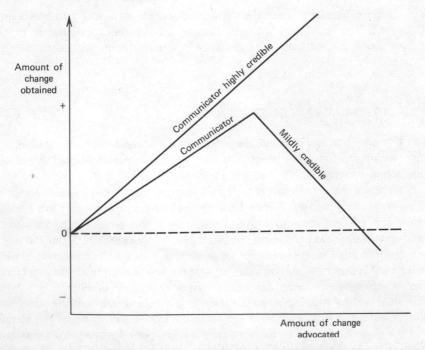

FIGURE 23.   The relationship between the amount of change advocated and obtained under two conditions of communicator credibility.

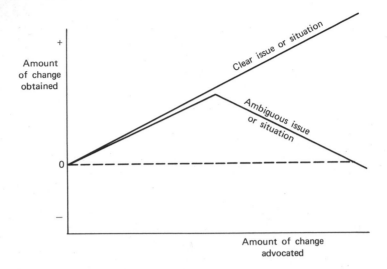

FIGURE 24.   The relationship between the amount of change advocated and obtained under two conditions of issue clarity.

that is a short distance outside the latitude of acceptance is likely to be accepted and to result in maximum attitude change; a communication that is too far removed from the latitude of acceptance is relatively ineffective in changing attitudes.

PROJECTS FOR ADVANCED STUDENTS

1. Examine the literature on the effects of ego-involvement and credibility of communicators on attitude change. In addition to the papers quoted in the text, study Johnson and Scileppi's (1969) paper on this topic.

2. What are the predictions made by dissonance theory and by social judgment theory concerning the relationship between the amount of advocated and obtained change and the influence of source credibility on this relationship? Review the studies that were mentioned above. Some of them support the predictions of one of these theories more clearly than the other. Sort out the studies according to which theory they support. In writing your paper, you should keep the following facts in mind. First, remember that dissonance theory makes no prediction about how dissonance will be reduced when a person is confronted with a highly discrepant communication. A highly involved subject might not attend, or might not comprehend the communication, or might reject the source, or might forget the communication at the earliest opportunity, *or* might change his attitudes. Second, there are usually other factors that have an influence on experimental results. For example,

in the Zimbardo study the highly ego-involved condition exposed the subject to the loss of his friend. Third, there is a difference between studies in which ego-involvement was found in the subjects (that is, field studies, such as those done by Sherif) and studies in which ego-involvement was experimentally manipulated. See Kiesler, Collins, and Miller (1969) for a discussion of these points.

Implications

Helson, Blake, and Mouton (1958) pointed out that under certain conditions the "big lie" technique can be exceptionally effective in changing attitudes. The approach is used in political (for example, Hitler), commercial (for example, advertising), and other situations. The advice given by Hitler's propaganda chief, Goebbels, can be paraphrased as: "If you are going to tell a lie, make it a whopper." Helson et al. showed that when a subject is exposed to the uniform opinions of a group of people, the more divergent the opinions of the group the more the subject changes his attitude.

When the state controls all the mass media, as is often the case in dictatorships, it is easy to create the impression that there is a uniformity of opinion on a given issue.

In predicting whether big lies will be more effective than small lies, it is necessary to consider the credibility of the source, the ego-involvement of the audience, and the clarity of the issue. The Soviets had little success in convincing their citizens that most important scientific discoveries were made by Russians, since that issue is not as ambiguous as some of the ones that were used by Hitler.

PROJECT FOR ADVANCED STUDENTS

Write an essay describing the nature of the interactions among the characteristics of the source and the message. A good beginning can be made by studying Tannenbaum (1956). A most important theoretical analysis and relevant data can be found in Kelman and Eagly (1965).

STUDY QUESTIONS

1. What is the relationship between the amount of fear in a message and the amount of attitude change that can be traced to this message?
2. Explain what is done in the fear-arousing role-playing procedure used by Janis and Mann. What are the long-term results of this experience?
3. What is the relationship between the amount of advocated change and the amount of obtained change under response-involvement? What is this relationship under issue-involvement? What is this relationship for different levels of communicator credibility?

4. Explain how the characteristics of the source and the message are likely to interact. What is meant by source orientation and by message orientation in Kelman and Eagly's paper?
5. Summarize the major findings about the effectiveness of different channels in facilitating attitude change.

FURTHER READINGS

McGuire (1969a); Hartmann (1936) in Rosnow and Robinson (1967); Janis and Feshbach (1953) and Leventhal (1965) both in Rosnow and Robinson (1967); Whittaker (1967); Bochner and Insko (1966); Zimbardo (1960).

An extensive review of mass media effects on attitudes can be found in Weiss (1969). An extensive review of propaganda and related issues can be found in Doob (1966).

References

ABELSON, R. P. A technique and a model for multi-dimensional attitude scaling. *Public Opinion Quarterly*, 1955, **19**, 405-418.

ABELSON, R. P. Modes of resolution of belief dilemmas, *Journal of Conflict Resolution*, 1959, **3**, 343-352.

ABELSON, R. P., & KANOUSE, D. E. Subjective acceptance of verbal generalizations. In S. Feldman (Ed.), *Cognitive consistency*. New York: Academic Press, 1966, 173-199.

ABELSON, R. P., & LESSER, G. S. The measurement of persuasibility in children. In C. I. Hovland & I. L. Janis (Eds.), *Personality and persuasibility*. New Haven: Yale University Press, 1959, 141-166. (a)

ABELSON, R. P., & LESSER, G. S. A developmental theory of persuasibility. In C. I. Hovland & I. L. Janis (Eds.), *Personality and persuasibility*. New Haven: Yale University Press, 1959, 167-187. (b)

ABELSON, R., & ROSENBERG, M. J. Symbolic psychologic: A model of attitudinal cognition. *Behavioral Science*, 1958, **3**, 1-13.

ABELSON, R. P., ARONSON, E., MC GUIRE, W. J., NEWCOMB, T. M., ROSENBERG, M. J., & TANNENBAUM, P. H. (Eds.), *Theories of cognitive consistency: A sourcebook*. Chicago: Rand McNally, 1968.

ADAMS, E. W., FAGOT, R. F., & ROBINSON, R. E. A theory of appropriate statistics. *Psychometrika*, 1965, **30**, 99-127.

ADAMS, J. S. Inequity in social exchange. In L. Berkowitz (Ed.), *Advances in experimental social psychology*. New York: Academic Press, 1965, Vol. II, 267-300.

ADELSON, J., & O'NEIL, R. P. Growth of political ideas in adolescence: The sense of community. *Journal of Personality and Social Psychology*, 1966, **4**, 295-306.

ADORNO, T. W., FRENKEL-BRUNSWIK, E., LEVINSON, D. J., & SANFORD, R. N. *The authoritarian personality*. New York: Harper, 1950.

AGER, J. W., & DAWES, R. M. The effect of Judges' attitudes on judgment. *Journal of Personality and Social Psychology*, 1965, **1**, 533-538.

AJZEN, I. & FISHBEIN, M. The prediction of behavioral intentions in a choice situation. *Journal of Experimental Social Psychology*, 1969, **5**, 400-416. (a)

AJZEN, I. & FISHBEIN, M. Prediction of behavior from attitudinal and normative variables. *Journal of Experimental Social Psychology*, 1970 (in press).

ALLPORT, G. W. Attitudes. In C. Murchison (Ed.), *Handbook of social psychology*. Worcester: Clark University Press, 1935, 798-844.

ALLPORT, G. W. The historical background of modern social psychology. In G. Lindzey (Ed.), *Handbook of social psychology*, Vol. I. Cambridge, Mass.: Addison-Wesley, 1954, 3-56. (a)

ALLPORT, G. W. *The nature of prejudice*. Cambridge: Addison-Wesley, 1954. (b)

ALLPORT, G. W., VERNON, P. E. & LINDZEY, G. *A study of values*. Boston: Houghton Mifflin, 1960.

ANDERSEN, K. (1961). Quoted in K. Giffin, The contribution of studies of source credibility to a theory of interpersonal trust in the communication process. *Psychological Bulletin*, 1967, **68**, 104-120.

ANDERSON, L. R. Belief defense produced by derogation of message source. *Journal of Experimental Social Psychology*, 1967, **3**, 349-360.

ANDERSON, L. R. & BASS, A. R. Some effects of victory or defeat upon perception of political candidates. *Journal of Social Psychology*, 1967, **73**, 227-240.

ANDERSON, L. R., & FISHBEIN, M. Prediction of attitudes from the number, strength and evaluative aspect of beliefs about the attitude object: A comparison of summation and congruity theories. *Journal of Personality and Social Psychology*, 1965, **3**, 437-443.

ANDERSON, N. H. Test of a model for opinion change. *Journal of Abnormal and Social Psychology*, 1959, **59**, 371-381

ANDERSON, N. H. Application of an additive model to impression formation. *Science*, 1962, **138**, 817-818.

ANDERSON, N.H. Averaging versus adding as stimulus-combination rule in impression formation. *Journal of Experimental Psychology*, 1965, **70**, 394-400.

ANDERSON, N. H. Component ratings in impression formation. *Psychonomic Science*, 1966, **6**, 279-280.

ANDERSON, N. H., & HOVLAND, C. I. The representation of order effects in communication research. In C. I. Hovland (Ed.), *The order of presentation in persuasion*. New Haven: Yale University Press, 1957, 158-169.

ANDERSON, N. H., & JACOBSON, A. Effect of stimulus inconsistency and discounting instructions in personality impression format. *Journal of Personality and Social Psychology*, 1965, **2**, 531-539.

ANDERSON, N. H., & NORMAN, A. Order effects in impression formation in four classes of stimuli. *Journal of Abnormal and Social Psychology*, 1964, **69**, 467-471.

APSLER, R., & SEARS, D. O. Warning, personality involvement and attitude change. *Journal of Personality and Social Psychology*, 1968, **9**, 162-166.

ARONSON, E. The psychology of insufficient justification: An analysis of some conflicting data. In S. Feldman (Ed.), *Cognitive consistency*. New York: Academic Press, 1966, 115-136.

ARONSON, E., & GOLDEN, B. W. The effects of relevant and irrelevant aspects of communicator credibility on opinion change. *Journal of Personality*, 1962, **30**, 135-146.

ARONSON, E., & LINDER, D. Gain and loss of esteem as determinants of interpersonal attractiveness. *Journal of Experimental Social Psychology*, 1965, **1**, 156-171.

ARONSON, E., TURNER, J., & CARLSMITH, J. Communicator credibility and communication discrepancy as determinants of opinion change. *Journal of Abnormal and Social Psychology*, 1963, **67**, 31-36.

ASCH, S. E. Effects of group pressure upon the modification and distortion of judgments. In E. E. Maccoby, T. M. Newcomb, and E. L. Hartley (Eds.), *Readings in social psychology*. New York: Holt, 1958, 174-182.

ATKINS, A. L., DEAUX, K. K., & BIERI, J. Latitude of acceptance and attitude change: Empirical evidence for a reformulation. *Journal of Personality and Social Psychology*, 1967, **6**, 47-54.

AVIGDOR, R. Etudes expérimentale des la genèse des stéréotypes. *Cahier International de Sociologie*, 1953, 154-168.

BARON, R. M. Cognitive bias of attitude change as a function of motivational, stylistic, and stimulus factors. *Journal of Personality and Social Psychology*, 1965, **2**, 219-230.

BASTIDE, R., & VAN DEN BERGHE, P. Stereotypes, norms and interracial behavior in Sao Paulo, Brazil. *American Sociological Review*, 1957, **22**, 689-694.

BAYTON, J. A., MC ALLISTER, Lois B., & HEIMER, J. Race-class stereotypes. *Journal of Negro Education*, 1956, **25**, 75-78.

BEM, D. J. An experimental analysis of self-persuasion. *Journal of Experimental Social Psychology*, 1965, **1**, 199-218.

BEM, D. J. Self-perception: The dependent variable of human performance. *Origins of Behavior and Human Performance*, 1967, **2**, 105-121.

BENNETT, E. B. Discussion, decision, commitment and consensus in "group decision." *Human Relations*, 1955, **8**, 251-274.

BERELSON, B., LAZARSFELD, P. F., & MC PHEE, W. N. *Voting*. Chicago: University of Chicago Press, 1954.

BERG, K. R. Ethnic attitudes and agreement with a Negro person. *Journal of Personality and Social Psychology*, 1966, **4**, 215-220.

BERGIN, A. E. The effect of dissonant persuasive communications upon change is self-referring attitudes. *Journal of Personality*, 1963, **30**, 423-438.

BERKOWITZ, L. The concept of aggressive drive: Some additional considerations. In Len Berkowitz (Ed.), *Advances in experimental social psychology*. New York: Academic Press, 1965, Vol. II, 301-329.

BERKOWITZ, N. H., & WOLKON, G. A forced-choice form of the *F* scale—free of acquiescent response set. *Sociometry*, 1964, **27**, 54-65.

BETTLEHEIM, B., & JANOWITZ, J. *Dynamics of prejudice*. New York: Harper, 1950.

BLAKE, R. R., SHEPARD, H. A., & MOUTON, Jane S. *Managing intergroup conflict in industry*. Houston, Texas: Gulf Publishing, 1964.

BOCHNER, S., & INSKO, C. Communicator discrepancy, source credibility and influence. *Journal of Personality and Social Psychology*, 1966, **4**, 614-621.

BOGARDUS, E. S. Measuring social distance. *Journal of Applied Sociology*, 1925, **9**, 299-308.

BOGARDUS, E. S. *Fundamentals of social psychology*. New York: Century, 1931.

BOSTROM, R., VLANDIS, J., & ROSENBAUM, M. Grades as reinforcing contingencies and attitude change. *Journal of Educational Psychology*, 1961, **52**, 112-115.

BREER, P. E., & LOCKE, E. A. *Task experience as a source of attitudes*. Homewood, Ill.: Dorsey, 1965.

BREHM, J. W. Comment on "counter-norm attitudes induced by consonant versus dissonant conditions of role playing." *Journal of Experimental Research in Personality*, 1965, **1**, 61-64.

BREHM, J. W. *A theory of psychological reactance*. New York: Academic Press, 1966.

BREHM, J. W. Attitude change from threat to attitudinal freedom. In A. G. Greenwald, et al. (Eds.), *Psychological foundations of attitudes*. New York: Academic Press, 1968, 277-296.

BREHM, J. W., & COHEN, A. R. *Explorations in cognitive dissonance*. New York: Wiley, 1962.

BREHM, J. W., & COLE, A. H. Effect of a favor which reduces freedom. *Journal of Personality and Social Psychology*, 1966, **3**, 420-426.

BREHM, J. W., & LIPSHER, D. Communicator-communicatee discrepancy and perceived communicator trustworthiness. *Journal of Personality*, 1959, **27**, 352-361.

BREWER, M. B. Averaging versus summation in composite ratings of complex social stimuli. *Journal of Personality and Social Psychology*, 1968, **8**, 20-26. (a)

BREWER, M. B. Determinants of social distance among East African tribal groups. *Journal of Personality and Social Psychology*, 1968, **10**, 279-289. (b)

BRIGHAM, J. C. & COOK, S. W. The influence of attitude on the recall of controversial material: A failure to confirm. *Journal of Experimental Social Psychology*, 1959, **5**, 240-243.

BROCK, T. C. Communication discrepancy and intent to persuade as determinants of counterargument production. *Journal of Experimental Social Psychology*, 1967, **3**, 296-309.

BROWN, R. W., & LENNEBERG, E. H. A study of language and cognition. *Journal of Abnormal and Social Psychology*, 1954, **49**, 454-462.

BRUNER, J. S. Social psychology and perception. In Eleanor Maccoby, T. M. Newcomb, and E. L. Hartley (Eds.), *Readings in social psychology*. New York: Holt, 1958, 85-94.

BUCHANAN, W., & CANTRIL, H. *How nations see each other*. Urbana: University of Illinois Press, 1953.

BUCKHOUT, R. Changes in heart rate accompanying attitude change. *Journal of Personality and Social Psychology*, 1966, 4, 695-699.

BUES, H. W. The construction and validation of a scale to measure attitude toward any practice. *Purdue University Studies in Higher Education*, XXVI, 1934, 35, 64-67.

BURSTEIN, E. Sources of cognitive bias in the representation of simple social structures: Balance, minimal change, positivity, reciprocity and the respondent's own attitude. *Journal of Personality and Social Psychology*, 1967, 7, 36-48.

BYRNE, D. Interpersonal attraction and attitude similarity. *Journal of Abnormal and Social Psychology*, 1961, 62, 713-715.

CALVIN, A. Social reinforcement. *Journal of Social Psychology*, 1962, 56, 15-19.

CAMPBELL, A. Civil rights and the vote for president, *Psychology Today*, 1968, 1, 26-70.

CAMPBELL, A. CONVERSE, P. E., MILLER, W. E., & STOKES, D. E. *The american voter.* New York: Wiley, 1960.

CAMPBELL, D. T. The indirect assessment of social attitudes. *Psychological Bulletin*, 1950, 47, 15-38.

CAMPBELL, D. T. Social attitudes and other acquired behavioral dispositions. In S. Koch, *Psychology: A study of science*, Vol. 6. New York: McGraw-Hill, 1963, 94-172.

CAMPBELL, D. T. Stereotypes and the perception of group differences. *American Psychologist*, 1967, 22, 817-829.

CAMPBELL, D. T., & FISKE, D. W. Convergent and discriminant validation by the multi-trait—multi-method matrix. *Psychological Bulletin*, 1959, 56, 81-105.

CAMPBELL, D. T., & LE VINE, R. A. Propositions about ethnocentrism from social science theories. (mimeographed, 1965)

CAMPBELL, D. T., & LE VINE, R. A. Ethnocentrism and intergroup relations. In R. P. Abelson, E. Aronson, W. J. McGuire, T. M. Newcomb, M. J. Rosenberg, & P. H. Tannenbaum (Eds.), *Theories of cognitive consistency: A sourcebook.* Chicago: Rand McNally, 1968, 551-564.

CAMPBELL, J. D., & YARROW, M. R. Perceptual and behavioral correlates of social effectiveness. *Sociometry*, 1961, 24, 1-20.

CAMPBELL, J. P., & DUNNETTE, M. D. Effectiveness of T group experiences in managerial training and development. *Psychological Bulletin*, 1968, 70, 73-104.

CAPEL, W. C. Continuities and discontinuities in attitudes of the same persons measured through time. *Journal of Social Psychology*, 1967, 78, 125-136.

CARLSMITH, J. M., COLLINS, B. E., & HELMREICH, R. L. Studies of forced compliance: The effect of pressure for compliance on attitude change produced by face-to-face role playing and anonymous essay writing. *Journal of Personality and Social Psychology*, 1966, 4, 1-13.

CARLSON, E. R. Attitude change through modification of attitude structure. *Journal of Abnormal and Social Psychology*, 1956, 52, 256-261.

CARTWRIGHT, D., & HARARY, F. Structural balance: A generalization of Heider's theory. *Psychological Review*, 1956, 63, 277-293.

CENTERS, R. *The psychology of social classes.* Princeton: Princeton University Press, 1959.

CHALMERS, D. K. Meaning, impressions, and attitudes: A model of the evaluation process. *Psychological Review*, 1969, 76, 450-460.

CHAPANIS, N., & CHAPANIS, A. Cognitive dissonance: Five years later. *Psychological Bulletin*, 1964, 61, 1-22.

CHEIN, I. Behavior theory and the behavior of attitudes: Some critical comments. *Psychological Review*, 1948, 55, 175-188.

CHRISTIANSEN, B. *Attitudes towards foreign affairs as a function of personality.* Oslo: Oslo University Press, 1959.

CHRISTIE, R., & COOK, P. A guide to published literature relating to the authoritarian personality through 1956. *The Journal of Psychology*, 1958, 45, 171-199.

CHU, G. C. Sex differences in persuasibility factors among Chinese. *International Journal of Psychology*, 1967, 2, 283-288.

CLARKE, P., & JAMES, J. The effects of situation, attitude intensity and personality on information seeking. *Sociometry*, 1967, **30**, 235-245.

COCH, L., & FRENCH, J. R. P. Overcoming resistance to change. *Human Relations*, 1948, **1**, 512-532.

COHEN, A. R. Some implications of self-esteem for social influence. In C. I. Hovland & I. L. Janis (Eds.), *Personality and persuasibility*. New Haven: Yale University Press, 1959, 102-120.

COHEN, A. R. Attitudinal consequences of induced discrepancies between cognitions and behavior. *Public Opinion Quarterly*, 1960, **24**, 297-318.

COHEN, R. A. A theoretical model for consumer market prediction. *Sociological Inquiry*, 1962, **32**, 43-50.

COLE, D., HARTRY, A., & BREBNER, L. Attitudes to Caryl Chessman as a function of his reprieve and execution. *Journal of Social Psychology*, 1962, **57**, 471-475.

COMREY, A. L., & NEWMEYER, J. A. Measurement of radicalism-conservatism. *Journal of Social Psychology*, 1965, **67**, 357-369.

COOK, S. W., & SELLTIZ, C. A multiple-factor approach to attitude measurement. *Psychological Bulletin*, 1964, **62**, 36-55.

COOPER, E., & JAHODA, M. The evasion of propaganda: How prejudiced people respond to anti-prejudice propaganda. *Journal of Psychology*, 1947, **23**, 15-25.

COOPER, J. B. Emotion in prejudice. *Science*, 1959, **130**, 314-318.

COOPER, J. B., & POLLOCK, D. The identification of prejudicial attitudes by the galvanic skin response. *Journal of Social Psychology*, 1959, **50**, 241-245.

CORROZI, J. F., & ROSNOW, R. L. Consonant and dissonant communications as positive and negative reinforcements in opinion change. *Journal of Personality and Social Psychology*, 1968, 8, 27-30.

COX, D. F., & BAUER, R. A. Self-confidence and persuasibility in women. *Public Opinion Quarterly*, 1964, **28**, 453-466.

CULBERTSON, F. M. The modification of an emotionally held attitude through role playing. *Journal of Abnormal and Social Psychology*, 1957, **54**, 230-233.

DAVIDSON, J., & KIESLER, S. Cognitive behavior before and after decisions. In L. Festinger (Ed.), *Conflict, decision and dissonance*. Stanford: Stanford University Press, 1964, 10-19.

DAVIS, E. E. A methodological study of behavioral and semantic differentials relevant to intercultural negotiations. Tech. Report No. 32. Urbana: Group Effectiveness Research Laboratory, 1966.

DAVIS, E. E., & TRIANDIS, H. C. An exploratory study of intercultural negotiations. Urbana: Group Effectiveness Laboratory Technical Report No. 26, 1965.

DAWES, R. M. Ordinal methods for evaluating the relationship between judgments of compound social stimuli and judgments of their components. Paper presented at the annual convention of the American Psychological Association, Chicago, 1965.

DAWES, R. M. Racial preference and social choice. *Science*, 1966, **151**, 1248.

DAWES, R. M. *Measures and indicators of attitude.* New York: Wiley, 1971.

DE FLEUR, M. L., & WESTIE, F. R. Verbal attitudes and overt acts: An experiment on the salience of attitudes. *American Sociological Review,* 1958, **23**, 667-673.

DIAB, L. N. Measurement of social attitudes: Problems and prospects. In Carolyn W. Sherif & M. Sherif (Eds.), *Attitude, ego-involvement, and change.* New York: Wiley, 1967, 140-158.

DIAZ-GUERRERO, R. Socio-cultural premises, attitudes and cross-cultural research. Paper presented at the 27th International Congress of Psychology, Washington, D.C. 1963.

DIAZ-GUERRERO, R., & PECK, R. F. Estilo de controntacion y aprovechamiento: un programa de investigacion. *Interamerican Journal of Psychology*, 1967, **1**, 127-136.

DILLEHAY, R. C., BRUVOLD, W. H., & SIEGEL, J. P. On the assessment of potability. *Journal of Applied Psychology*, 1967, **51**, 89-95.

DILLEHAY, R. C., BRUVOLD, W. H., & SIEGEL, J. P. Attitude, object label and stimulus factors in response to an attitude object. *Journal of Personality and Social Psychology,* 1969, **11**, 220-223.

DI VESTA, F. J., & BOSSART, P. The effects of sets induced by labeling on the modification of attitudes. *Journal of Personality,* 1958, **26**, 379-387.

DOLLARD, J. *Caste and class in a southern town.* New York: Anchor, 1957.

DOLLARD, J., DOOB, L., MILLER, N., MOWRER, O., & SEARS, R. *Frustration and aggression.* New Haven: Yale University Press, 1939.

DOOB, L. Some factors determining change in attitude. *Journal of Abnormal and Social Psychology,* 1940, **35**, 546-565.

DOOB, L. The behavior of attitudes. *Psychological Review,* 1947, **54**, 135-156.

DOOB, L. W. *Public opinion and propaganda.* Hamden, Conn.: Archon Books, 1966.

DULANY, D. E. Awareness, rules and propositional control: A confrontation with S-R behavioral theory. In T. R. Dixon and D. L. Horton (Eds.), *Verbal behavior and general behavior theory.* Englewood Cliffs, N.J.: Prentice Hall, 1967, 340-387.

DUSTIN, D. S., & BALDWIN, P. M. Redundancy in impression formation. *Journal of Personality and Social Psychology,* 1966, **3**, 500-506.

EAGLY, A. H. Involvement as a determinant of response to favorable and unfavorable information. *Journal of Personality and Social Psychology,* Monograph Supplement, 1967, **7**, whole of No. 643, 1-15.

EDWARDS, A. L. *Techniques of attitude scale construction.* New York: Appleton-Century-Crofts, 1957. (a)

EDWARDS, A. L. The social desirability variable in personality assessment and research. New York: Dryden, 1957. (b)

EDWARDS, A. L., & KENNEY, K. C. A comparison of the Thurstone and Likert techniques in attitude scale construction. *Journal of Applied Psychology,* 1946, **30**, 72-83.

EDWARDS, A. L., & KILPATRICK, F. P. A technique for the construction of attitude scales. *Journal of Applied Psychology,* 1948, **32**, 374-384.

EHRLICH, H. J. *The structure of stereotypes.* Mimeographed, 1967.

EHRLICH, H. J., & LEE, D. Dogmatism, learning and resistance to change: A review and a new paradigm. *Psychological Bulletin,* 1969, **71**, 249-260.

EHRLICH, H. J., & TUBERGEN, N. Social distance as behavioral intentions: A replication, a failure and a new proposal. *Psychological Reports,* 1969, **24**, 627-634.

EISINGER, R., & MILLS, J. Perception of the sincerity and competence of a communicator as a function of the extremity of his position. *Journal of Experimental Social Psychology,* 1968, **4**, 224-232.

EISMAN, B. Attitude formation: The development of a color preference response through mediated generalization. *Journal of Abnormal and Social Psychology,* 1955, **50**, 321-326.

ELMS, A. C. Influence of fantasy ability on attitude change through role playing. *Journal of Personality and Social Psychology,* 1966, **4**, 36-43.

ELMS, A. C. Role playing, incentive and dissonance. *Psychological Bulletin,* 1967, **68**, 132-148.

ELMS, A. C., & JANIS, I. L. Counter-norm attitudes induced by consonant versus dissonant conditions of role playing. *Journal of Experimental Research in Personality,* 1965, **1**, 50-60.

ENGLAND, G. W. Personal value systems of American managers. *Academy of Management Journal,* 1967, **10**, 53-68.

EPSTEIN, R., & KOMORITA, S. S. Prejudice among Negro children as related to parental ethnocentrism and punitiveness. *Journal of Personality and Social Psychology,* 1966, **4**, 643-647.

EYSENCK, H. J. *The structure of human personality.* London: Methuen, 1960.

FEATHER, N. T. A structural balance approach to the analysis of communication effects. In L. Berkowitz (Ed.), *Advances in experimental social psychology*. New York: Academic Press, 1967, 100-166.

FEATHER, N. T., & JEFFRIES, D. G. Balancing and extremity effects in reactions of receiver to source and content of communications. *Journal of Personality*, 1967, **35**, 194-213.

FEHLING, M. R., & TRIANDIS, H. C. Implicit attitude structures. Submitted for publication in 1970.

FELDMAN, R. E. The response to compatriot and foreigner who seek assistance. *Journal of Personality and Social Psychology*, 1968, **10**, 202-214.

FELDMAN, S. *Cognitive consistency*. New York: Academic Press, 1966.

FENDRICH, J. M. Perceived reference group support: Racial attitudes and overt behavior. *American Sociological Review*, 1967, **32**, 960-970.

FERGUSON, L. W. Primary social attitudes. *Journal of Psychology*, 1939, 8, 217-223.

FESTINGER, L. *A theory of cognitive dissonance*. Stanford, Calif.: Stanford University Press, 1957.

FESTINGER, L. Behavioral support for opinion change. *The Public Opinion Quarterly*, 1964, **28**, 404-417. (a)

FESTINGER, L. (Ed.) *Conflict, decision and dissonance*. Stanford, Calif.: Stanford University Press, 1964. (b)

FESTINGER, L., & CARLSMITH, J. M. Cognitive consequences of forced compliance. *Journal of Abnormal and Social Psychology*, 1959, **58**, 203-210.

FIEDLER, F. E. *A theory of leadership effectiveness*. New York: McGraw-Hill, 1967. (a)

FIEDLER, F. E. The effect of intergroup competition on group member adjustment. *Personnel Psychology*, 1967, **20**, 33-44. (b)

FISCHER, H., & TRIER, U. P. *Das Verhältnis zwischen Deutschschweizer und Westschweizer: Eine Sozialpsychologische Untersuchung*. Bern: Hans Huber, 1962.

FISHBEIN, M. An investigation of the relationships between beliefs about an object and the attitude towards that object. Technical Report No. 6. Los Angeles, Calif.: University of California, 1961.

FISHBEIN, M. A consideration of beliefs, attitudes and their relationship. In I. D. Steiner & M. Fishbein (Eds.), *Current studies in social psychology*. New York: Holt, Rinehart and Winston, 1965, 107-120.

FISHBEIN, M. (Ed.) *Readings in attitude theory and measurement*. New York: Wiley, 1967. (a)

FISHBEIN, M. Attitude and the prediction of behavior. In M. Fishbein (Ed.), *Readings in attitude theory and measurement*. New York: Wiley, 1967, 477-492. (b)

FISHBEIN, M. & HUNTER, R. Summation versus balance in attitude organization and change. *Journal of Abnormal and Social Psychology*, 1964, **69**, 505-510.

FISHBEIN, M., & RAVEN, B. H. The AB scales: An operational definition of belief and attitude. *Human Relations*, 1962, **15**, 35-44.

FLEISHMAN, E. A. Leadership climate, human relations training and supervisory behavior. *Personnel Psychology*, 1953, **6**, 205-222.

FOA, U. New developments in facet design and analysis. *Psychological Review*, 1965, **72**, 262-274.

FOA, U., TRIANDIS, H. C., & KATZ, Evelyn W. Cross-cultural invariance in the differentiation and organization of family roles. *Journal of Personality and Social Psychology*, 1966, **4**, 316-327.

FREEDMAN, J. Involvement, discrepancy and change. *Journal of Abnormal and Social Psychology*, 1964, **69**, 290-295.

FREEDMAN, J. L., & FRASER, S. C. Compliance without pressure: The foot-in-the-door technique. *Journal of Personality and Social Psychology*, 1966, **4**, 195-202.

FREEDMAN, J. L., & SEARS, D. O. Selective exposure. In L. Berkowitz (Ed.), *Advances in social psychology*. New York: Academic Press, 1965, Vol. 2, 57-97.

FREEDMAN, M. B. Changes in attitudes and values over six decades. *Journal of Social Issues*, 1961, **17**, 19-28.

GARDNER, R. C., WONNACOTT, E. J., & TAYLOR, D. M. Ethnic stereotypes: A factor analytic investigation. *Canadian Journal of Psychology*, 1968, **22**, 35-44.

GIFFIN, K. The contribution of studies of source credibility to a theory of interpersonal trust in the communication process. *Psychological Bulletin*, 1967, **68**, 104-120.

GILBERT, G. M. Stereotype persistence and change among college students. *Journal of Abnormal and Social Psychology*, 1951, **46**, 245-254.

GLENN, E. S. A cognitive approach to the analysis of cultures and cultural evolution. *General Systems Yearbook*, Ann Arbor, Michigan, 1966, 115-132.

GLENN, E. S. Learning theory and theory of social organization. Paper presented at a conference on cross-cultural interaction. Washington, D. C., 1968.

GOLIGHTLY, C., & BYRNE, D. Attitude statements as positive and negative reinforcements. *Science*, 1964, **146**, 798-799.

GOULDNER, A. The norm of reciprocity: A preliminary statement. *American Sociological Review* 1960, **25**, 161-178.

GREEN, B. F. Attitude measurement. In G. Lindzey (Ed.), *Handbook of social psychology*, **Vol. I** Cambridge, Mass.: Addison-Wesley, 1954, 335-369.

GREENWALD, A. G. Cognitive learning, cognitive response to persuasion, and attitude change. In A. G. Greenwald, T. C. Brook, & T. M. Ostrom (Eds.) *Psychological foundations of attitudes*. New York: Academic Press, 1968, 147-170. (a)

GREENWALD, A. G. On defining attitudes and attitude theory. In A. G. Greenwald et al. (Eds.), *Psychological foundations of attitudes*. New York: Academic Press, 1968, 361-390. (b)

GREENWALD, A. G. The open-mindedness of the counterattitudinal role player. *Journal of Experimental Social Psychology*, 1969, **5**, 375-388.

GREENWALD, A. G., & ALBERT, R. D. Acceptance and recall of improvised arguments. *Journal of Personality and Social Psychology*, 1968, **8**, 31-34.

GREENWALD, A. G., BROCK, T. C., & OSTROM, T. M. *Psychological foundations of attitudes*. New York: Academic Press, 1968.

GRUNER, C. R. An experimental study of satire in persuasion. *Speech Monographs*, 1965, **32**, 149-153.

GUILFORD, J. P. *Psychometric methods*. New York: McGraw-Hill, 1954, 2nd ed.

GUILFORD, J. P. *The nature of human intelligence*. New York: McGraw-Hill, 1967.

GUTTMAN, L. A basis for scaling qualitative data. *American Sociological Review*, 1944, **9**, 139-150.

GUTTMAN, L., A structural theory of intergroup beliefs and action. *American Sociological Review*, 1959, **24**, 318-328.

GUTTMAN, L., & SUCHMAN, E. A. Intensity and a zero point for attitude analysis. *American Sociological Review*, 1947, **12**, 55-67.

HAALOND, G. A., & VENKATESAN, M. Resistance to persuasive communications: An examination of the distraction hypothesis. *Journal of Personality and Social Psychology*, 1968, **9**, 167-170.

HACKMAN, J. R., & ANDERSON, L. R. The strength, relevance, and source of beliefs about an object in Fishbein's attitude theory. *Journal of Social Psychology*, 1968, **76**, 55-67.

HAIRE, M., & MORRISON, F. School children's perceptions of labor and management. *The Journal of Social Psychology*, 1957, **46**, 179-197.

HARDING, J. The conceptualization and measurement of prejudice. Paper presented on September 1, 1962 at the Annual Meetings of the American Psychological Association.

HARDYCK, J. A. Consistency, relevance and resistance to change. *Journal of Experimental Social Psychology*, 1966, **2**, 27-41.

HARMAN, H. H. *Modern factor analysis*. Chicago: University of Chicago Press, 1967.

HARTMANN, G. W. A field experiment on the comparative effectiveness of "emotional" and "rational" political leaflets in determining election results. *Journal of Abnormal and Social Psychology*, 1936, **31**, 99-114.

HARVEY, O. J. Personality factors in resolution of conceptual incongruities. *Sociometry*, 1962, **26**, 336-352.

HARVEY, O. J. Some cognitive determinants of influencibility. *Sociometry*, 1964, **27**, 208-221.

HARVEY, O. J. Some situational and cognitive determinants of dissonance resolution. *Journal of Personality and Social Psychology*, 1965, **1**, 349-355.

HARVEY, O. J. Conceptual systems and attitude change. In Carolyn and Muzafer Sherif (Eds.), *Attitude, ego-involvement and change*. New York: Wiley, 1967, 201-226.

HARVEY, O. J. & RUTHERFORD, J. Gradual and absolute approaches to attitude change. *Sociometry*, 1958, **21**, 61-68.

HARVEY, O. J., HUNT, D. E., & SCHROEDER, H. M. *Conceptual systems and personality organization*. New York: Wiley, 1961.

HEIDER, F. Attitudes and cognitive organization. *Journal of Psychology*, 1946, **21**, 107-112.

HEIDER, F. *The psychology of interpersonal relations*. New York: Wiley, 1958.

HELMREICH, R., & COLLINS, B. E. Studies in forced compliance: Commitment and magnitude of inducement to comply as determinants of opinion change. *Journal of Personality and Social Psychology*, 1968, **10**, 75-81.

HELSON, H. *Adaptation-level theory*. New York: Harper and Row, 1964.

HELSON, H., BLAKE, R. R., & MOUTON, J. S. An experimental investigation of the effectiveness of the "big lie" in shifting attitudes. *Journal of Social Psychology*, 1958, **48**, 51-60.

HESS, E. H., & POLT, J. M. Pupil size as related to interest value of visual stimuli. *Science*, 1960, **132**, 349-350.

HILGARD, E. R., & BOWER, G. H. *Theories of learning*. New York: Appleton-Century-Crofts, 1966.

HOBBS, D. J. *Factors related to the use of agricultural chemicals in Iowa farms*, M.S. Thesis, Ames, Iowa State University, 1960.

HOLMAN, P. A. Validation of an attitude scale as a device for predicting behavior. *Journal of Applied Psychology*, 1956, **40**, 347-349.

HOROWITZ, E. L. The development of attitude toward the Negro. *Archives of Psychology*, 1936, No. 194. Can also be found in H. Proshansky and B. Seidenberg (Eds.), *Basic studies in social psychology*. New York: Holt, 1965, 111-121.

HOVLAND, C. I. Effects of the mass media of communication. In G. Lindzey (Ed.), *Handbook of social psychology*. Boston: Addison-Wesley, 1954, 1062-1103.

HOVLAND, C. I. Reconciling conflict results derived from experimental and survey studies of attitude change. *American Psychologist*, 1959, **14**, 8-17.

HOVLAND, C. I., & JANIS, I. L. *Personality and persuasibility*. New Haven: Yale University Press, 1959.

HOVLAND, C. I., & MANDELL, W. An experimental comparison of conclusion-drawing by the communicator and by the audience. *Journal of Abnormal and Social Psychology*, 1952, 47, 581-588.

HOVLAND, C. I., & PRITZER, H. Extent of opinion change as a function of amount of change advocated. *Journal of Abnormal and Social Psychology*, 1957, **54**, 257-261.

HOVLAND, C. I., & SHERIF, M. Judgmental phenomena and scales of attitude measurement: Item displacement in Thurstone scales. *Journal of Abnormal and Social Psychology*, 1952, 47, 822-832.

HOVLAND, C. I., & WEISS, W. The influence of source credibility on communication effectiveness. *Public Opinion Quarterly*, 1952, **15**, 635-650.

HOVLAND, C. I., LUMSDAINE, A. A., & SHEFFIELD, F. D. *Experiments in mass communication*. Princeton: Princeton University Press, 1949.

HOVLAND, C. I., JANIS, I. L., & KELLEY, H. H. *Communication and persuasion*. New Haven, Yale University Press, 1953.

HOVLAND, C. I., MANDELL, W., CAMPBELL, E. H., BROCK, T., LUCHINES, A. S., COHEN, A. R., MC GUIRE, W. J., JANIS, I. L., FEIERABEND, R. L., & ANDERSON, N. H. *The order of presentation in persuasion*. New Haven: Yale University Press, 1957.

INSKO, C. A. Primacy versus recency in persuasion as a function of the timing of arguments and measures. *Journal of Abnormal and Social Psychology*, 1964, **69**, 381-391.

INSKO, C. A. Verbal reinforcement of attitudes. *Journal of Personality and Social Psychology*, 1965, **2**, 621-623.

INSKO, C. A. *Theories of attitude change*. New York: Appleton-Century-Crofts, 1967.

INSKO, C. A., & OAKES, W. F. Awareness and the "conditioning" of attitudes. *Journal of Personality and Social Psychology*, 1966, **4**, 487-496.

INSKO, C. A., & ROBINSON, J. E. Belief similarity versus race as determinants of reactions to Negroes by Southern white adolescents: A further test of Rokeach's theory. *Journal of Personality and Social Psychology*, 1967, **7**, 216-221.

IRWIN, J. V., & BROCKHAUS, H. H. The "teletalk project": A study of the effectiveness of two public relations speeches. *Speech Monographs*, 1963, **30**, 359-368.

JAHODA, G. Impressions of nationalities—an alternative to the "stereotype" approach. *British Journal of Social and Clinical Psychology*, 1966, **5**, 1-16.

JAHODA, M., & WARREN, N. *Attitudes*. Baltimore: Penguin Books, 1966.

JAMIAS, J. F., & TROLDAHL, V. C. Dogmatism, tradition and general innovativeness. A 1965 manuscript described by M. Rokeach, Attitude change and behavioral change. *Public Opinion Quarterly*, 1967, **30**, 529-550.

JANIS, I. L. Personality correlates of susceptibility to persuasion. *Journal of Personality*, 1954, **22**, 504-518.

JANIS, I. L. Effects of fear arousal on attitude change: recent developments in theory and experimental research. In L. Berkowitz (Ed.), *Advances in experimental social psychology*, Vol. III. New York: Academic Press, 1967, 166-224.

JANIS, I. L. Stages in the decision making process. In R. P. Abelson et al., *Theories of cognitive consistency: A sourcebook*. Chicago: Rand McNally, 1968, 577-588.

JANIS, I. L. *The contours of fear*. New York: Wiley & Sons, 1969.

JANIS, I. L., & FESHBACH, S. Effects of fear-arousing communications. *Journal of Abnormal and Social Psychology*, 1953, **48**, 78-92.

JANIS, I. L. & FIELD, P. B. A behavioral assessment of persuasibility: Consistency of individual differences. In C. I. Hovland & I. L. Janis (Eds.), *Personality and persuasibility*. New Haven: Yale University Press, 1959, 29-54.

JANIS, I. L., & KING, B. T. The influence of role playing on opinion change. *Journal of Abnormal and Social Psychology*, 1954, **49**, 211-218.

JANIS, I. L., & MANN, L. Effectiveness of emotional role playing in modifying smoking habits and attitudes. *Journal of experimental research in personality*, 1965, **1**, 84-90.

JANIS, I. L., & MANN, L. A conflict-theory approach to attitude change and decision making. In A. Greenwald, T. Brock and T. Ostrom (Eds.), *Psychological foundations of attitudes*. New York: Academic Press, 1968.

JANIS, I. L., & RAUSCH, C. N. Selective interest in communications that could arouse decisional conflict: A field study of participants in the draft-resistance movement. *Journal of Personality and Social Psychology*, 1970, **14**, 46-54.

JASPERS, J. M. F., VAN DE GEER, J. P., TAJFEL, H., & JOHNSON, N. *On the development of international attitudes*. Leiden, Netherlands: Psychological Institute, 1965.

JELLISON, J. M., & MILLS, J. Effect of public commitment upon opinions. *Journal of Experimental Social Psychology*, 1969, 5, 340-346.

JOHNSON, H. H. Some effects of discrepancy level on responses to negative information about one's self. *Sociometry*, 1966, 29, 52-66.

JOHNSON, H. H., & SCILEPPI, J. A. Effects of ego-involvement conditions on attitude change to high and low credibility communicators. *Journal of Personality and Social Psychology*, 1969, 13, 31-36.

JOHNSON, H. H., & TORCIVIA, J. M. Acquiescence response style and attitude change. *Journal of Personality and Social Psychology*, 1968, 8, 349-350.

JOHNSON, H. H., TORCIVIA, J. M., & POPRICK, M. A. Effects of source credibility on the relationship between authoritarianism and attitude change. *Journal of Personality and Social Psychology*, 1968, 9, 179, 183.

JONES, E. E., & ANESHANSEL, J. The learning and utilization of contravaluent material. *Journal of Abnormal and Social Psychology*, 1956, 53, 27-33.

JONES, E. E., & KOHLER, R. The effects of plausibility on the learning of controversial statements. *Journal of Abnormal and Social Psychology*, 1958, 57, 315-320.

KANOUSE, D. E., & ABELSON, R. P. Language variables affecting the persuasiveness of simple communications. *Journal of Personality and Social Psychology*, 1967, 7, 158-163.

KARLINS, M., COFFMAN, T. L., & WALTERS, G. On the fading of social sterotypes: Studies in three generations of college students. *Journal of Personality and Social Psychology*, 1969, 13, 1-16.

KATONA, G. *The powerful consumer*. New York: McGraw-Hill, 1960.

KATZ, D. The functional approach to the study of attitudes. *Public Opinion Quarterly*, 1960, 24, 163-204.

KATZ, D., & BRALY, K. W. Racial stereotypes of 100 college students. *Journal of Abnormal and Social Psychology*, 1933, 28, 280-290.

KATZ, D., & STOTLAND, E. A preliminary statement to theory of attitude structure and change. In S. Koch (Ed.), *Psychology: A study of a science*. New York: McGraw-Hill, 1959.

KATZ, D., SARNOFF, I., & MC CLINTOCK, C. Ego defense and attitude change. *Human Relations*, 1956, 9, 27-46.

KATZ, E. The two-step flow of communication: An up to date report on an hypothesis. *Public Opinion Quarterly*, 1957, 21, 61-78.

KATZ, E., & LAZARSFELD, P. F. *Personal influence*. Glencoe, Ill.: Free Press, 1955.

KAUFMAN, W. C. Status, authoritarianism, and anti-Semitism. *American Journal of Sociology*, 1957, 62, 379-382.

KELLY, G. A. *The psychology of personal constructs*, Vol. I. New York: Norton, 1955

KELLEY, H. H., & VOLKART, E. H. The resistance to change of group-anchored attitudes. *American Sociological Review*, 1952, 17, 453-465.

KELMAN, H. C. Attitude change as a function of response restriction. *Human Relations*, 1953, 6, 186-214.

KELMAN, H. C. Compliance, identification and internalization: Three processes of attitude change. *Journal of Conflict Resolution*, 1958, 2, 51-60.

KELMAN, H. C., & BARCLAY, J. The *F* scale as a measure of breadth of perspective. *Journal of Abnormal and Social Psychology*, 1963, 67, 608-615.

KELMAN, H. C., & EAGLY, A. H. Attitude toward the communicator, perception of communication content and attitude change. *Journal of Personality and Social Psychology*, 1965, 1, 63-78.

KELMAN, H. C., & HOVLAND, C. I. "Reinstatement" of the communicator in delayed measurement of opinion change. *Journal of Abnormal and Social Psychology*. 1953, 48, 327-335.

KENDALL, P. L., & WOLF, K. M. The analysis of deviant cases in communication research. In

P. F. Lazersfeld & F. N. Stanton (Eds.), *Communications research, 1948-1949.* New York: Harper, 1949, 152-179.

KERLINGER, F. N. Social attitudes and their criterial referents: A structural theory. *Psychological Review*, 1967, 74, 110-122.

KERRICK, J. S. The effect of relevant and non-relevant sources on attitude change. *Journal of Social Psychology*, 1958, 47, 15-20.

KIESLER, C. A. Commitment. In R. Abelson et al., *Theories of cognitive consistency: A sourcebook.* New York: Rand McNally, 1968, 448-455.

KIESLER, C. A., COLLINS, B. E., & MILLER, N. *Attitude change.* New York: Wiley, 1969.

KIESLER, C. A., & SAKUMURA, J. A test of a model of commitment. *Journal of Personality and Social Psychology*, 1966, 3, 349-353.

KIRSCHT, J. P., & DILLEHAY, R. C. *Dimensions of authoritarianism: A review of research and theory.* Lexington, Kentucky: University of Kentucky Press, 1967.

KISH, L. *Survey sampling.* New York: Wiley, 1965.

KIVLIN, J. E., & FLIEGEL, F. C. Differential perceptions of innovations and rate of adoption. *Rural Sociology*, 1967, 32, 78-91.

KLAPPER, J. T. *The effects of the mass media.* New York: Columbia University Bureau of Applied Social Research, 1949.

KLAPPER, J. T. *The effects of mass communication.* New York: The Free Press, 1960.

KLAPPER, J. T. Mass communication, attitude stability and change. In C. W. Sherif & M. Sherif (Eds.), *Attitude, ego-involvement and change.* New York: Wiley, 1967, 297-310.

KLECK, R. E., & WHEATON, J. Dogmatism and responses to opinion-consistent and opinion-inconsistent information. *Journal of Personality and Social Psychology*, 1967, 5, 249-252.

KLINEBERG, O. *Social psychology.* New York: Holt, 1954.

KLUCKHOHN, F. R., & STRODTBECK, F. L. *Variations in value orientations.* Evanston, Ill.: Row, Peterson & Company, 1961.

KOMORITA, S. S., & BASS, A. R. Attitude differentiation and evaluative scales on the semantic differential. *Journal of Personality and Social Psychology, 1967*, 6, 241-244.

KOSLIN, B. L., & PARGAMENT, R. Effects of attitude on the discrimination of opinion statements. *Journal of Experimental Social Psychology*, 1969, 5, 245-264.

KOSLIN, B. L., STOOPS, J. W., & LOH, W. D. Source characteristics and communication discrepancy as determinants of attitude change and conformity. *Journal of Experimental Social Psychology*, 1967, 3, 230-242.

KUTNER, B., WILKINS, C., & YARROW, P. R. Verbal attitudes and overt behavior involving racial prejudice. *Journal of Abnormal and Social Psychology*, 1952, 47, 649-652.

LAMBERT, W. E. A social psychology of bilingualism. *The Journal of Social Issues*, 1967, 23, 91-109.

LAMBERT, W. E., & KLINEBERG, O. *Children's views of foreign peoples: A cross-national study.* New York: Appleton-Century-Crofts, 1967.

LAMBERT, W. E., HODGSON, R. C., GARDNER, R. C., & FILLENBAUM, S. Evaluational reactions to spoken languages. *Journal of Abnormal and Social Psychology*, 1960, 60, 44-51.

LAMPEL, A. K., & ANDERSON, N. H. Combining visual and verbal information in an impression formation task. *Journal of Personality and Social Psychology*, 1968, 9, 1-6.

LANA, R. E. Three theoretical interpretations of order effects in persuasive communications. *Psychological Bulletin*, 1964, 61, 314-320.

LANGE, N. Beiträge zur theorie der sinnlichen aufmerksamkeit und der aktiven apperception. *Philosophische Studien*, 1888, 4, 390-422.

LA PIERE, R. T. Attitudes vs actions. *Social Forces,* 1934, 13, 230-237.

LA PIERE, R. T. Type-rationalizations of group antipathy. *Social Forces,* 1936, 15, 232-237.

LAWSON, E. D., & STAGNER, R. Group pressure, attitude change and autonomic involvement. *Journal of Social Psychology*, 1957, **45**, 299-312.

LAZARSFELD, P. F., BERELSON, B., & GAUDET, H. *The people's choice.* New York: Columbia University Press, 1948.

LEE, R. E., & WARR, P. (mimeographed, 1967).

LEMERT, J. B. (1963). Quoted by K. Giffin, The contribution of studies of source credibility to a theory of interpersonal trust in the communication process. *Psychological Bulletin*, 1967, **68**, 104-120.

LENSKI, G. Status crystallization: A non-vertical dimension of social status. *American Sociological Review*, 1954, **19**, 405-413.

LENSKI, G. Comment. *Public Opinion Quarterly,* 1964, **28**, 326-330.

LEVENTHAL, H. Fear communications in the acceptance of preventive health practices. *Bulletin of the New York Academy of Medicine*, 1965, **41**, 1144-1168.

LEVENTHAL, H., SINGER, R., & JONES, S. Effects of fear and specificity of recommendation upon attitudes and behavior. *Journal of Personality and Social Psychology,* 1965, **2**, 20-29.

LEVENTHAL, H., JONES, S., TREMBLY, G. Sex differences in attitude and behavior change under conditions of fear and specific instructions. *Journal of Experimental Social Psychology*, 1966, **2**, 387-399.

LEVINE, J. M., & MURPHY, G. The learning and forgetting of controversial material. *Journal of Abnormal and Social Psychology*, 1943, **38**, 507-517.

LE VINE, R. A. Socialization, social structure, and intersocietal images. In H. Kelman (Ed.), *International behavior: A social psychological analysis.* New York: Holt, Rinehart & Winston, 1965, 66-126.

LEWIN, K. Group decision and social change. In T. M. Newcomb & E. L. Hartley (Eds.), *Readings in social psychology.* New York: Holt, 1947. Can also be found in H. Proshansky & B. Seidenberg (Eds.), *Basic studies in social psychology.* New York: Holt, 1965, 423-437.

LIFTON, R. J. "Thought reform" of Western civilians in Chinese prisons. *Psychiatry*, 1956, **19**, 173-195.

LIFTON, R. J. Thought reform of Chinese intellectuals. *The Journal of Social Issues*, 1957, **13**, 5-20.

LIKERT, R. A technique for the measurement of attitudes. *Archives of Psychology*, 1932, **140**, 44-53.

LINDER, D. E., COOPER, J., & JONES, E. E. Decision freedom as a determinant of the role of incentive magnitude in attitude change. *Journal of Personality and Social Psychology*, 1967, **6**, 245-254.

LINN, L. S. Verbal attitudes and overt behavior: A study of racial discrimination. *Social Forces,* 1964/1965, **43**, 353-364.

LOCKE, E. A., & BRYAN, J. F. Goals and intentions as determinants of performance level, task choice and attitudes. Final Report to the Air Force. Silver Spring, Maryland: American Institutes for Research, 1967.

LOH, W. D., & TRIANDIS, H. C. Role perceptions in Peru. *International Journal of Psychology*, 1968, **3**, 175-182.

LOWIN, A. Approach and avoidance: Alternate modes of selective exposure to information. *Journal of Personality and Social Psychology*, 1967, **6**, 1-9.

LOWIN, A. Further evidence for an approach-avoidance interpretation of selective exposure. *Journal of Experimental Social Psychology*, 1969, **5**, 265-271.

LUCHINS, A. S. Primacy-recency in impression formation. In C. I. Hovland (Ed.), *The order of presentation in persuasion.* New Haven: Yale University Press, 1957.

LULL, P. E. The effectiveness of humor in persuasive speeches. *Speech Monographs*, 1940, 7, 26-40.

LUMSDAINE, A. A., & JANIS, I. L. Resistance to "counterpropaganda" produced by one-sided and two-sided "propaganda" presentations. *Public Opinion Quarterly*, 1953, **17**, 311-318.

LUND, F. H. The psychology of belief, IV: The law of primacy in persuasion. *Journal of Abnormal and Social Psychology*, 1925, **20**, 183-191.

MACCOBY, E. E., MACCOBY, N., ROMNEY, A. K., & ADAMS, J. S. Social reinforcement in attitude change. *Journal of Abnormal and Social Psychology*, 1961, **63**, 109-115.

MACCOBY, N., ROMNEY, A. K., ADAMS, J. S., & MACCOBY, E. E. "Critical periods" in seeking and accepting information. In *Paris-Stanford studies in communication*. Stanford Cal. Institute of Communication Research, 1962, 47-57.

MAHAR, P. M. A ritual pollution scale for ranking Hindu castes. *Sociometry*, 1960, **23**, 292-306.

MALPASS, R. Effects of attitude on learning and memory: The influence of instruction-induced sets. *Journal of Experimental Social Psychology*, 1969, **5**, 441-453.

MANIS, M. The interpretation of opinion statements as a function of message ambiguity and recipient attitude. *Journal of Abnormal and Social Psychology*, 1961, **63**, 76-81. (a)

MANIS, M. The interpretation of opinion statements as a function of recipient attitudes and source prestige. *Journal of Abnormal and Social Psychology*, 1961, **63**, 82-86. (b)

MANIS, M., GLEASON, T. C., & DAWES, R. M. The evaluation of complex social stimuli. *Journal of Personality and Social Psychology*, 1966, **3**, 404-419.

MANIS, M., HOUTS, P. S., & BLAKE, J. B. Beliefs about mental illness as a function of psychiatric status and psychiatric hospitalization. *Journal of Abnormal and Social Psychology*, 1963, **67**, 226-233.

MANN, L. The effects of emotional role playing on smoking attitudes and behavior. *Journal of Experimental Social Psychology*, 1967, **3**, 334-348.

MANN, L., & JANIS, I. L. A follow-up study on the long-term effects on emotional role playing. *Journal of Personality and Social Psychology*, 1968, **8**, 339-342.

MARTIN, J. G., & WESTIE, F. R. The tolerant personality. *American Sociological Review*, 1959, **24**, 521-528.

MARX, G. T. *Protest and prejudice.* New York: Harper, 1967.

McARTUR, L. A., KIESLER, C. A., & COOK, B. P. Acting on an attitude as a function of self-percept and inequity. *Journal of Personality and Social Psychology*, 1969, **12**, 295-302.

MC CLELLAND, D. C. *The achieving society*. Princeton, N.J.: Van Nostrand, 1961.

MC CLINTOCK, C. Personality syndromes and attitude change. *Journal of Personality*, 1958, **26**, 479-493.

MC CROSKEY, J. C. Scales for the measurement of ethos. *Speech Monographs*, 1966, **33**, 65-72.

MC GINNIES, E. Studies in persuasion: III. Reactions of Japanese students to one-sided and two-sided communications. *Journal of Social Psychology*, 1966, **70**, 87-93.

MC GINNIES, E. & ROSENBAUM, L. L. A test of the selective-exposure hypothesis in persuasion. *The Journal of Psychology*, 1965, **61**, 237-240.

MC GINNIES, E., & TURNAGE, T. W. Verbal association by Chinese and American students as a function of work frequency and mode of presentation. *Psychological Reports*, 1968, **23**, 1051-1060.

MC GUIRE, W. J. Order of presentation as a factor in "conditioning" persuasiveness. In C. I. Hovland et al. (Eds.), *The order of presentation in persuasion*. New Haven: Yale University Press, 1957, 98-114.

MC GUIRE, W. J. Cognitive consistency and attitude change. *Journal of Abnormal and Social Psychology*, 1960, **60**, 345-353. (a)

MC GUIRE, W. J. Direct and indirect persuasive effects of dissonance-producing messages. *Journal of Abnormal and Social Psychology*, 1960, **60**, 354-358. (b)

MC GUIRE, W. J. A syllogistic analysis of cognitive relationships. In M. J. Rosenberg & C. I.

Hovland (Eds.), *Attitude organization and change*. New Haven, Conn.: Yale University Press, 1960, 65-111. (c)

MC GUIRE, W. J. Inducing resistance to persuasion. In Len Berkowitz (Ed.) *Advances in experimental social psychology*. Vol I. New York: Academic Press, 1964, 192-229.

MC GUIRE, W. J. The current status of cognitive consistency theories. In S. Feldman (Ed.), *Cognitive consistency*. New York: Academic Press, 1966.

MC GUIRE, W. J. Theory-oriented research in natural settings. In Sherif and Sherif (Eds.), *Interdisciplinary relationships in the social sciences*. Chicago: Aldine, 1968. (a)

MC GUIRE, W. J. Personality and susceptibility to social influence. In E. F. Borgatta & W. W. Lambert (Eds.), *Handbook of personality theory and research*. Chicago: Rand McNally, 1968. (b)

MC GUIRE, W. J. Personality and attitude change: An information-processing theory. In A. G. Greenwald, T. C. Brock & T. M. Ostrom, *Psychological Foundations of Attitudes*. New York: Academic Press, 1968, 171-196. (c)

MC GUIRE, W. J. The nature of attitudes and attitude change. In Gardner Lindzey and Elliot Aronson (Eds.), *The handbook of social psychology*. Cambridge, Mass: Addison-Wesley, 1969, 136-314. (a)

MC GUIRE, W. J. Suspiciousness of experimenter's intent as an artifact in research. In R. Rosenthal & R. L. Rosnow, *Artifact in social research*. New York: Academic Press, 1969. (b)

MC GUIRE, W. J., & MILLMAN, S. Anticipatory belief lowering following forewarning of a persuasive attack. *Journal of Personality and Social Psychology*, 1965, **2**, 471-479.

MC GUIRE, W. J., & PAPAGEORGIS, D. The relative efficacy of various types of prior belief defenses in producing immunity against persuasion. *Journal of Abnormal and Social Psychology*, 1961, **62**, 327-337.

MEHRABIAN, A., & WIENER, M. Decoding of inconsistent communications. *Journal of Personality and Social Psychology*, 1967, **6**, 109-114.

MENZEL, H., & KATZ, E. Social relations and innovation in the medical profession: The epidemiology of a new drug. *Public Opinion Quarterly*, 1956, **19**, 337-352.

MESSICK, S. J. The perception of social attitudes. *Journal of Abnormal and Social Psychology*, 1956, **52**, 57-66.

MILLER, G. A. The magical number seven, plus or minus two. *Psychological Review*, 1956, **63**, 82-97.

MILLER, G. R., & HEWGILL, M. A. (1964) Quoted in McGuire, W. J. The nature of attitudes and attitude change. In Gardner Lindzey and Elliot Aronson (Eds.), *The handbook of social psychology*. Cambridge, Mass.: Addison-Wesley, 1969, 136-314. (a)

MILLER, N., & CAMPBELL, D. T. Recency and primacy in persuasion as a function of the timing of speeches and measurements. *Journal of Abnormal and Social Psychology*, 1959, **59**, 1-9.

MILLS, J., & JELLISON, J. M. Effect on opinion change of similarity between the communicator and the audience he addressed. *Journal of Personality and Social Psychology*, 1968, **9**, 153-156.

MITCHELL, J. C. The Kalela dance. Rhodes-Livingston Institute, Paper No. 27, Manchester: Manchester University Press, 1956.

MOULIK, T. K., HRABOVSZKY, J. P., & RAO, C. S. S. Predictive values of some factors of adoption of nitrogenous fertilizers by North Indian farmers. *Rural Sociology*, 1966, **3**, 467-477.

MYRDAL, G. *An American dilemma: The Negro problem and modern democracy*. New York: Harper, 1944.

NAIDOO, J. An inquiry into the structure of attitudes and behavior: A validation study. Technical Report No. 38, Group Effectiveness Research Laboratory, 1966.

NEWCOMB, T. M. *Personality and social change*. New York: Dryden, 1943.

NEWCOMB, T. M. An approach to the study of communicative acts. *Psychological Review*, 1953, **60**, 393-404.

NEWCOMB, T. M. The prediction of interpersonal attraction. *American Psychologist*, 1956, **11**, 575-586.

NEWCOMB, T. M. Persistence and regression of changed attitudes: Long range studies. *Journal of Social Issues*, 1963, **19**, 3-16.

NEWCOMB, T. M. *Persistence and change: Bennington College and its students after 25 years.* New York: Wiley, 1967.

NEWCOMB, W. W. Towards an understanding of war. In G. E. Dole and R. L. Carneiro (Eds.), *Essays in the science of culture*. New York: Crowell, 1960.

NISBETT, R. E. Taste, deprivation and weight determinants of eating behavior. *Journal of Personality and Social Psychology*, 1968, **10**, 107-116.

NISBETT, R. E., & GORDON, A. Self-esteem and susceptibility to social influence. *Journal of Personality and Social Psychology*, 1967, **5**, 268-276.

NOEL, D. L., & PINKNEY, A. Correlates of prejudice: Some racial differences and similarities. *The American Journal of Sociology*, 1964, **69**, 609-622.

NORMAN, W. On estimating psychological relationships: Social desirability and self-report. *Psychological Bulletin*, 1967, **67**, 273-293.

NOVAK, D. W., & LERNER, M. J. Rejection as a consequence of perceived similarity. *Journal of Personality and Social Psychology*, 1968, **9**, 147-152.

NUTTIN, J. M., JR. Attitude change after rewarded dissonant and consonant "forced compliance." *International Journal of Psychology*, 1966, **1**, 39-58.

OSGOOD, C. E. *Method and theory in experimental psychology*. New York: Oxford University Press, 1953.

OSGOOD, C. E. Cross cultural comparability of attitude measurement via multilingual semantic differentials. In I. S. Steiner & M. Fishbein (Eds.), *Recent studies in social psychology*. New York: Holt, Rinehart & Winston, 1965.

OSGOOD, C. E. Interpersonal verbs and interpersonal behavior. Urbana: Group Effectiveness Research Laboratory, 1968.

OSGOOD, C. E., & TANNENBAUM, P. H. The principle of congruity in the prediction of attitude change. *Psychological Review*, 1955, **62**, 42-55.

OSGOOD, C. E., SUCI, G. J., & TANNENBAUM, P. H. *The measurement of meaning*. Urbana: University of Illinois Press, 1957.

OSTROM, T. M. The relationship between the affective, behavioral and cognitive components of attitude. *Journal of Experimental Social Psychology*, 1969, **5**, 12-30.

OSTROM, T. M., & UPSHAW, H. S. Psychological perspective and attitude change. In A. C. Greenwald, T. C. Brock, & T. M. Ostrom (Eds.), *Psychological foundations of attitudes*. New York: Academic Press, 1968, 217-242.

PAPAGEORGIS, D. Anticipation of exposure to persuasive messages and belief change. *Journal of Personality and Social Psychology*, 1967, **5**, 490-496.

PAPAGEORGIS, D. Warning and persuasion. *Psychological Bulletin*, 1968, **70**, 271-282.

PEAK, H. Attitude and motivation. In M. R. Jones (Ed.), *Nebraska symposium on motivation*. Lincoln: University of Nebraska Press, 1955, 149-188.

PETERSON, P. D., & KOULACK, D. Attitude change as a function of latitudes of acceptance and rejection. *Journal of Personality and Social Psychology*, 1969, **11**, 309-311.

PETTIGREW, T. F. Regional differences in anti-Negro prejudice. *Journal of Abnormal and Social Psychology*, 1959, **59**, 28-36.

PETTIGREW, T. F., & CRAMER, M. R. The demography of desegregation. *Journal of Social Issues*, 1959, **15**, 61-71.

PODELL, J. E. The evaluative concept of a person as a function of the number of stimulus traits upon which it is based. *Journal of Personality and Social Psychology*, 1966, **4**, 333-336.

POPPLETON, P. K., & PILKINGTON, G. W. A comparison of four methods of scoring an attitude scale in relation to its reliability and validity. *British Journal of Social and Clinical Psychology*, 1964, **3**, 36-39.

PORIER, G. W., & LOTT, A. J. Galvanic skin responses and prejudice. *Journal of Personality and Social Psychology*, 1967, **5**, 253-259.

PROSHANSKY, H. M. The development of intergroup attitudes. In L. W. and M. L. Hoffman (Eds.), *Review of child development research*. New York: Russell Sage Foundation, 1966, Vol. 2, 311-371.

PROTHRO, E. T., & MELIKIAN, L. Studies in stereotypes, V: Familiarity and the kernel of truth hypothesis. *Journal of Social Psychology*, 1955, **41**, 3-10.

RAZRAN, G. Conditioned response changes in rating and appraising sociopolitical slogans. *Psychological Bulletin*, 1940, **37**, 481.

REISS, A. E. Personal communication, 1969.

REMMERS, H. H. *A scale for measuring attitudes towards any proposed social action.* Lafayette, Ind.: Purdue Research Foundation, 1960.

RETTIG, S. Relation of social systems to inter-generational changes in moral attitudes. *Journal of Personality and Social Psychology*, 1966, **4**, 409-414.

RHINE, R. J. A concept formation approach to attitude acquisition. *Psychological Review*, 1958, **65**, 362-369.

RHINE, R. J. The 1964 Presidential election and curves of information seeking and avoiding. *Journal of Personality and Social Psychology*, 1967, **5**, 416-423.

RHINE, R. J., & SILUM, B. A. Acquisition and change of a concept attitude as a function of consistency of reinforcement. *Journal of Experimental Psychology*, 1958, **55**, 524-529.

RICHEY, M. H., MC CLELLAND, L., & SHIMKUNAS, A. M. Relative influence of positive and negative information in impression formation and persistence. *Journal of Personality and Social Psychology*, 1967, **6**, 322-327.

ROBINSON, J. P. & HEFNER, R. Multidimensional differences in public and academic perceptions of nations. *Journal of Personality and Social Psychology*, 1967, **7**, 251-259.

ROGERS, E. M. *Diffusion of innovations.* New York: The Free Press, 1962.

ROGERS, E. M., & NEIL, R. E. *Achievement motivation among Columbian farmers.* East Lansing: Department of Communications, Michigan State University, 1966.

ROKEACH, M. *The open and closed mind.* New York: Basic Books, 1960.

ROKEACH, M. Attitude change and behavioral change. *Public Opinion Quarterly*, 1967, **30** 529-550.

ROKEACH, M. *Beliefs, attitudes and values.* San Francisco: Jossey-Bass, 1968.

ROKEACH, M., & MEZEI, L. Race and shared belief as factors in social choice. *Science*, 1966, **151**, 167-172.

ROKEACH, M., & ROTHMAN, G. The principle of belief congruence and the congruity principle as models of cognitive interaction. *Psychological Review*, 1965, **72**, 128-142.

ROKEACH, M., SMITH, P. W., & EVANS, R. I. Two kinds of prejudice or one? In M. Rokeach, *The open and closed mind.* New York: Basic Books, 1960, 132-168.

ROSENBERG, M. Psychological selectivity in self-esteem formation. In Carolyn W. & M. Sherif (Eds.), *Attitude, ego-involvement and change.* New York: Wiley, 1967.

ROSENBERG, M. J. Cognitive structure and attitudinal affect. *Journal of Abnormal and Social Psychology*, 1956, **53**, 367-372.

ROSENBERG, M. J. An analysis of affective cognitive consistency. In M. J. Rosenberg & C. I. Hovland (Eds.), *Attitude organization and change.* New Haven, Conn.: Yale University Press, 1960, 15-64. (a)

ROSENBERG, M. J. Cognitive reorganization in response to the hypnotic reversal of attitudinal affect. *Journal of Personality*, 1960, **28**, 39-63. (b)

ROSENBERG, M. J. A structural theory of attitude dynamics. *The Public Opinion Quarterly*, 1960, **24**, 319-340. (c)

ROSENBERG, M. J. When dissonance fails: On eliminating evaluative apprehension from attitude measurement. *Journal of Personality and Social Psychology*, 1965, **1**, 28-42. (a)

ROSENBERG, M. J. Some content determinants of intolerance for attitudinal inconsistency. In S. S. Tomkins & C. E. Izard (Eds.), *Affect, cognition and personality*, New York: Springer, 1965. (b)

ROSENBERG, M. J. Some limits of dissonance: Toward a differentiated view of counterattitudinal performance. In S. Feldman (Ed.), *Cognitive consistency*. New York: Academic Press, 1966, 137-172.

ROSENBERG, M. J., & ABELSON, R. P. An analysis of cognitive balance. In C. I. Hovland & M. J. Rosenberg, *Attitude organization and change*. New Haven: Yale University Press, 1960, 112-163.

ROSENBERG, M. J., & HOVLAND, C. I. Cognitive, affective and behavioral components of attitudes. In M. J. Rosenberg et al. (eds.), *Attitude organization and change*. New Haven: Yale University Press, 1960, 1-14.

ROSNOW, R. L. Whatever happened to the "Law of Primacy"? *The Journal of Communication*, 1966, **16**, 10-31.

ROSNOW, R. L., & ROBINSON, E. J. *Experiments in persuasion*. New York: Academic Press, 1967.

ROSNOW, R. L., & ROSENTHAL, R. Volunteer subjects and the results of studies of opinion change. *Psychological Reports*, 1966, **19** 1183-1187.

ROTTER, J. B. Beliefs, social attitudes and behavior: A social learning analysis. In R. Jessor & S. Feshbach (Eds.), *Cognition, personality and clinical psychology*. San Francisco, Cal.: Jossey-Bass, 1967, 112-140.

RUBIN, I. M. Increased self-acceptance: A means of reducing prejudice. *Journal of Personality and Social Psychology*, 1967, **5**, 233-238.

RUDIN, S. A. National motives predict psychogenic death rates 25 years later. *Science*, 1968, **160**, 901-903.

RYAN, T. A. *Intentional behavior: An approach to human motivation*. New York: Ronald Press, 1969.

SCHACHTER, S. The interaction of cognitive and physiological determinants of emotional state. In L. Berkowitz (Ed.), *Advances in experimental social psychology*. New York: Academic Press, 1964, Vol. I, 49-81.

SCHEIN, E. H. The Chinese indoctrination program for prisoners of war. *Psychiatry*, 1956, **19**, 149-172.

SCHRAMM, W. *The science of human communication*. New York: Basic Books, 1963.

SCHULMAN, G. I. The popularity of viewpoints and resistance to attitude change. *Journalism Quarterly*, 1968, **45**, 86-90.

SCHULMAN, G. I., & TITTLE, C. R. Assimilation-contrast effects and item selection in Thurstone scaling. *Social Forces*, 1968, **46**, 484-491.

SCHUMAN, H. Social change and the validity of regional stereotypes in East Pakistan. *Sociometry*, 1966, **29**, 428-440.

SCHUMAN, H., & HARDING, J. Sympathetic identification with the underdog. *Public Opinion Quarterly*, 1963, **27**, 230-241;

SCHUMAN H., & HARDING, J. Prejudice and the norm of rationality. *Sociometry*, 1964, **27**, 353-371.

SCHUTZ, W. C. *Firo: A three-dimensional theory of interpersonal behavior*. New York: Rinehart, 1958.

SCOTT, W. A. Attitude change through reward of verbal behavior. *The Journal of Abnormal and Social Psychology*, 1957, **55**, 72-75.

SCOTT, W. A. Cognitive consistency, response reinforcement and attitude change. *Sociometry*, 1959, **22**, 219-229. (a)

SCOTT, W. A. Attitude change by response reinforcement replication and extension. *Sociometry*, 1959, **22**, 328-335. (b)

SCOTT, W. A. International ideology and interpersonal ideology. *Public Opinion Quarterly*, 1960, **24**, 419-435.

SCOTT, W. A. Cognitive complexity and cognitive flexibility. *Sociometry,* 1962, **25**, 405-414.

SCOTT, W. A. Cognitive complexity and cognitive balance. *Sociometry,* 1963, **26,** 66-74.

SCOTT, W. A. Brief report: Measures of cognitive structure. *Multivariate Behavioral Research,* 1966, **1**, 391-395.

SCOTT, W. A. Attitude measurement. In G. Lindzey & E. Aronson (Eds.), *Handbook of social psychology* (revised edition), 1969.

SCOTT, W. A. Structure of natural cognitions. *Journal of Personality and Social Psychology,* 1969, **12**, 261-278.

SEARS, D. O. Effects of the assassination of President Kennedy on political partisanship. In B. S. Greenberg & E. B. Parker (Eds.), *The Kennedy assassination and the American public: Social communication in crisis.* Stanford: Stanford University Press, 1965, 305-326.

SEARS, D. O. Opinion formation and information preferences in an adversary situation. *Journal of Experimental Social Psychology,* 1966, **2**, 130-142.

SEARS, D. O. Social anxiety, opinion structure and opinion change. *Journal of Personality and Social Psychology,* 1967, **7**, 142-151.

SEARS, D. O., & FREEDMAN, J. L. Effects of expected familiarity with arguments upon opinion change and selective exposure. *Journal of Personality and Social Psychology,* 1965, **2**, 420-426.

SEARS, R. R. Comparison of interviews with questionnaires for measuring mothers' attitudes toward sex and aggression. *Journal of Personality and Social Psychology,* 1965, **2**, 37-44.

SEASHORE, S. E. *Group cohesiveness in the industrial work group.* Ann Arbor: Survey Research Center, 1954.

SELLTIZ, C., & COOK, S. W. Racial attitude as a determinant of judgments of plausibility. *Journal of Social Psychology,* 1966, **70**, 139-147.

SELLTIZ, C., EDRICH, H., & COOK, S. W. Ratings of favorableness of statements about a social group as an indicator of attitude toward the group. *Journal of Personality and Social Psychology,* 1965, **2**, 408-415.

SELOCK, D. P. Political perception at a Midwestern university. Study completed for honors social psychology seminar, University of Illinois, 1967.

SHAPIRO, D., & CRIDER, A. Psychophysiological approaches in social psychology. In G. Lindzey and E. Aronson (Eds.), *The handbook of social psychology.* Reading, Mass.: Addison-Wesley, Vol. 3, 1969, 1-49.

SHAW, M. E., & WRIGHT, J. M. *Scales for the measurement of attitudes.* New York: McGraw-Hill, 1967.

SHERIF, M. A study of some social factors in perception. *Archives of Psychology,* 1935, **27**, No. 187.

SHERIF, M., & HOVLAND, C. I. Judgemental phenomena and scales of attitude measurement: Placement of items with individual choice of number of categories. *Journal of Abnormal and Social Psychology,* 1953, **48**, 135-141.

SHERIF, M., & HOVLAND, C. I. *Social judgment.* New Haven: Yale University Press, 1961.

SHERIF, M., & SHERIF, C. W. The own category procedure in attitude research. From a symposium on *Attitudes and Attitude Change* organized by H. C. Triandis at the International Congress of Applied Psychology, Ljubljana, Jugoslavia, 1964. [Also reproduced in M. Fishbein (Ed.), *Readings in attitude theory and measurement.* New York: Wiley, 1967.]

SHERIF, M., & SHERIF, C. W. Attitude as the individual's own categories: The social judgmental approach to attitude and attitude change. In Carolyn W. Sherif & M. Sherif (Eds.), *Attitude, ego-involvement and change.* New York: Wiley, 1967, 105-139.

SHERIF, C. W., SHERIF, M., & NEBERGALL, R. E. *Attitude and attitude change.* Philadelphia: Saunders, 1965.

SHERIF, M., HARVEY, O. J., WHITE, B. J., HOOD, W. R., & SHERIF, C. W. Experimental study of positive and negative intergroup attitudes between experimentally produced groups. Robbers Cave Study. Norman: University of Oklahoma, 1954, (multilithed).

SHIBUYA, YURIKO. A study in the relationship between cognitive similarity and communication effectiveness. *Japanese Psychological Research,* 1962, **4**, 173-177.

SHIM, N., & DOLE, A. A. Components of social distance among college students and their parents in Hawaii. *Journal of Social Psychology,* 1967, **73**, 111-124.

SIEGEL, A. E., & SIEGEL, S. Reference groups, membership groups and attitude change. *Journal of Abnormal and Social Psychology,* 1957, **55**, 360-364.

SIGALL, H., & ARONSON, E. Affecting opinion change via the gain-loss model of interpersonal attraction. *Journal of Experimental Social Psychology,* 1967, **3**, 178-188.

SILVERMAN, I. Differential effects of ego threat upon persuasibility for high and low self-esteem subjects. *Journal of Abnormal and Social Psychology,* 1964, **69**, 567-572. (a)

SILVERMAN, I. Self-esteem and differential responsiveness to success and failure. *Journal of Abnormal and Social Psychology,* 1964, **69**, 115-119. (b)

SILVERMAN, I. Role-related behavior of subjects in laboratory studies of attitude change. *Journal of Personality and Social Psychology,* 1968, **8**, 343-348.

SINHA, A. K. P., & UPADHYAYA, O. P. Change and persistence in the stereotypes of university students towards different ethnic groups during Sino/Indian border dispute. *Journal of Social Psychology,* 1960, **52**, 31-39.

SINGH, Y. P., & PAREEK, U. I. Sources of communication, different stages of adoption of farm practices. *Indian Journal of Social Work,* 1966, **26**, 385-391.

SINGH, Y. P., & PAREEK, U. Interpersonal communication at different stages of adoption. *Indian Journal of Social Work,* 1967, **27**, 344-352.

SIZER, L. M., & PORTER, W. F. *The relation of knowledge to adoption of recommended practices.* Morgantown, West Virginia: Agricultural Experimental Station, Bulletin No. 446.

SMITH, M. B. The personal setting of public opinions: A study of attitudes towards Russia. *Public Opinion Quarterly,* 1947, **11**, 507-523.

SMITH, M. B., BRUNER, J. S., & WHITE, R. W. *Opinions and personality.* New York: Wiley, 1956.

SOLOMON, R. An extenstion of control group design. *Psychological Bulletin,* 1949, **46**, 137-150.

SPENCER, H. *First principles.* (Reprinted from 5th London edition.) New York: Burt, 1862

STAATS, A. W. An outline of an integrated learning theory of attitudes. In M. Fishbein (Ed.), *Readings in attitude theory and measurement.* New York: Wiley, 1967, 373-376.

STAATS, A. W., & STAATS, C. K. Attitudes established by classical conditioning. *Journal of Abnormal and Social Psychology,* 1958, **57**, 37-40.

STEIN, D. D. The influence of belief systems on interpersonal preference: A validation study of Rokeach's theory of prejudice. *Psychological Monographs,* 1966, **80**, No. 616.

STEIN, D. D., HARDYCK, J. A., & SMITH, M. B. Race and belief: An open and shut case. *Journal of Personality and Social Psychology,* 1965, **1**, 281-290.

STEINER, I. D. Ethnocentrism and tolerance for trait "inconsistency." *Journal of Abnormal and Social Psychology,* 1954, **49**, 349-354.

STEINER, I. D. Personality and the resolution of interpersonal disagreements. In Maher, B. (Ed.), *Advances in experimental personality research.* Vol. 3. New York: Academic Press, 1966, 195-239.

STEINER, I. D., & FISHBEIN, M. *Current studies in social psychology.* New York: Holt, Rinehart and Winston, 1965.

STEINER, I. D. & JOHNSON, H. H. Authoritarianism and "tolerance for trait inconsistency." *Journal of Abnormal and Social Psychology,* 1963, **67**, 388-391.

STEINER, I. D., & JOHNSON, H. H. Relationships among dissonance reducing responses. *Journal of Abnormal and Social Psychology*, 1964, **68**, 38-44.

STEINER, I. D., & ROGERS, E. D. Alternative responses to dissonance. *Journal of Abnormal and Social Psychology*, 1963, **66**, 128-136.

STEVENSON, H. W., & ODOM, R. D. Effectiveness of social reinforcement following two conditions of social deprivation. *Journal of Abnormal and Social Psychology*, 1962, **65**, 429-431.

STOTLAND, E., KATZ, D., & PATCHEN, M. The reduction of prejudice through the arousal of self-insight. *Journal of Personality*, 1959, **27**, 507-531.

STRAUS, M. A. Family role differentiation and technological change in farming. *Rural Sociology*, 1960, **25**, 219-228.

SUEDFELD, P., & VERNON, J. Attitude manipulation in restricted environments: II. Conceptual structure and the internalization of propaganda received as a reward for compliance, *Journal of Personality and Social Psychology*, 1966, **6**, 586-589.

SUGAR, J. An analysis of the relationship of attitudes and behavior. NSF Undergraduate Research Participation, Final Report, University of Illinois, 1967.

TANNENBAUM, P. H. Initial attitude toward source and concept as factors in attitude change through communication. *Public Opinion Quarterly*, 1956, **20**, 413-425.

TANNENBAUM, P. H. Mediated generalization of attitude change via the principle of congruity. *Journal of Personality and Social Psychology*, 1966, **3**, 493-499.

TANNENBAUM, P. H. The congruity principle revisited: Studies in the reduction, induction and generalization of persuasion. In L. Berkowitz (Ed.), *Advances in experimental social psychology*. New York: Academic Press, 1967, Vol. III, 272-320.

TANNENBAUM, P. H. The congruity principle: Retrospective reflections and recent research. In R. P. Abelson, E. Aronson, W. J. McGuire, T. M. Newcomb, M. J. Rosenberg & P. H. Tannenbaum (Eds.), *Theories of cognitive consistency: A sourcebook*. Chicago: Rand McNally, 1968, 52-72.

TANNENBAUM, P. H., & GENGEL, R. W. Generalization of attitude change through congruity principle relationships. *Journal of Personality and Social Psychology*, 1966, **3**, 299-304.

TAYLOR, I. A. Similarities in the structure of extreme social attitudes. *Psychological Monographs*, 1960, **74**, No. 489.

THIBAUT, J. W., & KELLEY, H. H. *The social psychology of groups*. New York: Wiley, 1959.

THOMAS, W. I., & ZNANIECKI, F. *The Polish peasant in Europe and America*, Vol. I. Boston: Badger, 1918.

THURSTONE, L. L. A law of comparative judgment. *Psychological Review*, 1927, **34**, 273-286. (a)

THURSTONE, L. L. Psychophysical analysis. *American Journal of Psychology*, 1927, **38**, 368-389. (b)

THURSTONE, L. L. Attitudes can be measured. *American Journal of Sociology*, 1928, **33**, 529-554.

THURSTONE, L. L. The measurement of social attitudes. *Journal of Abnormal and Social Psychology*, 1931, **26**, 249-269.

THURSTONE, L. L., & CHAVE, E. J. *The measurement of attitude*. Chicago: University of Chicago Press, 1929.

THURSTONE, L. L., & JONES, L. V. The rational origin for measuring subjective values. *Journal of the American Statistical Association*, 1957, **52**, 458-471.

TITTLE, C. R., & HILL, R. J. Attitude measurement and prediction of behavior: An evaluation of conditions and measurement techniques. *Sociometry*, 1967, **30**, 199-213.

TOMKINS, S. S., MC CARTER, R., & PEEBLES, A. Reactions to the assassination of President Kennedy. In S. Tomkins & C. E. Izard (Eds.), *Affect, Cognition and Personality*. New York: Springer, 1965, 172-197.

TORGERSON, W. S. *Theory and methods of scaling.* New York: Wiley, 1958.

TRIANDIS, H. C. Categories of thought of managers, clerks and workers about jobs and people in industry. *Journal of Applied Psychology,* 1959, **43**, 338-344. (a)

TRIANDIS, H. C. Cognitive similarity and interpersonal communication in industry. *Journal of Applied Psychology,* 1959, **43**, 321-326. (b)

TRIANDIS, H. C. Cognitive similarity and communication in a dyad. *Human Relations,* 1960, **13**, 175-183. (a)

TRIANDIS, H. C. Some determinants of interpersonal communication. *Human Relations,* 1960, **13**, 279-287. (b)

TRIANDIS, H. C. A comparative factorial analysis of job semantic structures of managers and workers. *Journal of Applied Psychology,* 1960, **44**, 297-302. (c)

TRIANDIS, H. C. A note on Rokeach's theory of prejudice. *Journal of Abnormal and Social Psychology,* 1961, **62**, 184-186.

TRIANDIS, H. C. Cultural influences upon cognitive processes. In L. Berkowitz (Ed.), *Advances in experimental social psychology.* New York: Academic Press, 1964, Vol. 1, 1-48. (a)

TRIANDIS, H. C. Exploratory factor analyses of the behavioral component of social attitudes. *Journal of Abnormal and Social Psychology,* 1964, **68**, 420-430. (b)

TRIANDIS, H. C. Towards an analysis of the components of interpersonal attitudes. In Carolyn W. Sherif & M. Sherif (Eds.), *Attitudes, ego-involvement, and change.* New York: Wiley, 1967, 227-270.

TRIANDIS, H. C. & DAVIS, E. E. Race and belief as determinants of behavioral intentions. *Journal of Personality and Social Psychology,* 1965, **2**, 715-725.

TRIANDIS, H. C., & FISHBEIN, M. Cognitive interaction in person perception. *Journal of Abnormal and Social Psychology,* 1963, **67**, 446-453.

TRIANDIS, H. C., & TRIANDIS, L. M. Race, social class, religion and nationality as determinants of social distance. *Journal of Abnormal and Social Psychology,* 1960, **61**, 110-118.

TRIANDIS, H. C., & TRIANDIS, L. M. A cross-cultural study of social distance. *Psychological Monographs,* 1962, 76, No. 21 (whole No. 540).

TRIANDIS, H. C., & TRIANDIS, L. M. Some studies of social distance. In I. D. Steiner & M. Fishbein (Eds.), *Recent studies in social psychology.* New York: Holt, Rinehart and Winston, 1965, 207-217.

TRIANDIS, H. C. & VASSILIOU, V. Frequency of contact and stereotyping. *Journal of Personality and Social Psychology,* 1967, 7, 316-328. (a)

TRIANDIS, H. C., & VASSILIOU, V. A comparative analysis of subjective culture. Urbana: Group Effectiveness Research Laboratory, 1967. (b)

TRIANDIS, H. C., DAVIS, E. E., & TAKEZAWA, S. I. Some determinants of social distance among American, German and Japanese students. *Journal of Personality and Social Psychology,* 1965, **2**, 540-551.

TRIANDIS, H. C., LOH, W. D., & LEVIN, L. A. Race, status, quality of spoken English, and opinions about civil rights as determinants of interpersonal attitudes. *Journal of Personality and Social Psychology,* 1966, **3**, 468-472.

TRIANDIS, H. C., TANAKA, Y., & SHANMUGAM, A. V. Interpersonal attitudes among American, Indian and Japanese students. *International Journal of Psychology,* 1966, **1**, 177-206.

TRIANDIS, H. C., VASSILIOU, V., & THOMANEK, E. K. Social status as determinant of social acceptance and friendship acceptance. *Sociometry,* 1966, **29**, 396-405.

TRIANDIS, H. C., FISHBEIN, M., HALL, E., SHANMUGAM, A. V., TANAKA, Y. Affect and behavioral intentions. *Modern trends of psychology.* Papers in honor of Professor Kuppuswamy. Bombay: Manaktala and Sons, 1967.

TRIANDIS, H. C., KILTY, K. M., SHANMUGAM, A. V., TANAKA, Y., & VASSILIOU, V. Cultural influence upon the perception of implicative relationship among concepts and analysis of values. Urbana: Group Effectiveness Research Laboratory, 1968.

TRIANDIS, H. C., MC GUIRE, H., SARAL, T. B., YANG, K., LOH, W., & VASSILIOU, V. A cross-cultural study of role perceptions. Urbana: Group Effectiveness Research Laboratory, 1968.

TRIANDIS, H. C., VASSILIOU, V., & NASSIAKOU, M. The cross-cultural studies of subjective culture. *Journal of Personality & Social Psychology, Monograph Supplement*, 1968, 8, No. 4, 1-42.

TUCKER, L. R. Systematic differences between individuals in perceptual judgments. In W. W. Shelly & G. L. Bryan (Eds.), *Human Judgments and Optimality*. New York: John Wiley & Sons, 1964. Can also be found in Fishbein, M., *Readings in attitude theory and measurement*. New York: Wiley, 1967, 157-162.

VASSILIOU, V., TRIANDIS, H. C. & ONCKEN, G. Intercultural attitudes after reading an ethnographic essay: An exploratory study. Urbana: Group Effectiveness Research Laboratory, 1968.

VASSILIOU, V., TRIANDIS, H. C., VASSILIOU, G., & MC GUIRE, H. Reported amount of contact and stereotyping. Urbana: Group Effectiveness Research Laboratory, 1968.

VERNON, J. *Inside the black room*. New York: Potter, 1963.

VIDULICH, R. N., & KAIMAN, I. P. The effects of information source status and dogmatism upon conformity behavior. *Journal of Abnormal and Social Psychology*, 1961, 63, 639-642.

VROOM, V. H. Some personality determinants of the effect of participation. *Journal of Abnormal and Social Psychology*, 1959, 59, 322-327.

WALY, P., & COOK, S. W. Attitude as a determinant of learning and memory: A failure to confirm. *Journal of Personality and Social Psychology*, 1966, 4, 280-288.

WATTS, W. A. Relative persistence of opinion change induced by active compared to passive participation. *Journal of Personality and Social Psychology*, 1967, 5, 4-15.

WEBB, E. J., CAMPBELL, D. T., SCHWARTZ, R. D., & SECHREST, L. *Unobtrusive Measures*. Chicago: Rand McNally, 1966.

WEBSTER, E. C. *Decision making in the employment interview*. Montreal, Canada: McGill University Industrial Relations Center, 1964.

WEICK, K. Promise and limitations of laboratory experiments in the development of attitude change theory. In C. W. Sherif & M. Sherif (Eds.), *Attitude, ego-involvement and change*. New York: Wiley, 1967, 51-75.

WEICK, K. E. Processes of ramification among cognitive links. In R. Abelson et al., *Theories of cognitive consistency: A sourcebook*. Chicago: Rand McNally, 1968, 512-519.

WEISS, W. Opinion congruence with a negative source on one issue as a factor influencing agreement on another issue. *The Journal of Abnormal and Social Psychology*, 1957, 54, 180-186.

WEISS, W. The relationship between judgments of communicator's position and extent of opinion change. *Journal of Abnormal and Social Psychology*, 1958, 56, 380-384.

WEISS, W. Effects of source, placement of sources, and persuasive communication on attitude, reason giving and action intentions. Technical Report No. 7. New York: Hunter College, 1966.

WEISS, W. Influence of source and number of exposures on communication effectiveness. Technical Report No. 10. New York: Hunter College, 1967.

WEISS, W. Effects of the mass media of communication. In G. Lindzey & E. Aronson (Eds.) *Handbook of social psychology* (revised edition). Cambridge, Mass.: Addison-Wesley, 1969, 77-195.

WEISS, W. & FINE, B. J. Opinion change as a function of some intrapersonal attributes of the communicatees. *The Journal of Abnormal and Social Psychology*, 1955, 51, 246-253.

WEISS, W., & FINE, B. J. The effect of induced aggressiveness on opinion change. *Journal of Abnormal and Social Psychology*, 1956, 52, 109-114.

WEISS, W., & STEENBOCK, S. The influence on communication effectiveness of explicitly urging action and policy consequences. Technical Report No. 3, Department of Psychology. New York: Hunter College, 1965.

WESTIE, F. R., & DE FLEUR, M. L. Autonomic responses and their relationship to race attitudes. *Journal of Abnormal and Social Psychology*, 1959, 58, 340-347.

WHITTAKER, J. O., Opinion change as a function of communication-attitude discrepancy. *Psychological Reports*, 1963, 13, 763-772.

WHITTAKER, J. O., Resolution of the communication discrepancy issue in attitude change. In Carolyn W. Sherif & M. Sherif (Eds.) *Attitude, ego-involvement and change*. New York: Wiley, 1967, 159-177.

WHITTAKER, J. O., & MEAD, R. D. Sex of the communicator as a variable in source credibility. *Journal of Social Psychology*, 1967, 72, 27-34.

WILSON, W., & MILLER, H. Repetition, order of presentation, and timing of arguments and measures as determinants of opinion change. *Journal of Personality and Social Psychology*, 1968, 9, 184-188.

WOODMANSEE, J. J., & COOK, S. W. Dimensions of verbal racial attitudes: Their identification and measurement. *Journal of Personality and Social Psychology*, 1967, 7, 240-250.

WORCHEL, P. Social ideology and reactions to international events. Technical Report for Contract Number 375-19, Austin, Texas, University of Texas, 1967.

YARROW, M. R. Interpersonal dynamics in a desegregation process. *Journal of Social Issues*, 1958, 14, 1-63.

ZAJONC, R. B. Structure and cognitive field. Unpublished doctoral dissertation. University of Michigan, 1954. Summarized in The Process of Cognitive Tuning in Communication. *Journal of Abnormal and Social Psychology*. 1960, 61, 159-167.

ZAJONC, R. B. The concepts of balance, congruity and dissonance. *Public Opinion Quarterly*, 1960, 24, 280-286. (a)

ZAJONC, R. B. The process of cognitive tuning in communication. *Journal of Abnormal and Social Psychology*, 1960, 61, 159-167. (b)

ZAJONC, R. B. The attitudinal effects of mere exposure. *Journal of Personality and Social Psychology, Monograph Supplement*, 1968, Part 2, 1-27.

ZIMBARDO, P. Involvement and communication discrepancy as determinants of opinion conformity. *Journal of Abnormal and Social Psychology*, 1960, 60, 86-94.

ZIMBARDO, P. G., WEISENBERG, M., & FIRESTONE, I. Communication effectiveness in producing public conformity and private attitude change. *Journal of Personality*, 1965, 33, 233-255.

Name Index

Subject Index

KING ALFRED'S COLLEGE
LIBRARY